EVERY GAME IS WON OR LOST

# Between The Ears

## HOW TO THINK LIKE A CHAMPION

**On the cover**

Athletes pictured (beginning with back cover) front row, left to right: Michael Pugh, Larkin Hatcher, Layne Hatcher, Justin Charette, Max Mendelsohn, Will Stafford, Zack Kelley, Mattie Hatcher, Haley Filat. Back row, left to right: Stephen Newell, Jonie Block, Julie Inman, Amanda Janton, Kelsey Hatcher, Annie DeCoursey, Haley Hatcher, Amanda Morris, Annie Stafford, Stefan Loucks, and Breanna Gordon.

"Ninety percent of the game
is half mental."

—YOGI BERRA

# MIGHTY BLUEBIRDS

100% of the proceeds from this book will go to the Mighty Bluebird Foundation to support their soccer and basketball teams.

2005 SOCCER STATE CHAMPIONS
Ranked #1 in the Nation in U-12 Girls

2005 BCI STATE CHAMPIONS and
SLAM-N-JAM NATIONAL CHAMPIONS

International Standard Book Number: 0-9676055-1-2

First Edition, 2006

12 11 10 9 8 7 6 5 4 3 2 1

Manufactured in the United States of America

The paper used in this book meets or exceeds the minimum requirements of the American National Standards for Information Sciences—Permanence of Paper for Printed Library Materials, ansi. 48 -1984.

Tiger Books, Inc.
Little Rock, Arkansas

I am often criticized for my zest for sports…
I read this poem to keep me going.

People are illogical, unreasonable, and self-centered.
LOVE THEM ANYWAY.

If you do good, people will accuse you of selfish ulterior motives.
DO GOOD ANYWAY.

If you are successful, you will win false friends and true enemies.
SUCCEED ANYWAY.

The good you do today will be forgotten tomorrow.
DO GOOD ANYWAY.

Honesty and frankness make you vulnerable.
BE HONEST AND FRANK ANYWAY.

The biggest men and women with the biggest ideas can be shot down
by the smallest men and women with the smallest minds.
THINK BIG ANYWAY.

People favor underdogs but follow only top dogs.
FIGHT FOR A FEW UNDERDOGS ANYWAY.

What you spend years building may be destroyed overnight.
BUILD ANYWAY.

People really need help but may attack you if you do help them.
HELP PEOPLE ANYWAY.

Give the world the best you have and you'll get kicked in the teeth.
GIVE THE WORLD THE BEST YOU HAVE ANYWAY.

# Foreword

## Athletics is a Training Ground

People often ask me why I spend so much time coaching all of my kids' sports teams. I have five children, four girls and a boy and I have coached every single one of their sports teams and will continue until they reach the junior high and high school level. In the end I believe that the time spent coaching them is the most important thing I can give them. I certainly care about school and their getting good grades, but anybody that knows me knows that I believe what I can teach them in sports is the difference maker later in life. I believe if I can help them be a success in sports, especially the mental side of it where they learn how to do the little extras and pay more of a sacrifice, have more discipline, and deal with the synergies of a team and the destructive things that can occur within a team such as jealousy, politics, and other things that are often unfair that they will be much better equipped for life after school and sports.

As I look at my own business that I run and the daily battles that I encounter, it's never what I learned in English class or math class that helps me win; it's the competitive and strategic things I learned in sports and simply the endurance to hang in there to the last second, never ever giving up, that allows me to be successful. In the end if I can give my kids that gift I won't have to worry about them nearly as much in their jobs or their marriages or anything else they may have to deal with. I truly love sports for all that it teaches and for the character it builds. Certainly all young men could learn these lessons, but oh how much stronger are women that have learned these lessons as well. I may enjoy coaching the women even more because I know how special they will be in the world and the confidence they will have as business persons, wife, mother, and even coach. I know that these girls will be less likely to do drugs or alcohol, or have a baby in their teenage years, and will just feel a lot better about themselves. They'll be less likely to be overweight, they'll be better looking, and just happier individuals.

One final aspect of sports is that money and power can't make you successful on the court. Only hard work and skill and athleticism can. I love the fact that you can't buy a championship; that it has to be earned. When I look at the screensaver on my computer each day and it has pictures of all my Mighty Bluebirds soccer and basketball players flashing across the screen I realize that my greatest joy in life is not the businesses I've built, but the sports teams I've coached; and I look forward to watching these little girls and boys grow up to be the winners that they most surely will be…tougher mentally and physically than almost any kid out there.

# Preface

My father said I should have been an evangelist preacher because I have for years tried to convince people to change and can really be committed when I believe in something and will try to spread the news.

My personal coach said if I came back in a second life in another profession I should come as a Trial Lawyer as no one would be more convincing or dig harder through all the details to try to win a case.

Probably the wisest quotation, however, I've ever read is this:

"When I was young and free and my imagination had no limits, I dreamed of changing the world. As I grew older and wiser, I discovered the world would not change, so I shortened my sights somewhat and decided to change only my country. But, it too seemed immovable. As I grew into my twilight years, in one last desperate attempt, I settled for changing only my family, those closest to me; but alas, they would have none of it. And now as I lie on my deathbed, I suddenly realize, if I had only changed myself first, then by example I would have changed my family. From this inspiration and encouragement I would then have been able to better my country and, who knows, I may have even changed the world."

—WRITTEN ON TOMB OF AN ANGLICAN BISHOP (1100 A.D.)
IN THE CRYPTS OF WESTMINSTER ABBEY

# How Coachable Are You?

The older I get the more my father was right when he said it's very, very hard to change people. He said it's a lot easier to just hire people that are already the way you want them to be or get players that are already the way you want them to be.

For me, I never stop trying to improve my players, employees, etc. just a touch. There's just too much of that evangelist preacher in me, but one thing that's a great compromise that I do believe is the old saying…

# When the student is ready the teacher will appear!

For all of you players out there who get to the point where you've had enough and you're ready to improve, this book was written to give you everything that I've learned over my lifetime as a player and as a coach to help you learn the 50% of the game that is simply won "Between the Ears." If you are the ready and willing student then this book, I hope, will be a good teacher for you and help you win a lot more games and be a lot more successful at whatever it is that you do.

# For My Children and Players

I want my children and my players to be Warriors. I want to develop a child that's a Warrior on the field and a sweetheart or gentleman off of it.

How do the personalities change so drastically?

The personality changes when they step over that line onto the playing field.

EVERY GAME IS WON OR LOST

# Between The Ears

HOW TO THINK LIKE A CHAMPION

# Acknowledgements

I can't write this book without acknowledging the true Warriors I've played with over the years. They come as players, coaches, teammates, and even a couple of business people. In the end, I can't be best friends with a person if they are not a Warrior, but thank goodness God has sent many Warriors my way and they are truly my closest friends.

1. Coach Bruce Dickey – My college soccer and wrestling and baseball coach. (6 Collegiate Conference Championships) Now the high school baseball coach at Bullock Creek High School. (Has won 15 of the last 16 Conference Championships.)

2. Coach Bill Klenk – My former college baseball coach, now retired.

3. Don Roescheise – A Warrior in anything he goes after.

4. Scott Loucks – Coach of over 20 State Championship teams in basketball, golf, baseball, and soccer, and frequent source for ideas for this book.

5. Kevin Kelley – State Champion coach in football, my movie buddy, and friend.

6. The Warriors on my college teams: Dan Coon, Bob Lovejoy, Gary Adam, Neil Tuomi, Chris Miller, Andy Beachnau, Steve Whitaker, Kyle Davidson, Sam Onekware, Ahmad Darvish, Obasi, Doug Fraser, and Jamie Harrison

7. Doug Fraser – The toughest athlete I've ever seen pound for pound. Great athlete, great coach, and now great businessman.

8. Morley Fraser – Coached Albion College football and baseball for 25 years, 14 Championships, my boss during four college summers, a Warrior against cancer who fought to the end.

9. Jim Foley – Nobody works harder. Played in college World Series, Warrior in business today.

10. My Hall of Fame teams. I'm proud to have played on more Hall of Fame teams than anyone in Alma College history. (Wrestling 1981, 1982, 1983, and Baseball 1980.)

11. Anthony School Basketball Team – A team I coached that had zero wins as 7th graders and we went undefeated as 8th graders.

12. Westside Warriors – My 8th grade football team that went unbeaten and unscored upon.

13. Adam Bettis – A former Westside Warrior. He walked on at Ole Miss and started his senior year at tight end.

14. Whitley McWilliams – the greatest male youth athlete I ever coached. He was amazing on the football field.

15. The Mighty Bluebirds Soccer Team—12 State titles. The toughest girls in Arkansas. Ranked #1 in the Nation in 2006.

16. Robert Farqua – My trainer; the toughest man I've ever known, but compassionate as well. He won't even step on a spider; he takes it outside.

17. John Russ – A counselor who helps others become better Warriors.
18. Softball Warriors, Jamie Harrison Curtis Bailey, Scott Allison, Phillip Wallace, Gary Flake, Ron Smith, Rick Angel, John Ford, Roland Pennington, and Terry Yamauchi.
19. My road racing buddies, Dr. Dale Burroughs, Larry Mabry, and Bill Torrey.
20. To my high school coaches: Coach Drysdale and Avery.
21. Chris Owen – My Bluebird co-head coach and friend. We have made many memories together. He is a fantastic teacher for the kids.
22. Ron Smith – The most positive player I ever played with. He made everyone better. I never heard him say a negative word.
23. Jamie Harrison – We played together in high school, college, and in our adult softball years, and moved to Arkansas together. A player you could always count on to make the effort play.
24. Bedford Camera & Video – John Rose and Jeff Beauchamp have produced thousands of pictures for the Mighty Bluebirds, Arkansas Belles, The Hatcher Agency, and all the charitable activities I'm in. They preserved the great memories.
25. Mighty Bluebird Soccer Coaches – Chris Owen, Mark Burr, Scott Loucks, Christy Smiley, and Chuck Ashburn.
26. To Coach Steve Quattlebaum and Andrew Brady, Back-to-Back State Champion Basketball Coaches at Central Arkansas Christian in appreciation for all they do for the kids at CAC.
27. Larry Waschka – my water skiing buddy and author. It's sad that he's not here to read this book since he's the one that encouraged me to write my first book, 55 Steps to Outrageous Service.
28. To Carter Lambert, the President of Central Arkansas Christian for setting up sports programs that support the kids and their coaches. Carter was an All-American in track and it shows.
29. To Adam May, for his efforts in filming hundreds of games for our teams and for handling our travel arrangements. God only knows how many times I would have gotten lost without him.
30. To Coach Shackleford, Coach Sullivan, and Coach Owen for their efforts in cross country, soccer, and track at CAC. They truly care about the kids.
31. To Doug Killgore, the Athletic Director at CAC, for running a first-class athletics program that is about the kids first.
32. To Rush Harding, my friend, who leads with his heart and has great passion and compassion. Although I never played alongside him, I'd want him on my team.
33. Thanks to my wonderful assistant, Shannon Wooley, who typed every word of this book.
34. To the Editor of all my books, Nancy Russ. Thanks for your creativity and for providing more clarity for the reader.
35. To Leah Dalton, my Vice-President, who has assisted in proofing this book and its design.
36. To John Naill, my running friend and mentor in running to my daughter Kelsey.

# Dedication

This book is written for my children, Kelsey, Haley, Larkin, Layne, and Mattie. It's written to help each of you become better than your father and hopefully help you learn from all the lessons and mistakes, trials and tribulations that I've learned from in my life.

It's not a blueprint that should necessarily be used to form your life, but I hope that you find a lot of wisdom in these words and that they help create a successful path for each of you to follow. Years later I hope these words are timeless and can even help my grandchildren and others become the very best that they can be.

# Special Appreciation

I want to thank my beautiful wife, Lee Hatcher, for her support in all the sports activities I've participated in and for supporting me as I coached all of my kids. You'd never know she was a "bleacher bum" by looking at her, but she's spent more weekends in the stands than we could ever count. She's also a Champion Hunter-Jumper at her horse shows. I love her very much.

# Teaching and Raising Warriors

This book is dedicated to my five children and all my other Mighty Bluebird players in hopes that they will gain a better mental understanding of competition in sports and life and that this book will help them compete better and eventually become Warriors. I enjoyed being a Warrior when I was a player more than anything else in my early years. I thought I would continue to play as long as my body would let me, but when I had kids, I found a greater joy than even competing myself, and that was to help teach all of you how to compete.

Dan Gable said it best upon retiring from the University of Iowa as wrestling coach. Sports Illustrated asked him which was more fun… to win 3 national championships and the Olympic Gold Medal that he had won as a wrestler, or to coach his team to 15 National Championship teams. His reply was, "It is a greater honor to teach someone to be the best, than to be the best yourself." Dan Gable won every match he wrestled in except one, however, he coached over 100 All Americans and led Iowa to 15 National Championships. It was also clear that he had a greater impact as a coach than as a wrestler. I learned from Dan Gable, and I consider it a greater honor to coach my kids than to play myself. I thank all of them for the great joy that I have had coaching and watching each of them grow.

# For the 1%

This book is written for the one percent of this world that desires to be the best and most importantly, will pay the price to get there. What you will find in life is that 100% of the world wants to be great but it is that 1% that will pay the price to get there. The other 99% will criticize you for trying to get there. Have courage and proceed anyway, even though you may be alone.

The reason I write this book is to help the 1% get a quicker education and to learn some things to help them get there more quickly and hopefully to convert a few people who never thought they could get there because they just simply didn't know how. Good luck, and I look forward to hearing from you as you make it to the top!

# A Magic Moment

There were 12.6 seconds left in the regional finals. My daughter Kelsey was a freshman, and as the team was in the timeout I thought of all the years I've been coaching her and said a little prayer for her. We have a poster in our gymnasium that says, "Victory is what happens when 10,000 hours of practice meet with one moment of opportunity." I got a lump in my throat as they came out of the timeout, but I prayed that Kelsey would get the ball and have an opportunity to help her team win.

Sure enough, with 5.1 seconds left on the clock the ball came to her and she shot the ball from about 3 feet behind the 3 point line. When she let it go I knew it was nothing but net. In fact, I never thought, nor did she, about the consequences of taking the shot and missing.

This child had worked since the second grade tirelessly and endlessly on her basketball skills, and I knew that this was that one moment of opportunity that the truly 10,000 hours of practice would pay off. It's really true that the harder you work the luckier you get. You see the rest of the time when you're winning by 40 points or losing by 40 points all the little things don't really seem to matter, but when it's really close it's all the little details and the work that you've done before the game that truly will decide it.

The shot swished the net, and I jumped to my feet and pumped my fist in the air 5 times as hard as I've ever swung. Kelsey showed no emotion and simply went to the bench when the other team called time out. She had made many big shots before, and as usual was very calm under pressure. Her coach called her "ice."

## Special Thanks To

# Bedford Camera & Video

## Thank You!

My photo sponsor for all activities I am involved in.

"You make memories last."

EVERY GAME IS WON OR LOST

# Between The Ears

## HOW TO THINK LIKE A CHAMPION

# Philosophy

# The Wall of Fame

As children we all have visions of what we want to become when we grow up. Some of us want to become sports stars, musicians, policemen, firemen, or dancers. Others want to be successful in business or a profession. As we get older we realize that while it is certainly good to dream, very few people end up achieving their childhood goals. There are two major reasons we don't fulfill these dreams. One is simply that our dreams change. The other is that we are not willing to work hard enough at the specific things we have to do to fulfill those dreams.

When I was a freshman in college I decided the kind of person I wanted to be. It was not profession-specific; I just designed a blueprint for the type of person I wanted to be, regardless of what I ended up doing for a living. My "Wall of Fame" helped remind me of the person I wanted to become. The person I wanted to evolve into was a combination of eight different people that I looked up to, or heroes that I thought were very important at the time. I believed that by taking the good qualities of these eight people I would evolve into the best person I could be.

The eight people were Pete Rose, Brian Piccolo, Roger Staubach, Morley Fraser, Tom Landry, my father, Rocky, and Jesus.

Let me tell you a little bit about each one of these eight people and the slogan that I had under each of their photos on my Wall of Fame which was located just above the top bunk of my bed in the college dorm. Each night before I went to sleep, I looked at the Wall of Fame, reminding myself of my goals.

## PETE ROSE

The quote under Pete Rose's photo read, "Leave behind no regrets. Give 100%." Pete Rose was a professional baseball player who played harder than any other player. He ran to first base when he walked; he dived into second base or third base head first on close plays; and he was always ready to play. He was the ultimate team player, giving his maximum effort everyday. Although Pete got in trouble later in his career for allegedly gambling on professional baseball, his work ethic was the trait I wanted to emulate.

## BRIAN PICCOLO

Brian Piccolo was a professional football player for the Chicago Bears. He had a good sense of humor, but he also had a great work ethic and was a real friend to his teammates. The movie Brian's Song was made about his life. Brian sat on the bench behind his best friend Gale Sayers. When Sayers got a knee injury, Brian Piccolo set up the weights in his basement and worked out with him to help him get back in shape. Brian was helping the person with whom he was competing for the starting position; but what happened was that as he worked to help Sayers get better, Brian got pretty good himself. The coach saw this and made a change and decided to start them both as running backs. (A lesson I learned in high school is that if you work hard enough the coach will find a way to play you somewhere.) Brian Piccolo got lung cancer shortly after he became a starting running back for the Bears. He fought hard to beat cancer, never losing his sense of humor. At the end of Brian's Song the narrator says, "Brian Piccolo died of cancer at the age of 26. He left behind a loving wife and three children. It was not the way he died for which he is remembered, but the way he lived – and how he did live!" Brian's picture is on my Wall of Fame with the slogan, "It's not the way he died for which he is remembered, but the way he lived." Every year that I live beyond age 26 I am thankful because I got more years than Brian Piccolo, the person I looked up to. I try to live my life as if it could end any day.

## ROGER STAUBACH

Roger Staubach was the quarterback for the Dallas Cowboys, America's football team for many years. Staubach was the ultimate team leader and a good Christian man. He could have gone out drinking and partying and picking up all kinds of girls, but Roger Staubach was the perfect example of a family man married to a wife that he loved and competing at quarterback for the Dallas Cowboys. Roger won the Heisman Trophy and is in the Pro Football Hall of Fame because of his unbelievable will to win. As quarterback he led the Dallas Cowboys to more fourth quarter comebacks after trailing than any other quarterback. His fellow players said they could be down by two touchdowns with two minutes to go and Roger Staubach still thought they were going to win. He literally willed his team to win over and over with his positive attitude and his "never say die" approach to the game. The quote under his picture, "Always be competitive", represents what I want to be in life.

## ROCKY

Rocky was a movie that starred Sylvester Stallone as a boxer. In the first Rocky movie, Rocky faced the world champion in boxing when he was just a little bit above an average boxer himself. When it got time to fight for the heavyweight championship of the world, Rocky knew he couldn't win; but he made up his mind never to quit and to see if he could just go twelve rounds with the champ without getting knocked out. At the end of those twelve rounds Rocky had a broken nose, two black eyes, and blood dripping from his face. As the champion continued to hit him, Rocky stood there and waved his arms asking for more. What Rocky proved in that fight was that you could be a winner without actually winning the match just by refusing to quit and by giving the very best you have to give. Under Rocky's photo are the words, "Never Say Die", to remind me that I wanted to grow up to be a person that would never ever quit.

## TOM LANDRY

Tom Landry was the coach for the Dallas Cowboys when Roger Staubach was a player. Landry had the winningest record of any coach in his time and led the Cowboys to five Super Bowls, winning two of them. Tom Landry was a Christian man who spent a lot of time with the Fellowship of Christian Athletes, but it was his sideline demeanor I most admired. He got his teams prepared and was calm and cool on the sidelines, always dressed in a suit with his famous trench coat and hat. As Tom Landry became famous and more and more successful, his demeanor and his attitude never changed. The mantra under Tom Landry's picture is "Never let fame and fortune change your character." I decided if I ever grew up to become extremely successful or famous, I would not let it go to my head; I would stay the same person I always was.

## JOE HATCHER

My father was a late entry on the Wall of Fame, as most of my heroes were sports figures. As I got older, I realized my father lived his life with solid principles. He is the most honest man I know. Under his photo is written: "Honesty is the best policy." Being honest and doing right frees you from a lot of worry and gives you an inner peace that always feels good.

## MORLEY FRASER

Morley Fraser was a college football coach at Albion College and my first boss in the summers during my college years. Morley was offered the head-coaching job at a lot of big colleges, but he turned them down to stay at small Albion College. He did that so he could be around to see his kids play high school and college football. Morley wasn't willing to sacrifice being with his family to take a job where he'd be on the road all the time and miss his kids' ballgames. I learned a lot of valuable lessons from Morley and one of them is what's written under his photo: "Always keep life in the proper perspective." There are some things that money can't replace, and time with your kids is one of them.

JESUS

The last person on the Wall of Fame is Jesus. Of all the people that have ever come into this world, nobody's sacrificed more than Jesus. Just when I think I'm working hard, just when I think I've made a pretty big sacrifice I think back to the fact that Jesus had nails driven through his wrists and through his feet; he was stabbed in the side;, and he hung on a cross for hours before he died so he could save the world from sin. He went through all that pain and agony to help other people. Under his picture is: "You must pay the price for success." Certainly Jesus paid the ultimate price. This also reminds me that whatever it is I'm trying to accomplish, if He can pay that price I can pay whatever price it takes to get there.

The Wall of Fame is my blueprint for success. I hope that you will get a blueprint for success in your life and then follow it with all the passion that is in you. If you do, you will achieve your dream.

## Questions/Discussion

1. Who would be on your Wall of Fame to build the person you want to become?

CHAPTER

# 2

# Little Bitty Details
# Determine Your Entire Career

There is no joy in Mudville.

Mighty Casey has struck out.

The fictional Casey was the team hero. He may have hit a hundred home runs for his team and assisted with hundreds of successful plays, but he was immortalized in a poem because he made the last out that lost the game.

It is amazing how an entire sports career can be affected by just one play. Nobody will ever forget Jackie Clark, the tight end for the Dallas Cowboys who dropped a wide-open pass in the end zone and gave the Super Bowl to the Pittsburgh Steelers. Every sports fan remembers that Dwight Clark jumped high up in the end zone to make the game-winning catch for the San Francisco 49ers against the Dallas Cowboys to send the 49ers to the Super Bowl. I will never forget when Rumeal Robinson went to the free throw line with no time left and his team down by one to shoot his one-and-one free throws for Michigan. He sank both shots to give Michigan the National Championship. Earlier in the year, Robinson had missed the front end of a one-and-one and cost Michigan a game; but he stayed after practice every day after that and shot 100 free throws. And oh, how it paid off when he again got the opportunity to shoot a one-and-one at the end of the game.

Finally, there is Bill Buckner. The first baseman for the Boston Red Sox who let a slow ground ball that would have been the third out of the inning go right through his legs at first base. The New York Mets scored the game-winning run, costing the Boston Red Sox the World Series.

Little details! What a difference they can make. You never know when that one play will define your entire career. In every sport there's the player who backs up the throw at first base or in center field or hustles down on defense on every play, who warms up properly every night, who is always on time, who is always in the game mentally. And there is also the player who is always a little late or rarely in the game mentally. These little details will show up when the pressure is on more than at any other time. When your team is down or up by 30 points you can make a little mistake or do something great and nobody will remember. The time the little details show up is when the game is on the line; it's super tight; and one little mistake or one little great play determines the ballgame. The people that are remembered for these tiny little details have been doing them all year, maybe all their lives. It's just that they show up at that defining moment and are remembered.

There's an old saying: "the harder I work the luckier I get." I don't believe much in luck. I think players develop good habits and bad habits, and those good or bad habits will show up in those close games. Develop great habits and pay attention to the little bitty details, and they'll show up to help you and save you someday.

## Questions/Discussion

1. What little detail have you forgotten that cost you something important?
2. What little detail did you do that made you successful?

CHAPTER

# 3

# Be a Copy Cat

"Copy cat!"

Coming from a sibling or a rival, this name calling has negative connotations. But I can't think of any better advice to give someone than, "Be a copy cat."

Every person you meet, every relative – including your mother and father – every friend, has some good trait that you can copy. If you can simply copy the good traits and ignore the bad ones, you can make yourself a pretty good and complete person. I have had many coaches over the years, and I like to think that I am a combination of the good things of all of those coaches. Certainly I have my faults; and as a constant work-in-progress, I try each day to get rid of my faults and copy the strengths of other coaches and friends. I replace my faults with their strengths.

As I write this chapter I think of the two biggest influences in my life – my mother and father. My father is a disciplined man, one of his favorite sayings is "moderation in all things." He is disciplined to the core. I mention in other chapters that he has a dessert every other day and he works out every day. For four hours each Saturday he plans his week. He is always on time. If you give him a job to do he takes responsibility and always comes through. I know no man more organized, more disciplined, or more reliable than my father.

My mother is the opposite in many ways. She would tell you that it is difficult for her to eat right, stay fit, and do the things she knows she needs to do. She can say it with a smile on her face because she's at peace with it. She is not moderate in anything. That's why she's great at whatever she wants to be great at. She's passionate! Presently, she's a world class quilter. She wins over $25,000 a year in prize money for her quilts. She's published over 15 books on quilting, is recognized as one of the top 100 quilters of the past century, has three quilts in the National Quilting Museum, and teaches quilting all over the world. She's the competitor in our family. Before she was the best quilter, she was the best school teacher, working lots of extra hours and coming up with all kinds of new teaching methods.

I try to copy my father's organization, discipline, and dependability and mix it with my mother's competitiveness, obsessive determination, and passion to be the best.

Copy the best traits of others and make yourself a better person.

## Questions/Discussion

1. What is a good trait that you could copy from someone else to make you better?
2. What is a trait you would get rid of from someone you admire?

CHAPTER

# 4

# A One Percent Improvement Every Day Adds Up

I always tell my kids to try to improve one percent at practice every day. Can you imagine if you got a little bit better at every practice? Day after day you'd be getting better and better and better. You can't get one percent better doing it the same old way everyday. You have to try new things in practice; you have to raise the intensity; and you have to increase the speed or increase the angle of the athletic maneuver you are working on.

I give members of my business staff a $2 bill for any one percent improvement they implement. We know that if you win 100 to 99, you're one percent better than the competition. If you can keep improving that one percent day after day, before long you'll be beating your opponent by 20 points. When you can beat them by 20 points you can have a bad day and still win. If you're only one percent better than the competition—doing just enough to get by—you may not win if you have a bad day.

Challenge yourself to get one percent better every day. If you truly put forth the effort, you'll find there are very few people who can stay with you because most people do it the same old way everyday and don't get much better.

## Questions/Discussion

1. What is a 1% improvement you could make?

2. Did you make a 1% improvement at your last practice?

> Courage does not always roar. Sometimes it
> is the quiet voice at the end of the day saying,
> "I will try it again."

# Pain: A Reason for Writing this Book

Pain was one of the main reasons I wrote this book. I don't want my kids or the kids I coach to go through the kind of pain I experienced as a college baseball player. I say that hesitantly because the pain made me a much tougher competitor. It taught me not to be satisfied with a "close one." I want to be so far ahead of the competition that I am sure of a win when I enter the game.

Growing up I was always a three-sport athlete. In junior high and high school I played every varsity sport at some time with the exception of golf and hockey. In high school I settled on cross-country, wrestling and baseball as my three sports. I was the top player in two of my three sports, the second best player in the other and captain of all three of my sports teams. When I went to college at Alma I was a four-year starter, captain, and all-conference wrestler and a three-year starter in soccer. But I never became the regular starter in baseball. The pain caused by my not getting into that lineup in baseball was excruciating. I never once thought about quitting. I did consider transferring, but I really believed I would get in that lineup and could get the job done. For a number of reasons, it didn't work out.

Several factors all came together to make things difficult for me to play baseball during my four years. I would not call them excuses; they are factors any player needs to be aware of because they could make the difference between winning and losing, between being on the bench or on the field. These were hurdles I was constantly fighting. Had just one of them changed, it might have put me in the lineup. I tell my kids that what you do in practice, your work ethic or putting in that little bit of extra time might make the difference. I've lived firsthand through most of the challenges they face, and I experienced quite a few of them during my baseball career.

The four-years that I played baseball at Alma College were the most successful in Alma College's 100-plus years of baseball. While this certainly was a blessing for Alma, it proved to be a disadvantage for me. The teams during my four years won three Conference Championships, finished second in the other year, and missed going to the College World Series by one game one year. There is only one Alma College baseball team in the Alma College Hall of Fame; it's the baseball team I played on. When I was a freshman I didn't make the traveling team to Florida because I was not a standout freshman with a super strong arm, nor was I a big power hitter. I also was not a star recruit coming in. When the team returned from Florida, I played on the J.V. team my freshman year and did well, but I was not outstanding and had no long home runs. I did have a solid year, however, and was looking forward to coming back my sophomore year and earning a spot on the varsity. My sophomore year I had become a pretty good athlete, starting in soccer and being a second year starter on our MIAA Championship wrestling team. (One thing I've learned in sports is that if you become a good athlete in other sports coaches pay a little more attention to you in their sport.) Unfortunately, I double-dislocated my elbow toward the end of the wrestling season, and when baseball season came I could not throw the baseball for the entire season. I showed up at baseball practice every day of my sophomore year, catching ground balls and rolling them underhanded to first base or second base for the double play. My sophomore year was lost for all practical purposes due to injury, but I still participated in every practice. That year our baseball team won their first of three consecutive MIAA Championships; and the entire infield, which was my position, was named either First Team All-Conference or Second Team All-Conference. When I came back as a junior, we had the entire All-Conference Infield returning, and I was now a junior who had no playing experience. When it came time to pick the team for Florida I was passed over for two freshmen. Although I was a good player I was the same age as the rest of the starting infielders, and it made more sense to groom a couple of freshmen to take over for these players' starting positions when the freshmen became juniors. As a coach today I certainly understand the thinking: you have to build your program for the future. Nevertheless, I was devastated, and I knew I had to work harder.

By the end of my junior year I'd had quite a successful college career, with one exception. I was President of Fellowship of Christian Athletes; I was President-Elect for the Student Body the next year; I had been named Captain of the wrestling team my senior year; I would be going into my third starting season in soccer. I had had a lot of success. But my only goal for my senior year of college was to be a starter on the baseball team. To do this I couldn't be just one of the top nine players. I had to be, in my opinion, the best player on the team. That summer I went away and played 80 baseball games, learned to switch hit, and came back to Alma College for my senior year. I went to soccer practice in the fall, but as soon as soccer practice was over I was down in the batting cages hitting; I was in the weight room doing a workout specifically for baseball; and I arrived at the gymnasium – if you can believe this – every morning at 7:00 a.m. to take ground balls by myself. How does a person take ground balls by himself? Well, only a person who wanted to get off the bench bad enough could come up with such an invention. I took one of those little trampolines that cheerleaders run and jump on and tilted it on its side so it would throw a baseball back to me on the ground. I would then catch the baseball and throw it to one of two contraptions I had built and put at the first and second bases in the gymnasium. These contraptions were made with 2 x 4s, stood about six feet tall by 3 feet wide, and each had a hanging net. The hanging nets were the first and second basemen. Every day I took ground balls, worked on my double play turns from both second base and shortstop, and practiced throwing the ball across the gym. As my coach would later say, I didn't have the strongest arm but I certainly had the most accurate one. That accuracy was developed from my taking thousands and thousands of ground balls before anybody else got out of bed in the morning.

My determination was fueled by the fact that one of the infielders had left, and there was one infield spot open. I made myself a promise that I would work harder than anybody that had ever lived would work for that starting position. And, I decided I would not talk to the coach about the position but would earn it the old fashioned way. What I didn't know was that when that player graduated our coach thought, "All I have is one player coming back for his senior year with no playing experience." He had the opportunity to recruit a player from a division I school at nearby Central Michigan. The player was friends with a couple of starters on our team because they had gone to the same high school. The coach had told the player that if he transferred for his junior and senior years he would have the open spot. As the baseball season started it became obvious that the shortstop position was his. I never gave up because I knew that sometimes injuries or poor play by a particular player could still give me a chance. I made the spring trip to Florida and did particularly well when given opportunities in a couple of games. I hit the ball well, and I fielded it better than anyone else on the team—as you might imagine after all the practice. The third base coach from the opposing team told me when I was out there and had made a couple of plays that it looked like the team had a new shortstop or third baseman. But my name never got penciled into that starting lineup.

My goal was to start on the baseball team my senior year and to make First Team All Conference, although those sounded like big goals for somebody that had struggled those first three years. Some of the struggle was due to the exceptional talent on the team; some was due to injury; and some was just due to being a senior that was too close to the finish line. As the season progressed I was the top hitter in the junior varsity games. I was playing extremely well, and we were two games away from our first conference game. I couldn't stand it anymore. A couple of the players in the infield on the varsity team were not hitting very well, and I thought I deserved a chance to play. I went into the coach's office and told him that I deserved to start and that I could perform better than some of the players who were starters. The coach told me that the people ahead of me were former All-Conference players and Division I transfers and that they would eventually break out of their slumps.

I told him it didn't matter what they'd done in the past, that I was performing better now and that I did two things far better than they. One was that I never struck out. Another was that I had not made an error in the field this year in junior varsity, and I was a superior fielder. When I went out the next day I found myself in the starting lineup. The coach realized that I did deserve a chance to play.

In that game I struck out for the first time that year. Over my entire career in high school and college baseball I rarely struck out—only twice in my high school senior season and very little in my college at bats. Later in that game I was hit a ground ball. I knocked it down but was so intent on trying to prove that I deserved to be in the lineup that I simply couldn't pick up the ball. I must have picked it up two or three times and, due to the intensity of the moment, just simply couldn't hold the ball. After all those years of hard work and the grueling regimen of this senior year, I lost it. I threw my glove on the ground in disgust knowing that I had done the two things that I had told the coach I would never do, and I knew my baseball career at Alma College was over. Following the game, with tears running down my face I went to my coach and said, "I will never say another word to you again" regarding my position on the team. I continued to do my workouts after practice every single day and push the other players to be the best they could be.

The two players who were struggling went on to hit very well at the end of the season and made All Conference again. That was okay because they were teammates and friends of mine, and I was happy for them. I started a few more non-conference games and actually performed pretty well – even getting the game-winning hit in one game; but I was never able to get a starting position for the season. The baseball team went on to win their third consecutive championship, and I felt that I at least pushed these other players to be the best that they could be and helped the team win. At the banquet I was voted the Most Improved Player as a senior non-starter, almost an impossible feat to accomplish; but there was no player on the team that didn't know how hard I worked and how much I had improved.

Upon graduation I was named my college's Outstanding Senior, and my fraternity's Top Man. I also won a host of other accolades, but I did not achieve the one goal I was shooting for – to be an All-Conference baseball player.

After graduation I went into the work world and about four months later I called my old baseball coach and told him I was coming back. The year that I lost because of the dislocated elbow made me eligible to play another year, and now all but one of the infielders had graduated, and there were a couple of outfield positions open. Our team had lost the star players that had won those three championships, and it would have been easy for me to start. My coach told me I could come back, but he thought it would be an embarrassment for someone who had accomplished so much in my college career just to come back to play that one season of baseball when I had already graduated.

He was right, and I decided instead to take a job as baseball coach at the University of Notre Dame to get it out of my system. I was also a Player/Coach on a summer team with major college baseball players from the University of Notre Dame, Purdue, and Indiana, with me as the starting shortstop. I was good enough to play at that level because I had worked so hard the year before.

It has taken 20 years for me to get over not getting that starting position. Today, the baseball coach and I are the very best of friends and have the utmost respect for each other. The situations that occurred were not his fault. Some of them were just bad circumstances for me, but I learned from them. Since then I have tried to make sure things would never be close again when I was in a competitive battle. I try to teach my kids that it's the little tiny things that can cost you. I understand not being good enough. I understand that injuries can put somebody else in front of you and you may not be able to get your job back. I understand college athletics and the commitment by a coach to bring in a transfer player; I understand that when two players are equal, the coach has to go with the younger player because it helps to develop the program; and I understand that you can put so much pressure on yourself that it can hinder your performance. I understand how important it is for the coach to have enough confidence to play you even if you're not playing your best. I also understand how important it is as a coach to let players know they have your confidence even when they are not performing well. I realized that all of these things made sense and learned not to be upset with my coach. The experience made me a better player and coach.

Probably the most important lesson I learned is that there will also be obstacles if you want to be the best in anything you do and that to be able to overcome all these obstacles you must be all that you can be. If 70 is required to pass the test, I don't study to score a 71; I study to score 100. Instead of shooting for a starting position, or to win a game, or to win over an account in my business I don't ever prepare to do just enough to win; I prepare to do everything I can to make our team perfect or to score 100. I don't want the game to be close; I don't want to rely on referees to make the right calls; I don't want to have to rely on my team being healthy; I don't want to rely on a certain star player to perform; I want to get everything in order so that on a very, very, bad day we can still win.

Hopefully you can learn from my pain too. There's no better teacher than adversity and pain in life.

Note: In 1999 the Alma College 1982-1983 baseball team was inducted into the Alma College Hall of Fame, and the baseball field was named for my coach, Klenk Field. At the dedication ceremony there was a presentation and video showing and highlighting Coach Klenk's baseball coaching career and the many greats that played at Alma College over the past 100 years. A slide show highlighted All-Americans and 10 or 15 of the greatest careers at Alma College. In that slide show popped up a slide of me in my baseball uniform. Coach Klenk said Greg Hatcher was not a great baseball player, but my slide was included because I was the hardest working baseball player in Alma College history, a player that he would always remember as a part of the great Alma College Baseball team. Doug Fraser, my best friend in college, was a three time All-Conference player and M.V.P. of the baseball team, and his picture was not in that slide show. He said, "Hatcher, you finally beat me at something in baseball."

In the end the coach and the player can have a great respect for each other even if you're not in the lineup. Things didn't work out for Coach Klenk and me to team together as I had hoped we could during those four years, but I consider him one of the greatest coaches I ever played for.

Today, Coach Klenk and I work closely together on our TKE Fraternity's Alumni Association. Although he is at least 20 years older than I, today I consider him a friend.

## Questions/Discussion

1. It is said we learn more from our losses or failures than your wins or successes.
   Can you think of a failure you've had that changed you forever?

> The thrill is not just in winning,
> but in the courage to join the race.

# Life Is a Competition

I love competition, I guess, as much as anybody. I get up each day and look forward to competing to get more business in my insurance agency. And I look forward to competing in the games that I will coach during the course of the week. I even love practice to prepare the kids to get ready for those competitions. As a young athlete, sometimes you ask yourself, "Am I tired of competing? Do I really want to compete all my life? Can't I just relax and watch some T.V. and not have to compete anymore?" I have asked some of those questions over time and I finally figured out that, really, you are competing in everything you do until you die. Sometimes I even think that may be what dying is about. When you are 95 years old and you don't have any energy left to compete, I guess that's when you die.

Actually, we all compete every single day. When children go to school, they are competing for grades to see who can get the As, the Bs, the Cs, and the Ds. When you go out for a sport at your school, you are competing every day to try to be the starting player on the team. And, there is someone on that team trying to get better to take your position. If you are a starter, then you are competing to be the most valuable player on the team, and every day someone else is also trying to win that award. When you practice all week and prepare for games, there is another team in another city trying to beat you and become the conference champion. You think when you graduate high school you won't have to compete anymore, but the competition only gets more serious! You go to college and you compete again in the classroom. They have class rankings, and they name the top student in the college. If you are trying to go to Medical School or Law School, they literally rank you based on your academic performance in the classroom; and the best Law Schools and Medical Schools get first pick of the students who scored the highest in college.

You might think, "Well, love is something you don't have to compete in." But sure enough, you find the guy or the girl you like, and guess what? Somebody else likes him or her too. You may be competing to see who that person will choose as their boyfriend or girlfriend.

You get out of college, and competition gets even fiercer. Now you try to get a job. Everybody out there is competing for the best-paying jobs so they can make money, buy a house and a car, and put clothes on their back and food in their stomachs. The individuals who don't compete well and don't get a job you will literally see living on the streets. Can you imagine not being good at getting a job and having to live under a bridge with no money for a toothbrush or toothpaste?

This world is pretty cruel at times, but competition is everywhere. If you think it's pretty cruel to have to live under a bridge, how would you like to live in Africa and be an animal? As the late Sam Walton once said, "In the jungle, when you wake up, you'd better be running. Because, no matter what animal you are, you have to kill something else to eat that day, and there is another animal trying to kill you for his breakfast." Even the king of the jungle has to get up and run. Although the lion is chasing a zebra for its breakfast, there are hunters out chasing the lions for their pretty pelts and for their meat. Walton, one of America's wealthiest businessmen, said he really enjoyed that analogy because it helped him understand that that was the way God made the world. We all had to get up and hit the ground running in order to eat, or we would be eaten.

It took me many years to finally understand competition and why God put it there. I finally understood that if we didn't have competition for everything, nothing would ever get done. We would be a society that lies around unmotivated, not trying to get better, and with no purpose or goal in mind. I have learned to embrace competition, and I have learned that the only way to protect myself from all this competition is to make myself the best I can be and better at what I do than almost anyone else out there. When I do that, I am as close as I can get to feeling some peace and relaxation, knowing I have paid the price. I have prepared myself to be better so that I can win those games, whether in sports, in business, or in the jungle in Africa. Then, after a good day of competition, I can enjoy a good night's rest. What really sets me free is simply enjoying the competition, which I certainly do. The thrill for me is not just in winning the race, but also in preparing, practicing, and actually running the race.

The movie, The Last Samurai, focuses on the samurai Warriors who, from the time they get up in the morning until they go to bed at night, are constantly preparing themselves and perfecting themselves in the art of war and self-defense. They get up each day and work on fighting with swords, knives, and bows & arrows. They try to perfect their art so that they are the very best because their lives depend on it. In their world someone everyday is trying to kill them and take their property and their food and their land, so they must prepare themselves to defend it. The ultimate in competition is when you have to be good at something or die, and this is what The Last Samurai was all about.

Today's world is much more civilized in that we compete in all things, and we don't stab each other with swords. However, the warfare is still very similar… if you are not successful in the working world, you may not have a house or a car, or good food to eat. Likewise, if you are not a competitor on the sports team you play on, you may sit on the bench and be upset the entire season. The only way to deal with this competition thing is to work hard enough and get good enough that you become the best at whatever it is you decide to do. Most of all, you must learn to enjoy the preparation for competition and the competition itself, because that's life.

I'll never forget a motivational speech I watched on television before the annual Army-Navy football game. A former football player and soldier who is now retired and doesn't play any more came into the locker room and talked to the boys about the big game they were going into and the big battle they would be fighting. He told them that even though they were nervous about the outcome of the game and their preparation, their greatest fear should not be of losing, but of waking up one day with no more battles to fight. For the competitor, waking up without competition is truly the saddest day of all.

Learn to be a competitor; learn to be the best at what it is you are doing; and you will have great satisfaction in your life. It is a way of life.

## Questions/Discussion

1. Do you enjoy competition, or dread it?
2. Should competition be a way of life?

CHAPTER

# 7

# Biscuits, Fleas, and Pump Handles

One of my favorite authors is motivational speaker Zig Ziglar. I've read all his books and listened to his tapes over and over, and they have had a profound influence on my life. I just wish I had learned about Ziglar when I was a high school kid so he could have impacted my sports career as he influenced my career as a businessman. Zig's messages are rarely aimed at making an impact on the athlete but are geared more toward adults and their roles at work and raising a family. One of my all-time favorite videotapes and audiotapes is his "Biscuits, Fleas, and Pump Handles." This little story could help any athlete better understand what it takes to make things work. Zig says in his story that if you understand Biscuits, Fleas, and Pump Handles, then you can become a great success. He is talking about business and personal success, but I think the principles work in sports as well. Zig's rendition of Biscuits, Fleas, and Pump Handles is much longer, but following is a short version of the message.

He described a neighbor lady who had a house next door to him when he was growing up. He said the biscuits she made were the best. But one day she said her biscuits got "cooked in the squat." Ziglar explains that biscuits, before they are cooked, are pretty thin. As they begin to cook, they kind of squat down before they actually rise and become nice plump biscuits. This particular day the biscuits got cooked in the squat and never became the plump, light biscuits the neighbor was known for. Zig said that many of us are like those biscuits. We intend to get out and do things, but sometimes we just get cooked in the squat and never get around to getting started. He says the key to achieving your goals in life is not to get cooked in the squat, but to get started and not to procrastinate. The hardest part of a three-mile run is the first step; the hardest part of achieving your goal many times is just simply to get started.

Then Zig compared us to fleas. He said you can put a bunch of fleas in a glass jar and put a piece of saran wrap over the top of it. Those fleas will bounce around in the jar and hit their heads on the top of that saran wrap for a while. Then they will learn how to jump just high enough not to hit the saran wrap because they get tired of hitting their heads. After a while you can take the saran wrap off the top of the jar; and the fleas, which now have freedom right above them, will never jump out of the jar. They have trained themselves to jump only so high. Ziglar says the same thing happens to all of us in life. We condition or train ourselves to be only so good; we decide that certain things are impossible. Then when the jar lid is wide open and our potential is unleashed we never achieve it because we simply don't try to jump out of the jar. He explains that the greatest flea trainer in the world was Roger Banister because Roger was the first man to break the four-minute mile. For years nobody ever thought the four-minute mile barrier could be broken. People ran race after race trying to do it, but nobody broke the four-minute barrier. Scientists and physiologists said the human body just couldn't do it, that nobody was born with a big enough oxygen intake, heart, etc. There were a million "reasons" why it couldn't be done.

Then Roger Banister devised a plan that ignored the "reasons." He got four people to each run a mile lap with him with a goal of 59 seconds a lap. He used the other runners to pace himself so he could be sure he'd get under the four-minute mile. He was the first to run the four-minute mile in an official race and prove that it could be done. Later that year several other runners broke the four-minute mark. Today, if you go to a college race at the major college level, eight people in one race will run a mile in under four minutes. As Zig said, "The human body didn't get that much better. It's just that people figured out that the flea could jump out of the jar, so now everybody was doing it.

The last analogy is that old water pump. Sometimes, you can just pump the handle up and down, and water will come out. At other times, you have to prime the pump by pouring water in before you start pumping that handle. Again, isn't it true in life that sometimes you have to put a little in before you get something out? The theory behind the pump handle is that you never know how many times you are going to have to pump to get the water to come out, but once you get the water coming out you barely have to put any pressure at all to keep it coming. That principle holds true in so many things we do. We never know how long or how hard we're going to have to work to get things going, but once they get going all we have to do is apply a little steady pressure and we'll get all the water we ever wanted. It's like a snowball building momentum. Once you get it going, success is pretty easy. The problem is that a lot of people don't have the patience, the discipline, or the persistence to stay in there and keep pumping that water pump until the water comes out. We never know if that water is one inch from the top or 100 yards down deep in the well, but if we just keep pumping hard enough and long enough and enthusiastically enough, we will eventually get water. And once we get water, all you have to do is apply a little steady pressure and you will have all the water you ever wanted.

Remember the Biscuits, Fleas, and Pump Handles story in life. Zig Ziglar's little story has been an inspiration in every area of my life, and I think you will find it helpful too.

## Questions/Discussion

1. What is the Biscuit a reminder of?
2. What does the flea teach us?
3. What is the point of the pump handle?
4. Have you ever been Cooked in the Squat? If so, what?

# Do What You Say You're Going to Do

In the movie Forrest Gump, Lieutenant Dan promised to be Forrest's first mate if he became a shrimp boat captain. Gump became a shrimp boat captain; and sure enough, the Lieutenant became his first mate. Why were we surprised when he kept his word?

It's amazing how many people say they're going to do something and then don't do it. This is a pet peeve of mine that will get me in a battle with a player, my wife, my kids, or friends quicker then anything. We all depend on each other to do what we say we're going to do. I am writing this chapter on the evening of Christmas dinner at the home of my brother-in-law. He had ordered lobsters from Maine for Christmas dinner and had talked to the people to make sure that they would arrive on Christmas day. Sure enough, at 5:30 on Christmas Day they were not there. After calling the company and realizing they just dropped the ball, he drove to Red Lobster and bought lobsters from them in order to get Christmas dinner prepared. Needless to say he was a little frustrated, but he did a great job of winning the ball-game and getting dinner on the table for Christmas.

This little example inspired this chapter: Do What You Say You're Going To Do. As a teammate, as a coworker, a student, or a friend you will gain a reputation in a heck of a hurry as a person that can be counted on to do something when you say you're going to do it.

A friend once made me a promise and then played a joke on me and pretended not to do what he said he would do. When I fell for the joke he told me I was a fool because I should have known that if he said he was going to do something he always came through. He was right. I should have known better. This friend had never let me down when he promised to do something. I remember thinking, "Gosh, this is odd that he didn't come through." His batting average was 100 percent.

Doing what you say you will do will earn you respect with your family, your friends, your teammates, and your clients. It will also establish your reputation in the community as someone who can be trusted. Not coming through will be something that the people you let down will never forget, and you may have to take years rebuilding their confidence.

I try to be the kind of person about whom people say: "If Greg said he would do it, it will be done."

## Questions/Discussion

1. When you say something, do you back it up? Are you good on your word?
2. Would your friends say you fulfill your promises?
3. As an employer, would you hire someone who doesn't do what they say they are going to do?

"I can't imagine looking back and
knowing I didn't give my best."
—BILL TRANUM, MY FATHER-IN-LAW
All Southwest Conference Arkansas Razorback Football Player

# No Regrets

"I wish I had done that."

"I wish I could do this over again."

"If only I had known then what I know now".

All of us have heard these laments over and over again:

Most of us have regrets about the way we've done some things in the past. There's nothing quite as wonderful as finishing a chapter in your life then looking back and having no regrets, knowing that you gave it your very all.

As a youth soccer coach, football coach, and basketball coach over the years I've had a lot of parents come to me and wonder if I'm pushing the kids too hard or if the pressure is too intense – or just too much work for kids in the fourth, fifth, sixth, seventh, and eighth grades. I always ask them to think back to the best teacher or coach they ever had. I tell them that I always know the common denominator of those teachers and coaches: they're the ones that pushed you the hardest; the ones that weren't always your favorites at the time because they were tough; but when you look back, they are the ones that made a difference.

When I look back as a coach I know I won't be a perfect coach for all the kids I've been involved with, but I don't think I'll have regrets about setting the bar high enough for them and challenging them and even demanding and pulling them, dragging them to be the very best they could be. I always say a great coach is someone that can pull you further than you could ever have gone by yourself. In the end, however, no coach can do it without a kid that wants to do it for himself or herself.

There will be many chapters in your life. What I encourage you to do is to lay it all on the line, to work your hardest, leave no regrets and be the best that you can be. Skipping that party to go to practice, getting a good night's sleep, eating the right food, doing your extra 20 minutes workout, being the first one to practice and the last one out will all be worth it.

Some people will say, "Why would you want to do all those things?" You're missing out on all the fun. I can only promise you one thing: those very people who are telling you that you are missing out on all the fun will look back years later at you who paid the price, and they will be the ones with the regrets. They will be the ones saying, "If only I had had someone to push me a little more; if only I had worked a little harder, I could have been great."

In the end, paying a great price to be the best that you can be has been, and always will be, worth it. Play like one of my members of the Wall of Fame, Pete Rose. Give 100 percent and leave behind no regrets.

(Okay, Pete has some regrets, but not for the effort he gave on the field.)

## Questions/Discussion

1. What regrets do you have:

2. With your family?

3. With your school?

4. With your sports?

5. With your job?

6. Have you ever done anything where you have no regrets? How does it feel?

CHAPTER

# 10

# Just Win the Damn Ballgame!

I began learning the principles of Outrageous Service in my first job after high school graduation. Along with three other college students, I was hired to work for the summer for Morley Fraser, who was head football and baseball coach for Albion College and one of the greatest motivators of all time. Morley was the kind of fiery coach about whom books are written and movies are made.

But Morley never made it to "the big time" because he chose to stay at an NCAA Division III school in Michigan, Albion College. He and his wife had three sons and three daughters, and Morley passed up many offers to coach Division I and II schools. He chose to stay in this small Michigan town where he had the time to see his kids play sports and where he could coach his own athletes. Each of his three sons quarterbacked the high school football team. One was killed in a car wreck in high school, and the other two went on to play in college and become head football coaches. The girls were also athletes, and all three married coaches. It is an understatement to say that the Fraser family was competitive.

During the summer, Morley served as Director of Continuing Education for Albion College. The program included approximately 40 different camps and conferences that ranged from cheerleading camps to IBM business conferences, and from church groups to sports camps.

Morley's "Big Four," as we were called, were on call 24 hours a day, and our job description was to do whatever it took to keep the campers and staff happy. The ultimate goal was to ensure that every contract would be renewed for the next summer.

The Big Four, all under age 22, were armed with master keys to the college campus. Our primary responsibility was to plan the leisure and sports activities. But, we were also responsible for seeing that conference rooms were set up, the residential rooms were clean, the laundry was picked up and any other task that affected the campers' satisfaction.

We often had as many as four conferences in the same week. At the beginning of each conference, Morley called us in to outline the game plan and assign responsibilities to each of the Big Four. The duties were broad, but the mission was simple: "Do whatever it takes to make these campers happy and Win the Damn Ballgame."

As a football coach, Morley knew that there are many ways to win a game. You can pass; you can run; you can play great defense; you can have great special teams play; you can make wonderful play calls. But Morley also knew that all that matters when the game is over is who has the winning score. He didn't care what method we chose as long as we played by the rules and won.

Morley often told us that each of us had a different set of skills, and we were to utilize those skills to make the customers happy. We took little old ladies to church; we took men's groups to taverns; sometimes we rushed people to the airport; other times we went to the local diner to get special food for someone or to the drug store to get a prescription filled. There was no job too big or too small for us to do, and any hour of the day or night was "convenient" for us.

I remember picking up hundreds of bags of dirty linen from the dormitories and loading them on the linen truck in 85-degree heat. The smell was unbelievable.

I also remember getting to have a few beers with the instructors from the cheerleading camps. This was quite a treat for a 19-year-old boy.

In the first couple of years with Morley, I would go into his office and ask a question about what to do about some problem at one of the conferences. Sometimes he would give me suggestions and help me decide what to do. However, if I brought him a problem he thought I could solve on my own, he would simply look me in the eye and say, "Hatcher, get out of my office and Win the Damn Ballgame." It was a unique style of coaching and development, but a very effective one that I have incorporated in my business. In almost all situations, employees can figure out how to solve the problems if we allow them to use their initiative.

I was not always the brightest or the most talented member of Morley's Big Four, but I will never forget what he told me when I left after working for him for four summers. He said that I did not always do things exactly the way he would do them, but that he had never had anyone work for him who was as good at figuring out a way to win the ballgame. That was high praise coming from Morley Fraser.

The most important thing I learned from Morley and Albion College was that good customer service is an attitude. Fraser taught me that every detail is important, and no detail is too big or too small to take care of it if it helps win the ballgame. The coach helped me develop the ability to probe, ask questions, listen to people and figure out what they want – then go get it for them. That was the beginning of my concept of Outrageous Service and, for you in sports, to "Winning the Damn Ballgame."

## Questions/Discussion

1. Are you the kind of person that figures out what it takes to win?
2. Can you think of a situation when you went outside the box to win the ballgame?

# 11

# Red Shirt Your Freshman Year

I've learned a lot from people who are older and wiser than I. One of the main reasons they are wiser is that they have had more experiences, and they've had more time to look back on those experiences and see how they might have done it differently. If I were advising any of my kids on playing Division I college sports I would advise all of them to red shirt their freshman year in almost all situations. No matter how good you are, and even if you get a lot of playing time your freshman year, it's hard to believe that anybody wouldn't be a better athlete after getting a year's experience.

It's a difficult adjustment to go from living at home with your parents to living on a college campus and traveling on a sports team that's highly competitive. It takes a while to get to know your new coaches and teammates and to learn all the new systems. That's why very, very few freshmen ever start in that first year or get anywhere near the amount of playing time they do in future years.

I remember as a college athlete the magical sophomore year I was no longer intimidated by any of the athletes on my team, and I understood the system; and everything just seemed to come a lot easier. I was a better student and knew the ropes of college life, and all of that affected my athletic career positively. Certainly if had taken a red shirt, and my sophomore year could have been my freshman year on the team I would have been a lot better athlete. The problem is most freshman come in cocky and want to play right away. They don't want to wait, or they don't have the discipline to wait and go through that red shirt year.

You only get to go to college once, and it can be the best four or five years of your life. So why not stretch it out a little bit, learn your way around the college, get accustomed to the coaches, possibly even let your body mature. (I grew 30 pounds my freshman year, as I was a late bloomer). All these things considered, taking that first year to learn the system, understand college, and get to know your teammates will help you have a better career. And, the coaches will love it when they know they can get four good starting years out of you because you spent a year being patient and getting prepared. Waiting takes discipline, and discipline gets rewarded. If you've got the discipline to put up with not getting to play that first year, there will be a lot of rewards for the next four.

## Questions/Discussion

1. They say discipline is delaying personal gratification. Would you be willing to practice hard for a full year and redshirt if you knew you would be better the next year, or would you rather play now even if you wouldn't be as good in the long run?

CHAPTER

# 12

# On Your Worst Day You Must Still Be Very Good

In sales and customer service, on your worst day you must still be very good. Customers operate on the principle of "What have you done for me lately?" You can take care of a customer for years and then fail to deliver what he wants just once and put that account in jeopardy. This is the flip side of "Outrageous Service." One bad experience can negate years of extraordinary service.

Think about it in your own life. Have you ever had a bad experience in a store where you had done business for years? Someone was short with you, didn't treat you right, or had a poor attitude toward you? You may have made a decision never to go in that store again. Furthermore, you may have told your friends about your experience, causing them to think twice before doing business with that store.

The bottom line is that a company simply cannot afford "bad days" that affect customer service. Regardless of how bad the employee feels or how many things have gone wrong, the employee must remember that every contact with the customer is crucial. One failure to render good service could mean the loss of that account.

Customers who get the kind of service they expect from a business are not likely to talk about it. A customer who is irate, or even slightly annoyed, with the service is almost certain to tell someone. People talk loudly and passionately when their emotions are involved. If our customers are going to be excited, we want them to be excited about the "outrageously positive" service we've delivered.

It takes a super-special effort to get customers to take the time and make the effort to tell others about the service they received from our company. The great news is that the extra effort it takes to make customers happy also makes employees feel good. And, it is a lot more effective and less expensive way to get new customers than advertising on the radio, in the newspapers, or on TV.

Be very good on your worst days, and you will get free advertising. Your customers will be walking billboards for you.

Now, what does this have to do with sports? In sports, just as in business, you have to be better than your competition on your worst day, or they'll be starting some games you wanted to start.

For you or your team to win championships you're going to have to win games without your best efforts…in other words, on your worst day you must still be very good. For example, if you want to win the state cross country championship or if you want to win the Tour De France seven times like Lance Armstrong, you had better prepare yourself so well that even on a bad day when you are ill or just don't feel up to par, you can still beat your opponent.

Michael Jordan scored 55 points in an NBA finals game moments after throwing up all day. Lance Armstrong won a Tour De France after a bad bike crash during the race and after overcoming cancer; and Walt Garrison played a Super Bowl with a broken ankle.

On their worst days they were all still very good.

## Questions/Discussion

1. What are you like on your worst day?
2. On your worst day do you whine and complain, or make the most of the circumstances?

# 13

A hundred years from now it will not matter what my bank account was, the sort of house I lived in, or the kind of car I drove... but the world may be different because of the way I treated people.

# Keep Things in the Proper Perspective

As I got in the car after visiting with my old boss, friend, mentor, and one of the most famous coaches in the state of Michigan's history, I thought how important it is to keep things in the proper perspective. The man I had just visited was Morley Fraser, age 82. I had chatted with him, prayed with him, and wished him the best of luck just a couple of days before he would undergo chemotherapy treatment. Morley gave me his last life lesson that day: he taught me how to die. He had been diagnosed with terminal cancer two weeks earlier, and they wanted to start treatment immediately. He said no, he wanted to go home and sit in his chair and get his house in order before his battle with chemotherapy and cancer. He wrote out his funeral arrangements, named his pallbearers, pulled out all his life insurance policies and had meetings with his wife and children just in case things didn't work out. He wanted to tell his friends and his family goodbye should he not make it through chemotherapy. Driving back to the airport to come back to Arkansas after my visit I thought of Morley and how he always taught me to keep things in the proper perspective.

Certainly the sporting events that we play seemed like the most important thing in the world to us at the time, but they really don't mean much in the overall scheme of life. What matters are our relationships—with God, our family, and with other people. It reminded me of my own little prayer that I said before every athletic contest when I was in college. The prayer was short and sweet and went like this, "Lord, help me to behave like a Christian, be as competitive as possible, and give it my very best." The prayer reminded me that there were a lot of people watching and that I needed to behave like a Christian and be a good example. It reminded me that it was okay to be as competitive as possible while being a Christian, and that it didn't matter so much whether I won or lost but whether or not I had given my best effort for the day.

That prayer carried me through a lot of losses and a lot of victories. It gave me the courage to compete sometimes in wrestling matches against opponents who were All-Americans when I was a freshman and really didn't stand much of a chance. It allowed me to battle on the field and be a good Christian as soon as the match was over. It also took a lot of pressure off me. You see, when you have things in the proper perspective, you understand that God is the most important, your relationship with your family and your friends is next, and you are third. That helps you to worry less about whether you made the shot or missed the shot or whether you won the match or lost because you know that you gave it your absolute best. Win, lose, or draw I was always able to live with that, and it helped take the pressure off.

Go out there and have fun in the games you play; give it your very best and leave behind no regrets. Just play hard and everything will work out.

I still have a Fellowship of Christian Athletes poster on my wall with a picture of a little six-year-old boy in a football uniform watching the bigger boys in a huddle. The message is clear: every time you walk out on an athletic field there's a little boy or a little girl who is watching and looks up to you. Make sure you set a good example and behave like a Christian on the field. This picture motivated me to always have good sportsmanship on the field.

Keep things in the proper perspective. The pressure will come off; and you'll realize that it's only a game. But, it's also a game worth giving your best.

NOTE: Morley made it through the first round of chemotherapy a victor, but two weeks later the cancer came back, and the second round of chemotherapy killed him. He survived heart bypass surgery, a pacemaker, a hip replacement, and a round of chemotherapy. As courageous and honorable as he was in dying, it's the courage, passion, and compassion in the way he lived his life that I remember.

## Questions/Discussion

1. What types of things have you let get out of perspective?

2. If you died today, how would others describe you? Would you like their description?

CHAPTER

# 14

# Setting Goals My Way

When I was growing up, especially by the time I got to high school, I was always setting goals. The goal might be to be first team All-Conference in wrestling or to be the most valuable player on the baseball team. My goal might have been to make the National Honor Society, or to be named the Outstanding Senior Graduate. Sometimes my goals might have been to lead the team in batting average or to win the cross-country race. It seems like all my goals had something to do with receiving an award or getting some kind of accolade. During those high school years what I learned was that when I set my goal to be first team All-Conference I'd end up getting second team All-Conference. When my goal was to win the cross-country race, I might end up finishing second. When my goal was to make the National Honor Society and it required a 3.5 grade average, I ended up with a 3.46; and when my goal was to be the most valuable player in baseball, I'd end up getting the second most votes.

The problem with setting goals that are based on awards or accolades is that we tend to work just hard enough to reach that level and invariably something always goes wrong along the way. Maybe somebody has a better day that day; you have a bad game or two along the way; but the number one thing that goes wrong along the way is that when you set a goal like these you tend to work just hard enough to get there instead of working hard to shoot way past the goal. The other problem is that the goal you set may have been lofty but still short for your potential. After having a series of near misses on goals as a younger man I decided to change my goals to a very simple one. That goal was to do the best I could at everything I did, to absolutely lay it all out on the line and in each game I played to be the best that I could be.

In college I actually ended up becoming a better athlete than I was in high school. I don't think it was that my body changed; I think it was that my goal changed. When I changed my goal to simply be the best I could be I ended up achieving the goals I would have set plus so much more. I actually accomplished things that I would have never even thought I could achieve simply by just deciding to be the best that I could be and unleashing my entire potential.

It's tempting when you're young to want those accolades and those awards, but in the end the greatest goal and the most satisfying goal is to lay it all on the line and be the best that you can be. The goal of being the best you can be is not a cop out, as it is so many times after you play a bad game and a parent or somebody will say, oh, you played well; you did your best. No, this is the kind of best that only a Warrior and a competitor can understand. Holding yourself accountable for maximum effort on every play and doing your best at this level is much, much harder than just playing well or winning any particular award. The funny thing is when I wasn't shooting for all those awards I ended up winning them anyway and a few extra I never would have even thought of. Doing your very best, achieving your maximum potential, is the hardest goal you'll ever achieve.

## Questions/Discussion

1. When you study for a test, do you study to score a 100% or to get a certain grade?

2. Is perfection something you should strive for? (Hint: John Wooden always strove for it, but knew it was unattainable)

# Organization and Preparation

CHAPTER
# 15

# Write It Down

When I was a collegiate wrestler at Alma College in Michigan I had a great coach. His name was Bruce Dickey, and he understood that little details made a difference. He had come to Alma College to take over the wrestling program, which literally had won no matches the year before his arrival. Coach Dickey was a solid collegiate wrestler, but his ability as a coach was not totally based on his ability as a wrestler. He was a great coach because of his intensity, hard work, and desire to be the best. Coach Dickey went to clinic after clinic, continuing to learn how to be a wrestling coach. He took his note cards with him and his notepad and he wrote everything down. He read books; he studied videotapes; he did everything he could do to improve himself. He also spent a lot of time recruiting good wrestlers.

It only took him five years to build a wrestling program that not only was ranked nationally, but more importantly, stopped Olivet College's streak of nine consecutive Conference Championships. I'll never forget Olivet College's T-shirts that said "Do it again for 10". Because of Coach Dickey they never got there. When Coach Dickey broke the streak, he not only won his first conference title, but he won three conference titles in a row and never lost another conference match until he retired at Alma after those three years.

Coach Dickey would show us new moves on the wrestling mat – one or two new moves each day. He told all of us to get a little 3 x 5 note card box and have some note cards in it so that when he showed moves we could write down the moves and how to execute them, step by step. Most people would think this a little ridiculous to have all these athletes with their pen and note card in hand. He told us if we wanted to be great we needed to do it. At the beginning all the wrestlers had their note card boxes, but as the weeks passed the number of boxes got down to two or three. After a month or so I was the only one who still had my note card box. You see, I was a freshman eager to get better, and I was not the star wrestler. I was willing to do anything to become a better wrestler so I did exactly what Coach Dickey asked us to do.

Four years later that forest green plastic note card box had athletic tape wrapped all around it, and it was full of moves I had learned over those four years. I learned then the importance of writing things down. I could go back through my note cards at night, re-review the moves, visualize them in my head, and become a better wrestler. It has been 20 years since I wrestled at Alma College, but I still have my green note card box. It is a symbol of the blood, sweat, and tears and hard work I put in as an Alma College wrestler.

Today I employ with my children many of those techniques that Coach Dickey taught me with the note cards. For example, I've learned that if you write something down you're a lot more likely to remember it. If you write it down 10 times in a row you're really likely to remember it. If you're trying to change a bad habit you may need to write it down 50 times.

One of the things I've learned from coaching girls is that it's not their nature to be physical and rough. You have to constantly do drills and encourage girls to be physical whereas you don't have to say anything to boys and they're in there battling right from the get go. Many times after coaching my daughter when she hasn't been physical enough I'll ask her to write down ten times before the next game: "I will be physical today." I may ask her to write another sentence that says, "I will dive on the floor for the loose ball," or "I will help my team by rebounding," or "I will go to the hole in basketball and I will create contact versus avoiding it." These are many of the sentences that she's written repeatedly over the years. What I've found is that when we take the time to write these sentences over and over and over just before a game, she executes very well in the areas we have written about.

Zig Ziglar says that a person that has a To Do List written down at the beginning of each day will make twice as much money on average as the person who doesn't. Given equal ability between two athletes, the one who writes things down and studies them—and more importantly, keeps track of and maintains them, will be twice the athlete as the one who doesn't do those things. The more I coach sports, the more I do business, and the more I deal with people, the more I find that success is as much about desire and hard work as it is about anything else. If you are truly an athlete that desires to be the best, you will write down the things you need to improve on and change in games; you will write your sentences over and over and over to help yourself change; and you may even have a little "to do" list that you read over reminding you of the things you need to do each game day.

It has been said that the difference between a winner and a champion is that a winner wins some of the time, and a champion wins all of the time. I would say there are many people who can write things down some of the time, but the champion will be the one who writes things down and studies them every single day and every single game to get better. It's a simple blueprint for success; but even as you read this chapter, fewer than one in 100 of you will ever get around to doing it on a regular basis. If you are the one in 100, I can assure you we will see you at the top. The choice is yours...write it down if you want to be great.

## Questions/Discussion

1. Do you write ideas down when they cross your mind?
2. Do you have a "To Do" list today?
3. Do you know anyone that writes down new ideas when they hear them?
4. Do you know anyone who has a "To Do" list each day? Are they successful?

CHAPTER

# 16

# Getting Organized

One of the most frustrating things about being a coach and parent with young players is trying to help them get organized. It's just not natural for them to worry about details, since their parents drive them everywhere, pack their bags in many situations, make their meals, take them to school and pick them up from school. Parents get them to the places they need to go and get them there on time. As a result, kids don't learn a lot of responsibility. Most of them don't even wake up to an alarm clock; their parents tap them on the shoulder and give them a kiss on the cheek when it's time to get up. Making the transition from Mommy and Daddy taking care of everything to doing it on their own can be a big adjustment if the parents haven't pushed them a little bit along the way.

By the time my oldest daughter was in the seventh grade, I had purchased her a Palm Pilot and was encouraging her to enter all her stuff into the Palm. This embarrassed her because none of the other kids at school worried about these things, and she didn't want to look like a geek. I explained to her that if she wanted to be great she wouldn't worry about what others thought. It was not easy to get her to make the transition. Eventually I bought her a small day planner so she could enter in her basketball games, soccer games, etc. and list her friends' phone numbers, fax numbers, e-mail addresses, and cell phone numbers. Again, this was not really a cool thing to do and certainly not a habit she was used to. At the time I write this she is not nearly as organized as she'll want to be some day, but she is probably more organized than most tenth graders. You see, people who are well organized will know what they need to pack for this basketball practice or soccer practice or tennis match, and they will know when they need to pack it. They will be able to look at a planner and know whether they need some energy bars or an extra water in the backpack, and they will know if they need to pack a uniform. When kids have to worry and call mom about the uniform they forgot, the soccer cleats that are missing, or the shin guards they don't have, it is very stressful and it will detract their attention away from the game. There will be less time for visualization; there may be no quiet time to get ready for the game if you have to figure out where your shoes or your warm-ups are. Furthermore, coaches tend to get tougher and tougher if you come to practice without your practice jerseys or your game uniform. You may get penalized and not be able to play in a game. Eventually, kids learn the hard way; but they've wasted a lot of warm-up time and dealt with a lot of stress that they wouldn't have had if they had just gotten organized. If you want to be a champion in anything, get more organized than anyone else.

To this day you'll never find me without my cell phone and my Palm Pilot on my hip. It will be there whether I'm wearing sweats, a suit, or casual clothes. The only time it comes off is when I go to bed. I'm amazed at how much more I can get done with these tools than a person who is unorganized. You can always identify the people who are unorganized because they are the ones who call you and say, "Can you give me so-and- so's phone number?" "What time is the game?" or "Can you call and remind me?" If you have your planner or palm pilot you'll never have to do any of these things because when they come up you simply log them in and you have them forever. Can getting organized help you win a championship? You bet it can! And being organized gets even more important as you move up the chain of command to coach, General Manager, or owner.

## Questions/Discussion

1. Do you have an organizational system? Why or why not?

2. Do you feel more at ease when you're organized? Why or why not?

If you don't know where you're going,
you will end up somewhere else.
—YOGI BERRA

CHAPTER

# 17

# Your Mission Statement

You would never ever think of building a house without a floor plan. You wouldn't drive from California to New York without a road map. Why in the world would you go through life without a set of goals and a mission statement to guide you on your way? Every person needs to take the time to write their own mission statement and set a plan so they can sail through life directly on course to achieve their mission. If you put a boat in the water and try to sail across the sea and you get just a few degrees off, you could end up far away from your destination. The same is true for all of us in our lives. When we are young we hope that we will live to be 100, that we will stay fit, be in great shape, have a wonderful job, a loving spouse, and wonderful children, and make plenty of money. Somewhere along the way most of us end up struggling with our health and fitness; marriage can be a challenge; and very few people ever reach the success they had once hoped for in the business world.

I believe the key to achieving your goals is to have a mission statement, which is a list of your life goals with a line drawn in the sand. Just a list of goals is not enough. A mission statement also identifies what you are willing to give up and what you are not willing to give up along the way. It has a moral compass and a philosophy. In fact, your mission statement could be referred to as your philosophy of life. Take some time now and write out your mission statement; have it laminated; and put it in your school notebook, your briefcase, your purse, your Palm Pilot, your planner, your organizer, or whatever it is that you carry around everyday so that you can refer to it frequently. If you check your mission statement from time to time you'll see when you're off course and you can make the right decisions to get you back on course so that you'll reach your destination. If you don't follow your plan and if you don't check it regularly, you'll end up at another destination, one you will not be proud of and one you will regret.

Following is my mission statement that I don't mind sharing with all of you. Take the categories that I have and write your own mission statement. If there's something missing in my mission statement that applies to your life, add a couple of new categories. Of all the chapters in this book, this one may be the most important because if you don't take the time to write your mission statement right now, unfortunately, you have a 99% chance of not reaching your potential and your goals. Zig Ziglar says that people who write things down, that have a "to do" list each day make twice as much money on average as those who don't. As Nike says, "Just Do It!"…and I mean now.

## Questions/Discussion

1. Are you going to write your mission statement after reading this chapter? Why or why not?

# Mission Statement

<u>Son of God</u> – My mission is to become more spiritually active, attend church regularly, take time to read the Bible each day, and strive to keep my life in proper perspective. It is important that I ask God for forgiveness on a regular basis and live more of a model life not for others to perceive, but for God to perceive.

<u>Life, Family, Children</u> – It is my desire to put my wife as the #1 person in my life and to have her to come before all other things. I always need to be available for my children, both in person, by phone, and simply being there for the important functions in their life. In regard to my family, I need to have contact with my immediate family members at least every month and set up a special family reunion each year, just like I have a Musketeers reunion.

<u>Be a Good Neighbor-Community Leader</u> – My goal in life is to continue to help other people better themselves and make improvements in their life. This could be done as a youth coach, a community speaker, through donations to certain charities, and by playing an active role with special individuals that need help.

<u>President of the Hatcher Agency</u> – My goal is to have vision and take time to plan for the future so that The Hatcher Agency will continue to grow and prosper and provide better opportunities for all of those that work with me. My goal is to provide the best customer service in America and eventually write books on our agency and become a household name when it comes to customer service.

<u>Motivator-Teacher within The Agency</u> – My job is to have people that come to the Hatcher Agency leave as better human beings and better workers. Our goal is not only to teach how to do insurance, but to keep things exciting through special challenges, trips for employees, events, and training sessions.

Salesman – My goal is to never stop being a salesman, but to always stay active with our accounts. I will need to continue to stay out in the field in order to keep our agency growing. The Agency should grow through my sales and continue to be serviced by the very best staff.

Staff – Continue to hire only All-Star Staff, and pay them very well.

My Body – My goal is to push my body to its absolute limit without breaking it. I will be committed to staying in great shape and taking time to work out regularly to reduce stress and to feel and look better.

Social Affairs – Friends - My goal is to take time to spend with friends and not talk about work so that I will become a more well-rounded individual and make my wife and children happy people. All work and no play will not give me a well-rounded life.

Education – My goal is to read one book per month, attend 3 workshops a year and take one professional test a year. Also, I need to read the paper prior to 6:40 each morning.

Vacation – I should take 3 family vacations a year: One that I plan, one that my wife plans, and one that the kids plan.

This mission statement updated on August 17, 2005.

CHAPTER

# 18

# Be On Time

I know of no one who is stricter about being on time than a coach, a customer, or your boss. My recommendation is that you set your watch 15 minutes fast so you'll always be alerted to be on time. At The Hatcher Agency we have "Hatcher Time", which requires all clocks on all phones, watches, etc. to be 15 minutes fast as I expect everybody to be where they're supposed to be 15 minutes early. This way if something goes wrong along the way you'll still be on time. People who are chronically late always try to get there right at the last second; and then if something goes wrong, as it always does – an extra phone call, the urge to use the bathroom, misplaced keys, etc. – they'll be late.

The other good thing about being a little early is it takes away the stress of worrying about being late. There is nothing as comforting as getting someplace 15 minutes early and having time to arrange your thoughts, go to the bathroom, and get ready for your practice, your appointment, or whatever it is you might be going to.

Finally, I've never known anyone who was elected Captain of his or her sports team, President of his or her company, or any other leadership position who did not value being on time. Nobody really respects people who are late, nor do they trust them as leaders or with important responsibilities. You'll meet people who are chronically late all their lives, and you'll meet people that are always on time. Those who are on time respect other people's time enough to be on time. People who are chronically late do not respect that time, and therefore are not respected as much by others. Being on time is an attitude; and regardless of what age you are, it's time to get it right. Wear a watch and be sure to be at practice on time.

Note: I have a player on my basketball and soccer teams who has already figured this out. She absolutely starts watching the clock before a practice or a game and makes sure that whoever is driving her gets her there 15 to 20 minutes early. You can always count on her being on time, as she obsesses about being late. This little detail allows us to trust her, to give her more responsibility on the team.

## Questions/Discussion

1. Are you a person who is on time, or usually late?
2. When you arrive 10 - 15 minutes early do you feel less stressed in your life? Why?

# If You're Late, Walk in Like You Own the Place

In spite of the emphasis in the previous chapter on being on time, and as much as I value punctuality, there have been circumstances when I have had to be late to certain meetings, practices, etc. There have been situations where I had to choose between cutting off an appointment with somebody who was very upset or needed me desperately and being late for another meeting. I may have been riding with someone else who made me late. Or, some catastrophe happened with the kids that even my 15-minute advance didn't fix. When these situations occur, it's important not to walk in late with sweat running down your face and looking embarrassed. Learn to walk in as if you own the place and you are late because you had something very important going on and everybody in the world knows that.

I learned this trait from my old boss at Blue Cross Blue Shield, who when he walked in late to a meeting, made it seem like he had just been closing a sale on Wal-Mart, and that's why he was five minutes late to the meeting.

My boss was six foot, six inches tall, and when he walked in he commanded a presence; but he never let you see him sweat in those difficult situations. I have had to walk in late to a Rotary meeting, a board meeting, a staff meeting, and even a game I was coaching. In these situations I walk confidently and act confidently when there is nothing else to do. If you haven't made a practice of being late, people will understand; and they will believe that something urgent happened. It's important not to be arrogant, but you can acknowledge that you're ready to go and leave no room for bantering on about why you are late. Your attitude can say, "Let's get to the subject matter and make things work."

## Questions/Discussion

1. When something is wrong, are you better off to make a big production or give an excuse, or is it better to be courteous but move forward?

CHAPTER

# 19

# You Need a Fitness Diary

Measuring things is extremely important to success in anything. Businesses keep track of every sale they made and every expense incurred, and they keep score at the end of the year to see if they've had a better year than the year before. Your teachers give you grades, and they keep a scholastic record on each of you. These report cards and transcripts are basically scorecards of your performance over all your years in school. They determine whether you get into a good college.

If a person wants to be a great athlete or be in shape, the same holds true. You need to start a Fitness Diary—possibly a calendar that keeps track of the fitness activities that you do each day to make yourself better. When you are a young person, this calendar may need to be on your bathroom sink, and after you brush your teeth each morning or night you can record what you did the previous day. As your journal gets more and more filled with entries, you can be sure that you're improving as an athlete. Keep track of your workouts and your game performances in this calendar; and you may find that when you had a particularly good game, it followed two or three types of specific work-outs, or even a day off, that helped make you successful. It's your scorecard.

Runners keep track of their mileage on logs, and it's interesting that as they get in more miles or more quality miles their times drop as well. This is a good piece of information to keep track of and something that will help each athlete get better. Simply by keeping score of your workouts you'll be able to monitor your success and compare month to month and year to year. Keep score, and it will motivate you to put in more time and effort which will make you a better player.

## Questions/Discussion

1. Is there anything in your life that you track or keep statistics or records of?
   Is this particular item important to you? Why do you track this item?

You wouldn't put cheap motor oil in a
Ferrari or feed a race horse fried food.

# Eating Right

We've all heard in computer terminology that "garbage in equals garbage out." The same thing really applies to your body as well. When we are kids our taste buds and just our age dictate that we'll like sweets more than at other times in our lives. Our body also has such a high metabolism that we can eat just about whatever we want and we won't get fat. The problem is, we develop habits of eating too much junk food or a lot of sweets, and these habits don't go away. That's why people, as they get older, continue to gain weight. The bad eating habits continue while the body's metabolism changes and doesn't burn all those calories as fast.

Once we were in the middle of a basketball tournament, and it was kind of a unique weekend in that our fourth grade girls' team would play nine games over a course of a Saturday and Sunday. The reason for this was that we played in two leagues, the fourth grade league and the fifth and sixth grade league, so our fourth graders got to play five games on Saturday and four on Sunday. Obscene by almost any parent's standard, but for the true Warrior we all understand that this would put a smile on anybody's face. Every now and then people run marathons or 100-mile races, or they do something else extreme. After accomplishing the task I have never heard anybody say, "I wish I hadn't done that great feat that I just finished." They may be in pain; they might even say they might not do it again; but they'll never tell you that they regret doing something that was a worthwhile accomplishment. Sure enough, none of my fourth graders have looked me in the eyes and said, "I regret playing nine games that weekend." Of course, I did get a few comments from parents that maybe that seemed like a bunch, but in the end hard work is always worth it.

One thing that happened during that tournament as we were trying to get our kids energized between games, we had a couple of the kids who drank Coca-Cola and Cherry Coke just before they were to play. Let me assure you being smart about what you eat and drink is just as important as being smart about how well you train. Soft drinks have a ton of sugar in them, and that sugar goes right to the stomach; and it pulls a lot of the water from the body to help digest that sugar. Nobody knows this better than Jimmy Connors who drank a Pepsi just before the semifinal match of the US Open and ended up throwing up and having all kinds of cramps during his match. Be sure to drink water, Gatorade, and maybe eat an energy bar if you're in the middle of a big time athletic event. You have to learn what foods work for you, as making a mistake can be fatal.

One reason to eat right when you're growing up is so that you'll have good habits when you get older, and you'll have a better quality of life. If you're a sports person, there is another reason, however; and that is that eating right will improve your performance. The most critical times to eat right are the two days before an athletic activity. When you're young, eating a lot of pasta two nights before and the night before the game is a way of carbohydrate loading, or carb loading as it is often called. Spaghetti and pasta turn to sugar while the body is processing them, and that produces energy. This will help a runner run longer or faster and help any athlete have more strength and endurance. Athletes also need to eat more protein because protein is needed to help build muscle. And, more importantly, protein helps us recover from muscle soreness associated with playing sports.

In summary, there are two types of eating right for the athlete. One is avoid eating sweets and instead load your body up with lots of protein to build muscle on a consistent basis and help with recovery. The other is carb-loading and fueling your body prior to an event to get your very best performance. We all know that there are some days that we feel great and have a great day playing on the field; and there are other days when we didn't feel so good, and we don't know why we feel good from one day to the other. Feeling good or feeling bad is determined most by what we eat prior to our workout. Different sports may require different foods, so be sure to consult with your coach, personal trainer, or dietician to find out what you should eat. It is also true that different people's bodies respond to foods differently, and you may have to experiment to find out what works for you.

Athletes have to be extremely careful about taking medications before or during a performance. My daughter and I learned this the hard way. She had been running cross country races for a couple of years and had always had excellent times, winning almost all her races. A few days prior to one race, she fell and bruised her butt bone while horsing around, and it had been hurting all week. About 30 minutes prior to the race, I told her she should take some Aleve, and that might make her feel better. We found out that Aleve with water on an empty stomach before a two-mile race was not a good idea. She threw up four or five times at about the half-mile mark and had her worst race ever. To her credit, she still gutted it out, but it wasn't her normal performance. I learned then that experimenting with any type of medication shouldn't be done for the first time prior to a race, but should be tried first at practice.

I talked to my personal trainer about my daughter's diet, and he recommended spaghetti and fruit for breakfast in the morning prior to a cross-country race. The spaghetti would give her carbohydrates that turn to sugar; the fruit is a natural source of sugar to help give her extra energy. That combination with a lot of water seemed to work best for her. Don't kid yourself, what you eat will make a huge difference in your performance and might be the difference between winning and losing.

## Questions/Discussion

1. Is eating right a goal or a way of life? Why?

There's a reason Division I football players
still have a curfew and lights out time.

CHAPTER

**22**

# Getting Enough Sleep and Spending the Night with a Friend

I have five kids, and I have dealt with the question, "Dad, can I have a friend spend the night?" or "Dad, can I sleepover at so-and-so's house?" In the early years as a coach you notice a substantial difference in kids when they've spent the night out and when they haven't. I could almost tell you on a Saturday game which kids spent the night away from home and which ones didn't based on their performance. For a kid, staying in another house, in a different bed, staying up late, watching T.V. and then getting up early and having pancakes, etc. will certainly have an effect on how he or she plays.

In the early years I tried to have my kids not spend the night away from home before a game; but as they got older and they had games almost every weekend, there had to be a balance between sports and having some social time with friends. After all, most of the time the people they wanted to spend the night with were their teammates. We learned to teach our athletes to get to bed by 9:00 or 10:00, depending on their age; and then if they didn't handle things properly, they wouldn't be allowed to do it in the future. There was no sense telling us a fib about what time they went to bed because we'd be able to tell it by the way they played the next day.

Sometimes the entire sixth or seventh grade has a sleepover at the church or on the gymnasium floor. When this happens, you know that it's impossible for the kids to go to sleep at 10:00 because somebody will wake them up. What we learned in those situations is let them go for the social part and have fun, and then when it's bed time we just pick them up and get them home so they have a good night's sleep before their game. That way they really don't miss anything except the time they would have or should have been sleeping. Helping educate yourself and your kids on these issues is part of the one percent improvements that can help them become better performers at game time.

## Questions/Discussion

1. What commercial do we see on T.V. that emphasizes the importance of a good night's sleep? How important do they portray a good night's sleep?

> It takes talent to become great,
> but desire is the most important.

# Twenty Minutes
# in the Morning

Twenty minutes in the morning! If I could go back to high school and junior high and know what I know now I can't imagine how much better an athlete I would be. One of the things I would do differently is I would set my alarm clock 20 minutes earlier and get up and do some kind of work out each day. It might be a two or three mile jog; it might be juggling a soccer ball; it might be working on some special shots in basketball, doing some receiver routes for football or jumping rope; but I would put in my 20 minutes every day.

Twenty minutes of extra practice time multiplied by 365 days a year is 7,300 extra minutes, or 121.6 extra hours of practice. Assuming a typical practice lasts an hour and a half, that is like getting in 81 extra practices per year. Considering the fact that a normal season is approximately 3 months long, and you only practice 5 days a week, then 5 days a week times 12 weeks would be 60 practices a season. So, by creating those 81 extra practices a year, you're basically getting an extra season and a half of practices just by working on your own. I can assure you that an extra season and a half of practices will make almost anybody better than someone that doesn't put in the extra time.

Success is a choice; being great is a choice; and the choice is yours. The question is, are you really willing to pay the price for success? If you go back to chapter one you will see that on the Wall of Fame, the seventh honoree is Jesus and under his name it says "Are you willing to pay the price for success?" More than anything else in life, it is your desire and your ability to be disciplined to pay that price that will make you successful.

On the next page you will find a true story about Ron Burton who was a football player. This true story is told by Oscar Rowan, an All-Pro tight end for the Cleveland Browns. I think you will find that Ron was lucky—he had a coach that believed in him early enough and gave him the challenge early enough to make him great. I hope that you will take the Ron Burton Challenge as well and that you have read this book early enough that it could really help you.

## Questions/Discussion

1. What does "it's a cinch by the inch" mean?
2. Read the following story about Oscar Rowan and discuss what made him successful.
3. Are you willing to pay the price to become a champion?

# The Making of a Champion

A true story as told by Oscar Rowan, former All-Pro tight end with the Cleveland Browns at the Fellowship of Christian Athletes Summer Conference in Oklahoma City, Oklahoma.

Is it worth working to be a champion? Maybe this story about a man from Gettysburg, Pennsylvania named Ron Burton can help you make up your mind.

Ron Burton, when he was in high school his freshman year, was the 46th man on a 45-man football squad, which means he didn't suit up. He didn't play at all. He was a little guy, about 5'6" and 135 pounds, but he had a desire to play the game of football.

One day after practice, his coach called him over and talked to him. He said, "Ron I see something special in you that I don't see in very many young men." He said, "Ron, do you want to be a champion? Do you want to be the finest football player this High School has ever had? Do you want to be a high school All-American?" And here was this kid who wasn't even suiting up saying, "yeah coach, yeah." And his coach told him, "I want you to do exactly as I say; don't ask any questions; just do what I say and in three years you will be a high school All-American."

"From this day on, I don't want you to ever eat another piece of junkfood. No more hamburgers, french fries, candy bars - get rid of all of it - eat good solid food; eat lots of protein and if you have to have desert, have ice cream." He said, "Ron you will find that you will get stronger." Ron said, "I can do that coach, that's no problem." His coach then replied, "Ron, from this day forward, I want you to get up at 5:30 in the morning, put two pairs of warm-ups on, put a towel around your neck so none of the heat will get out, put on a pair of combat boots, and I want you to run seven and one half miles. If you will do it, you will be a High School All-American.

For the next three years of Ron Burton's life, that skinny little running back got up every morning of his life and he ran seven and one half miles. It didn't matter if it rained or snowed; it didn't matter if he was tired, sore, or sick - Ron Burton ran seven and one half miles. Some days that was all he could do; sometimes he ran and spent the rest of the day in bed. But Ron Burton never missed his morning run.

By the time Ron Burton was a senior in High School, he not only had made the traveling squad, added 50 pounds to his physique, and led the state of Pennsylvania in rushing; but he was named a First Team All-American halfback. He still holds every rushing record at Northwestern University and holds most of the rushing records for the New England Patriots. He played six years of professional football for the Patriots - never got injured one time, and never missed one football game.

Just last summer, Oscar Rowan visited Ron Burton and spent the night at his home. He is now 46 years old; he got up at 5:30 a.m., put on two pairs of warm-ups, put a towel around his neck, put on a pair of combat boots, and he ran seven and one half miles. Champion habits are hard to break and that is exactly what Ron Burton is and always will be... A CHAMPION.

ARE YOU WILLING TO PAY THE PRICE TO BE A CHAMPION?

# You Must Watch the Game to Become A Student of the Game

Anson Dorrance, the great soccer coach for the University of North Carolina, has coached a lot of great soccer players. He commented once that Brandi Chastain, who did not play at North Carolina was one of the greatest students of the game he had ever known.. He said it is not necessarily a coach that makes players great students of the game, but it is the players themselves. Brandi became an expert of the game by watching pro men's soccer on T.V. She learned to play the game by watching others. It's not enough to just go to practice and play the games you're involved in. Great Warriors and great students of the game learn by watching others play not only their sport, but other sports as well.

One of the things that has helped our Mighty Bluebird soccer team more than anything else is that I didn't grow up playing just soccer, but had played virtually every sport in junior high and high school, with the exception of golf and hockey. (I jokingly tell my golfing friends that you can't call golf a sport if you can drink beer and smoke while playing). I participated in football, cross-country, wrestling, basketball, swimming, tennis, soccer, baseball, volleyball, and track. I learned a little bit from all these sports and encompass a lot of cross training methods in our practices to help make our players better. For example, I can guarantee you that we're the only girl's soccer team that has a football-blocking sled. We have our kids hit the football sled just like they are football players to get tougher and get used to taking a pounding so that when we play boys' teams in soccer we're not intimidated by the bumps and hits we may take. We also have our kids wrestle from time to time during the season. There is nothing that gets your blood going quicker than having to wrestle somebody to the ground. After all, if a girl can get used to wrestling, she certainly isn't going to be intimidated by any little bump or bruise she may take on the soccer fields.

We employ a lot of the running drills that I learned in cross country and track and use a lot of passing drills used in basketball to help cross train in soccer. Most of all, I learned a lot about mental toughness from watching athletes in other sports. After all, a competitor is a competitor, regardless of the sport. If you want to be the best, be a student not only of your sport, but of a wide range of sports in general and learn from the champions in every field.

I'm not a golfer, but watching Tiger Woods compete helps me in my other sports. I'm not a basketball player today, but watching Allen Iverson's heart and his ability to compete with giants on the court teaches me a lot about courage. I bike a little, but watching Lance Armstrong in the Tour de France can't help but add motivation to anything I compete in. Watch the best in your sport and become a student of the game, and you'll become a better player.

## Questions/Discussion

1. Who watches more sports on T.V., men or women? Why?
2. Do you think reading and watching can help you learn more about something, anything?
3. Why is it that some of the best coaches in the world were not necessarily the best players?

Mighty Bluebird Welcome sign

## How Mighty Bluebird Field Came to Be

Frustrated with only having the practice field once a week and having to share the field making it hard to scrimmage, Coach Hatcher began looking for a flat piece of land that he could put a couple of soccer goals on and make a soccer field. By putting his feelers out his wife Lee found an old friend in Rush Harding who was willing to sell some farm land to be used exclusively for Mighty Bluebird Soccer only. Rush gave us a very good deal on the land and Lee got a place to ride her horses as well.

Mighty Bluebird Field was purchased in October of 1999 and hosted its first game in April of 2000. Mighty Bluebird Field is equipped with a press box, a team room, a locker room for the girls, a concession building, a soccer kick board, three scoreboards, two full size soccer fields, along with a U10 soccer field and a U7 soccer field, and an outdoor grill. Mighty Bluebird Field was designed to give girls and boys a chance to have the best practice facilities in the nation in order to make them the best players.

The national anthem is played before games and the starting lineups introduced over the P.A. system as they run onto the field. This is part of the Mighty Bluebird Field experience.

Mighty Bluebirds State Championships

**Mighty Bluebird**
**Motivational signs**

The Race is Not Always to the Swift But to those who Keep on Running

It's A Lot Easier To Get To The Top Than It Is To Stay On Top

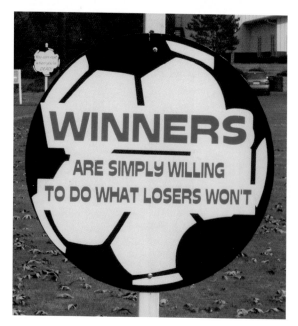

**WINNERS** ARE SIMPLY WILLING TO DO WHAT LOSERS WON'T

On my Tombstone I want it to read... Here Lies a Great Competitor

NOBODY EVER DROWNED IN SWEAT!

MIGHTY BLUEBIRDS

Jealousy Has Killed More Championships Than Any Other Disease.

HISTORY Is written by the WINNERS

Are You Willing To Work Hard Enough To Be The Best?

MIGHTY BLUEBIRDS

**clockwise from top left**

Press Box

Mighty Bluebird Grill

Mighty Bluebird
Gymnasium Floor

HOME OF THE MIGHTY BLUEBIRDS

B-BIRDS    GUESTS

SHOTS    PERIOD    SHOTS

STATE CHAMPIONS 1999
C.A.S.A. CHAMPIONS 1998,1999
YMCA CHAMPIONS 1995,1996,1997,1998

**clockwise from top left**

Study room

Locker room

Mighty Bluebird
trophy case

Scoreboard

# Being a competitor runs in the family.

## Kelsey

The original Mighty Bluebird Kelsey Hatcher. She named the team when she was 4 years old. She is the Bluebirds all time leader in goals, assists, and total scoring.

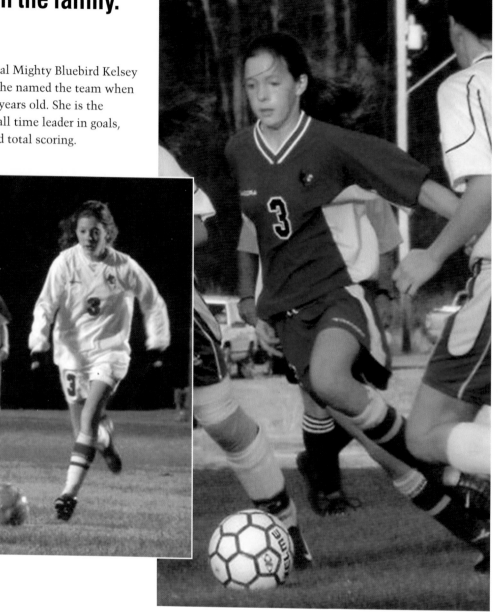

## Haley

We're always used to playing against bigger players as we play up and Haley shows just how she competes. Haley is a phenom averaging more than 3 goals per game per her lifetime. She's been playing competitive soccer and playing up an age group or against boys since she was 3.

# Larkin

Although 5 inches shorter than her twin sister, Larkin is a referee favorite. Intense and hard working she is the Bluebirds second leading scorer, and a solid defender. She has delivered more assists than any other player.

# Layne

At age 5, Layne shows that he's going to use a little brute force along with finesse for his soccer career.

**below left**

Layne scores with a sliding kick.

**below right**

Layne has a commanding lead in the 2006 Kids Marathon.

## Mattie

Although she has not yet played her first game, she'll be more than ready.

**below** Mattie with Toby gives us a hint that she may have horse riding in her future, too.

## Lee

I call her Elly Mae
because she loves
animals so much.
We have five dogs,
two goats, chickens,
ducks, cats, and
yes, several horses...
Lee's true love.

**right** Lee and Romanze

**left** Riding Too Much

Flashpoint ©2006

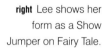

**right** Lee shows her form as a Show Jumper on Fairy Tale.

I guess you could say my kids come by it honestly as Haley, Larkin, and Layne all show their moves with their tongue hanging out just like their daddy did and their grandfather before them.

# Start Weight Training in the Eighth Grade

When I was growing up I always played three sports in high school: cross-country, wrestling, and baseball. These sports were not quite as weight-training oriented as other sports. College wrestlers spend a lot of time in the weight room; but high school wrestlers who play spring and fall sports don't do as much weight training because they are already involved in another sport. So I did very little weight training. Today it just doesn't work to try to be an athlete without weight training. What I have found from talking to trainers and from watching the athletes I coach is that eighth grade is about the right time to start some form of weight training.

I recommend that you get with a counselor or with a good trainer, and either pay a fee to work out with them on a regular basis or get a program and get started on your own. My oldest daughter's trainer started her off on plyometrics, which is a form of weight training without using many weights. It involves a lot of callisthenic type movements— pushups, ab work, stretching exercises, and exercises such as lunges, etc. to get going. After several months of plyometrics, her trainer, Robert Farqua, who is probably one of the best in the country, then started moving her into light weights and building up. I've also watched him work out other young athletes, some of whom I also coach. What athletes get from this weight training is strength that will certainly help them in their sport, but there is an added dimension of the training that is hard to measure. Athletes who do weight training develop a confidence that comes from knowing they're looking better, getting stronger, and getting started early. It's so important that they get a trainer that has a positive outlook on life and that gives them good information, not just about their workouts, but about their outlook in general. What Robert has done for them has given them a vision to really be better athletes and people as they continue to grow. You might say it is 50 percent weight training and 50 percent motivation.

Actually, it may be 33 percent weight training, 33 percent motivation, and 33 percent eating right. Before Robert will work out with us, he requires all of us to write down everything we've eaten for the last week. He then devises a diet for us that is high in protein. He asks us to eat right five days a week and then on the weekend we can take two off days to eat whatever we want. What we have found is that after eating right for five days, the crappy food just doesn't taste quite as good on Saturday and Sunday. In some cases, the "poor diet" can actually make you sick after you have eaten right for long periods of time.

Weight training coupled with the proper diet gives young athletes a huge edge and gets them started off right at an early age. The habits they develop now will serve them well through their athletic careers, as well as later in life. Find your trainer and get started! The longer you wait the harder it gets, especially when it comes to eating right. Forming those habits early is the easiest way.

## Questions/Discussion

1. Why is weight training so important? Wouldn't you just be better to play the sport you do during the hours you would be lifting weights? Why?
2. Will it make any difference if you start lifting weights years after everyone else?

CHAPTER

# 26

# No Deposit, No Return

I grew up in several states throughout the U. S. I was born in Texas and spent kindergarten through seventh grade in Baldwin, Kansas; went to eighth grade in Parkville, Missouri; and spent my high school years in Albion, Michigan. Throughout the moves in my childhood, I loved to drink Coca-Cola and other soda pops. One of the things that was interesting as we moved from state to state was that some states had return policies on their soda bottles and cans, and others didn't. For example, in the state of Michigan, when you bought a soda pop, you could take the can back to the store and they would give you a 10-cent deposit return. If a soda was 50 cents, you actually paid 60 cents; and you got your dime back when you returned the can. The reason for this deposit on drinks was to make sure people didn't throw their cans away or litter the highway. Since the cans were worth money, street people would pick up the cans on the side of the street and take them back to the store. Also, families would store empty bottles and cans until they could take them back to the store for a substantial return. This also helped with the recycling of paper, aluminum, and glass, all of which the soft drinks were bottled in.

In some of the other states where I lived, the drinks said, "No Deposit, No Return" on the outside, which meant they would not take the containers back when you were finished with the drink.

This "No Deposit, No Return" idea can be applied to a lot of areas in life: marriage, sports, work, and school. If you don't make a deposit, you don't get anything in return. This is true of your savings account: if you don't put any money in the bank, you can't get a return on your money. In today's world, a lot of people want success without a deposit. They want a return without investing. I can assure all of you that there is no shortcut to success. Just as those "miracle diets" for weight loss never work out over the long haul, no "quick fix" will get you in shape. The only way to stay fit in life is to eat right and work out. The only way to be successful in sports, work, marriage, and friendships is to take some time and energy and make a deposit. If you do this, you'll have a nice return. The greater the deposit you put in, the greater the return. Each season we give our Mighty Bluebirds T-shirts that have "Mighty Bluebirds" and their logo on the front. On the back we have a different saying each year. One year, the shirt read, "No Deposit, No Return" to help our kids understand the very simple concept that you get out of life what you put into it. Work hard, and remember: "No Deposit, No Return."

## Questions/Discussion

1. What does "No Deposit, No Return" mean?
2. How often have you had huge results without much effort?

CHAPTER

# 27

# First In and
# Last Out

First In and Last Out. Five little words that can make a big difference in your life. Be the first to arrive at sports practice and the last to leave. Begin working when you get there and work after everyone else is gone. Arrive at least 15 minutes early each day unless the practice begins immediately after school and it is impossible to get there early. When you arrive, get dressed quickly and go out and work 15 minutes on your skills. They may be skills that need improvement, or perhaps there are some skills you are already good at but you need to do them more quickly, with more intensity, or with more power. This extra time before practice will add up each day, and by the end of the season you will have had a lot more practice time than the other players.

When practice is over, stay on and shoot some extra free throws; run some extra sprints; take some extra batting practice or some extra ground balls; or get in an extra lap.

When coaches talk about the outstanding players they have had over the years, they will tell you that the great ones were the ones who were the first in for practice and the last to leave after practice. It is not surprising that the words "hard work" and "great players" so often show up in the same sentence. It is almost impossible to be better than everyone else without outworking them.

The beauty of the "First in, last out" habit is that it will serve you as well in other areas of your life as it does in sports. If you are the first one in and the last one out in your first job, you won't be long in getting a promotion. People who put in more, who do a little bit extra, end up being more successful and getting more recognition. One of the things I have always tried to teach my children is that the difference between winning and losing is just a fine little bit. If the whole world is willing to spend "X" amount of time or put forth "X" amount of effort, then you can win by putting forth just a little more than "X" amount of time and effort. You only have to be one percent better than your competition to win almost every game or match. It just takes that little extra showing up first and leaving last to separate the field. Be First In and Last Out at everything you do, and you will be successful at everything you do.

## Questions/Discussion

1. Who is the first person to your practice each day?
2. Who is the last to leave?
3. Are they good players?

# Outwork Them

Wouldn't it be awful if, in order to be the best basketball player, football player, soccer player, swimmer, runner, or whatever your sport might be, you had to be born the best in the world at it? That would give only one person the chance to be the best in this entire universe. There would be no incentive to get in the gym and work to be the best at your particular sport or craft. The United States was founded on the principle that you can have anything in life you want if you work hard enough for it. In fact, in this country we reward people for putting in the work and producing results. We are a very incentive- based society, and we respect and look up to those who pay the price for success.

One of the interesting dynamics about any team is that there will always be some jealousy and some competition over who is going to start at a particular position on the team. What is neat about sports is than even though there is jealousy and competition, it is very possible for the athlete who works extremely hard to earn the respect and even admiration of the very person that they are competing against. This principle is also true in business and in any other competitive battle; the person who loses admires the person who did it better. But sports are different from other areas because it is easier to measure achievement in sports. While promotions in business are sometimes based on numbers, such as the amount of sales in a given month; the decision on who to promote to be the next manager or president of a company is more subjective. Sports are decided a little more objectively through competition on the field. For the most part, when you're practicing and competing with someone every-day in practice, not only does the coach know who the best player is, but so do the players themselves. It's obvious to everyone on the team who is putting in the work and who is putting in the extra effort to be the best they can be. I can guarantee you that Michael Jordan was not born with the best body ever to play basketball. He was born with an outstanding body, but it was his attitude and his work ethic that made him the best player ever to live. There are plenty of 6'6" athletic young men in this world, but Michael Jordan put in the time and strove for excellence and became the best at his game.

I don't know what God-given ability each of you has, and I will never have a ranking system that says you're a 9 on a scale of 1 to 10. But, I can tell you that if you outwork your opponent, you will beat everybody who was born with less of a gift athletically, and you will beat most of the people who were born with better genes than you just by outworking them. Coming to practice early, staying late, putting in extra time on the weekends, watching your sport on TV, reading books on other successful athletes in your sport, and even watching and reading about sports figures in other sports you may never play will help you outwork your competition, and most importantly, make you the best that you can be.

There are so many mine fields out there waiting to destroy you and your opponent along the way to success. These mine fields include drugs, alcohol, lack of focus, pregnancy, not making grades, bad boyfriend or girlfriend relationships, and overeating. But the biggest mine fields of all are apathy, procrastination, and failure to focus on your goals. If you're willing to outwork everybody else, there's no question there will always be room for you at the top.

## Questions/Discussion

1. How hard do you work compared to others on your team?
2. Could you work harder? If yes, why aren't you?

section 3

# Practice

# When Practicing Always Visualize the Defender In Front of You

Visualize a defender, and your practice will be more effective.

Some people say, "I can't practice; I don't have anybody to practice with."

Others just go through the motions when they're shooting baskets, playing catch with a football, or shooting a soccer ball.

If you visualize yourself playing against a defender, it will improve your moves and add intensity to your practice.

When I'm practicing as if I have a defender in front of me my facial expressions change, my intensity goes up and everything I do is quicker or more precise. When you're warming up before a basketball game, when you step in the batter's box to take batting practice, when you're throwing and catching a football, visualize a defender out there. Your practices will be much more game-like and you will be better prepared for the real thing when it is game time.

Visualize when you practice and both your practices and games will be more productive.

## Questions/Discussion

1. Have you ever just gone through the motions on a drill simply to get by?
2. Who are you cheating, yourself or the coach?

# Be a Complete Player, Not a One Dimensional Player

In all sports there are players who focus on one particular dimension of the game and forget to develop themselves in all phases of the game. These one-dimensional players may be successful at the high school level, possibly at the college level, but they are rarely successful at the professional or world-class level. You'll see the basketball player who just wants to shoot the ball but doesn't want to play any defense or rebound or take the charge. You'll see the running back in football that's a good runner but is not good at blocking or catching the pass out of the backfield. You'll see the tennis player who has a great serve and a good net game but can't play the baseline and you'll see the baseball player who is a good hitter but just is not very good in the field. Many times the players that develop one dimensional type games develop them because when they are young they are so focused on being the hero. They want to hit the homerun, score the points in basketball, or run the football in for a touchdown. It's the complete player, however, that coaches at the next level are looking for, and it's the complete player that helps his or her team win at all levels.

Becoming a complete player is very simple. You work on all aspects of the game, trying to perfect your skills in each area. Getting a rebound in basketball is critical to helping your team to win, even though it's not a glorious statistic. You can keep track of the number of rebounds each team gets in a basketball game, and the one that gets the most rebounds will almost always win. This is because the team that gets the most rebounds has the ball the most, and therefore gets the most shots. And the team that gets the most shots will most likely win the game.

In a sport like baseball, having a great batting average is wonderful; but if you make errors in the field, that's like giving hits to the other team, which nullifies the hits you get. Knowing how to run the bases in baseball, communicating out on the field, making a great heads up play, can be just as important in the outcome of the game as hitting a homerun.

I can't tell you how many players had great statistics in high school but couldn't make the college-starting lineup because they weren't complete in all phases of the game. The very best players can do it all; the coach does not consider them a liability in certain situations of the game; and he has the confidence to keep them in the game.

I have seen players average 30 points a game in high school basketball, but they sit at the end of the bench in college basketball because they can't play man-to-man defense. The coaches have plenty of players that can score baskets, but they can't afford to put a liability on the floor who allows an opponent to score against them on a regular basis. Therefore, despite being maybe the best shooter on the team, a player may find himself not just on the bench, but at the end of the bench.

As a young player you must develop all your skills, listen to your coach and not be satisfied with just being the top scorer, top hitter, top receiver, running back, or tackler. You must develop all parts of your game. You'll find your team will win more, and the coaches will notice you for the little things when it comes time to pick a college team or a professional team. One of the players that come to mind more than any other is Derrick Fisher who played for the Los Angeles Lakers and now plays for the Golden State Warriors. In high school he was the fifth best player on his team according to recruiters, but because he had a complete game he started all four years at the University of Arkansas at Little Rock; and in his last two years he made All Conference despite averaging decent scoring numbers but nothing magnificent. His senior year he averaged 17 points and was named Player of the Year because the coaches recognized him for all his other abilities such as passing the ball, getting rebounds from the guard position, and his incredible defense. Because he was a complete player the Los Angeles Lakers drafted a little 6'2" guard from a small Division I school ahead of all the other big stars at the big schools. He still plays professional basketball today because of his well-rounded abilities.

## Questions/Discussion

1. What are the best parts of your game?
2. What are the worst parts of your game?
3. Are you interested in improving your weaknesses and capitalizing on your strengths or are you happy where you are?

# 31

# Going to Practice is not Enough

The practice required by the coach at your school is never going to be enough to make you a great player. After all, everybody else on your team is going to that same practice and putting in the same amount of work. If going to practice and going through the drills your coach designed for you was enough to make you great, then every player on every team in America would be great because they are all going to practice. Greatness is achieved by putting forth effort that is extraordinary and beyond what everyone else is willing to do, in addition to having a lot of athletic talent. The truth is, there are a lot of people out there in this world that have enough talent to become great at something; the ones that truly end up being great are the ones who combine extra work ethic with the talent.

When coaches design practice, they have to spend a lot of time going through plays and coordination to get the team to work together and understand its mission. Your coach doesn't have time to focus 90 percent of the practice on your learning how to do a left handed lay-up or a double clutch reverse lay-up in basketball. The football coach can't spend much time helping you practice catching the sideline route as a receiver, and the baseball coach doesn't have a lot of time to spend on helping you improve your footwork at turning the double play in baseball. While these coaches spend a little time showing you the fundamentals, it's up to you to take the fundamentals they showed you and then get in hundreds of repetitions perfecting that particular maneuver on your own after practice.

When I was a player in college I loved practice; in fact practice was never long enough for me. After virtually every soccer practice, wrestling practice, and baseball practice I had in college I stayed for at least 15-30 minutes to work on some of the fundamentals of my sport. I just decided from the beginning that it was a price I was willing to pay in order to become better. If you want to be the best that you can be, it's a real simple formula: you have to work extra on your own; and if you're lucky enough to have talent to go with that, you may find yourself being the very best at what you do. If you don't have that talent, then you'll find yourself being the best that you can be. Either one sounds pretty good to me.

## Questions/Discussion

1. What do you do outside of practice to improve your game?

# Play the Best (Players)
# In Practice

When I was a high school wrestler I was one of the best wrestlers on the team my freshman, sophomore, and junior years. By the time I was a senior, I was the best wrestler on the team at any weight class despite wrestling at 145 pounds. In other words, I could beat everybody below 145 pounds, and I could beat everybody on my team all the way up to heavy weight. My wrestling team won no matches my senior year, and I was just a little bit above a .500 wrestler, which means I won just a couple more matches than I lost.

My freshman year in college, I was the worst wrestler of the ten in the starting lineup. I couldn't beat any of the starters on our team who were bigger than I, yet I had a record that was better than .500. By the time I was a senior, Captain of my Wrestling Team and an All-Conference wrestler, I still could only beat about half the wrestlers on my team; and my record was well over .500. My college wrestling team did not lose a match my last three years and was nationally ranked, and I wrestled against the toughest guys I would see all year right in my own practice room. The moral here is that "Iron sharpens iron, as one man sharpens another." Wrestling against my better teammates challenged me and sharpened my skills.

If you want to get better, wrestle with the best person on your wrestling team; play one-on-one with the best player on the basketball team; work out with, or do your blocking and tackling drills against, the best weight lifter on your football team. The bottom line is: who you practice against everyday will have a lot to do with how good you become. Good tennis players and players of any individual sport that requires head- to-head combat know that playing against someone better will raise the level of their game. Runners need to run with runners that can challenge them in practice each and every day. Many of us, when we go to practice, want to go against somebody that's not as good as we are so we can feel the confidence of having a good practice and winning. But this does not necessarily make you better.

When my oldest daughter was growing up, she and a good friend were the two best dribblers and defenders on the basketball team. These two always went against each other in the offensive/defensive dribbling drills when at practice. As they practiced against each other, both girls continued to get better and better, distancing themselves more and more from the competition. It's wonderful if you can have a great friend who is a great player, and the two of you can work each other out and push each other so both can be your best. Play the best players in practice; play the best players you can find in pick up games; and try to find some-body that can beat your rear end on a regular basis. You'll find that you'll get a lot better fast.

## Questions/Discussion

1. Do you often look to play the best in practice? Why or why not?
2. If you are already the best player on your team, in what ways can you challenge yourself in practice?

CHAPTER

# 33

# One on One…It's Where the Game is Played

In all team sports players are tempted to work on a different fundamental part of the game but often they avoid playing one-on-one. Playing one-on-one puts the player in an arena where it is completely their fault if they win or lose, and a lot of players don't like this. This is especially true in girls' sports. I have a coaching friend who has said, "If you put a basketball at a goal, two girls will show up and play 'horse,'" and if two boys show up they will play one-on-one." That truly is the case.

Whether it is soccer, football, or basketball the game really is broken down into a bunch of one-on-one scrimmages. Anson Dorrance, the great soccer coach at North Carolina who has won 20 of the last 24 national championships, says the key or the keys to his team's unbelievable winning record is the majority of his practices are focused on having players go one-on-one. Even though a soccer game consists of 11 players against 11, it is broken down into a bunch of one-on-one scrimmages that have to be won by his players in order to advance the ball down in front of the goal. Once it is in front of the goal, he has to have an offensive player that can beat the defensive player one-on-one, and the goalie to put it in the goal.

In basketball you can be a decent player in high school and maybe in college by hitting an open three-point shot without the ability to go one-on-one. But for the most part, at the major college level, coaches are looking for players that can beat somebody one-on-one and go to the hole. If you can't do that in college, you have no chance of playing in the pros because professional basketball is all about one-on-one.

The great thing about playing one-on-one in practice is that you get the most repetition and the most touches, and you can learn the most in the shortest amount of time. Even a sport like football is broken down into one-on-one match-ups. The defensive lineman versus the offensive lineman with the defensive lineman trying to get to the quarterback and the offensive lineman trying to keep him from getting there. The receiver versus the cornerback with the receiver trying to get open and the cornerback trying to keep the receiver covered. The running back versus the linebacker: the linebacker making the open field tackle and the running back making a move to beat him.

The bottom line is if you want to be great, play one-on-one because it incorporates offense, defense, game situations, and moves necessary to beat each other. It is the most intense, strenuous part of a workout you can have. Play one-on-one and play it well and advance to the next level.

## Questions/Discussion

1. Do you play a lot of one-on-one in your sport?
2. Have you ever shied away from playing one-on-one because you thought you would lose?

> The distance is nothing…
> the first step is tough.

# Get Started

Most of us have set goals at some time, often around the first of a new year, for something we wanted to accomplish. We all have things we intend to do when we get around to it, but we just can't seem to get started.

We all know that the hardest part of a three-mile run is the first step. You have to set the alarm clock, get out of that nice warm bed, put on your sweats, and then start the jog. Once you've done the hard part of getting up and getting dressed, once you take that first step, the rest of it is pretty easy; and you're glad you got out there and got started. The same thing is true of all the things you want to do; you just have to get started.

It is really difficult to change an old habit and start something new. However, it gets easier once you have taken the first step. If you can just get started and stay with your commitment for 30 days, you will develop a new habit, perhaps replacing an old one. That's right. Whatever it is you're trying to do—whether it's eating right, getting in an extra workout, putting extra time in on your shooting skills in basketball, or getting in an extra sprint or an extra jog to be more fit for your sport—whatever it is, if you'll do it for 30 days it will become habit and you won't have to work so hard to get it done anymore. The key is to be religiously determined and dedicated for those first 30 days.

In the end you will find that successful people have successful habits. In sports you can practice a particular athletic maneuver over and over again so that when you get into a game you will just naturally perform the skill perfectly without even thinking. In other words, you've practiced the skill enough that it just becomes habit to do it right. The same is true in everything else you do in life: If you can develop enough good habits, or successful practices that you don't even have to think about, you will become a successful person. Imagine how successful you can be. You can take a negative habit you have and turn it into a positive one. It only takes 30 days of making that change, and you'll have a positive habit for life. Get started. Don't procrastinate. Do it today.

## Questions/Discussion

1. Can you think of something you've accomplished where actually getting started was the hardest part?

CHAPTER

# 35

# Don't Make the Same Mistake Twice

There is only one thing worse than walking in late to a Christmas church service with your entire family and being unable to find a seat. What is worse is walking into a Christmas church service late with your entire family for the second year in a row. Both times we had called a friend to ask what time the service was and were told the wrong time. After the first time, one would think we would have gone to a different source or triple checked the time before we went.

We've all had situations occur with a client, a friend, or a coach where we made the same exact mistake twice. These situations are extremely embarrassing and generally cause a person of authority to raise the level of punishment so that we get it through our thick heads and don't make a mistake the third time.

As a coach, I know that every athlete makes mistakes. But I believe the player who recognizes a mistake when it is pointed out and never makes that mistake again will become a great athlete. The best athletes and the most successful people make a note of the error they've made and take action to change the way they do things so that it does not happen again. We all tend to do things over and over the same way, and because that's our nature, we're very likely to make the same mistake again. It's important to understand your nature and make changes or take precautions to make sure you don't repeat mistakes.

One mistake I have made over and over was forgetting about my regular haircut appointment, which is scheduled once every three weeks. Although I had it in my Palm® digital planner, many times I would look at the important items for the day, and when I got to the haircut I wouldn't think about it as important. When the time came that was logged right in on my Palm, I would forget all about the 2:30 appointment and simply not go for my haircut. I did this two or three times, and it was embarrassing. Of course, I paid the beautician to compensate for the inconvenience and wasted time. To make sure I didn't continue to make this mistake I began entering the time in my Palm with a 30-minute alarm and a one-day prior alarm to make sure I didn't forget. Paying for the appointments I missed was a good financial lesson that helped motivate me to make a change so I would absolutely not overlook the appointment again.

To break your bad habits, or even harder, to change your nature, you may have to take some extreme measures. The easiest way to make these changes is to have a burning desire to change and to be very coachable. If you can learn after the first mistake and not repeat that behavior, you'll be way ahead of the pack. If you want to be successful, don't do the same bone-headed thing over and over again.

## Questions/Discussion

1. Can you think of something in which you have repeated the same mistake?
2. Can you think of a situation in which you made a mistake once, learned from it and never made it again? If yes, then you were very coachable.

CHAPTER

# 36

> Sometimes you have
> to get your hands dirty.

# Be a Blue-Collar Worker

In the work world a blue-collar worker is someone who does a lot of the hard work and doesn't get much glory. It may be the person that cleans the floors; the person that runs the office behind the scenes, typing the letters and getting the mail out; it could be a person in the plant moving the heavy machinery; or the person changing tires on the car. A blue-collar worker is not the one who gets the credit or who is in the limelight dressed in the fancy suit or appears on T.V. or in the newspaper. The blue-collar workers, however, are some of the most important people in any company when it comes to getting the job done. My assistant and office manager is rarely ever seen by my customers, but it would be hard to run the agency without her. The courier who delivers to our customers all day might be considered blue-collar, but he is as important to our day-to-day business as our account managers. They put in a lot of important work without a lot of the credit.

If your coach refers to you as a blue-collar worker, you should consider it the ultimate compliment. The blue-collar worker in sports is the one who gets the rebound, who does the blocking for the quarterback or the running back, who dives on the floor for the loose ball, who takes the charge in basketball to help get a turnover, and who plays good defense. Blue-collar workers aren't so concerned with scoring all the points, getting the touchdown, or being the quarterback on the team.

If you're a blue-collar worker, your coach will appreciate you very much and you'll most likely find yourself in the starting lineup in a heck of a hurry, as all teams need great blue-collar workers. The ultimate compliment is to be a great offensive player who scores a lot of points or maybe even be a quarterback and still be referred to as a blue-collar worker. A quarterback can be a blue-collar worker if he's out there blocking on the reverse play for his running back, if he's doing all the little things that can help his team win.

Actually, I believe you can never be a complete player if you don't have a lot of blue-collar worker in you. All winners understand how important it is to do the things that might be described as "grunt work" to help your team win, even if you don't get a lot of credit for it. Be a blue-collar worker, and you'll be noticed by your coach and people who really understand the game.

## Questions/Discussion

1. In what areas are you a Blue-Collar Worker?
2. In what areas are you a White-Collar Worker?

CHAPTER

# 37

# The 45-Minute Warm-Up Should be an Extra Practice

The soccer and basketball teams I've coached over the years have always arrived at the games 45 minutes prior to start time. During this warm up period I run my players through all kinds of drills to get them game ready. Most other coaches on other teams have the kids stretching out, chitchatting, taking a little jog, and for the most part slowly- but-surely getting ready for the game during their pre-game warm up. Most of these teams arrive 20-30 minutes prior to game time.

We use our 45 minute warm up period as an additional practice. In soccer we'll play four to five games during a tournament weekend. We don't use our 45 minutes as a time to take it easy even though we might be tired from a previous game. Instead, we use it as a 45-minute practice, working to improve different aspects of our game. I demand that the kids work to actually improve their skills during this pre-game warm up. The cumulative effect of these 45-minute practices is that our kids have up to twice as many practices as a normal team. This will give them an advantage over the course of a season and over the course of a career. It is important as athletes that we be fit enough, but a warm up does not make us tired for the game, and we can use this time to actually get better.

One of the results of this strategy is that our soccer team has won over 90 percent of all the games we've ever played. Most of the time when we're going into a game we already know we're going to win it, so why not spend the time in pre-game warm up actually challenging our players and getting better? Then, when we do get in the tough game we've been improving all along the way, and we'll be ready. In addition, by using this 45-minute warm up to get game ready, we are creating a greater distance between us and the competition we play because we're getting better with every little pre-game practice session.

When I played high school and college baseball, I realized that the pre-game warm up was more important than the game for developing my skills. I played shortstop and third base; and on a normal day I might get three or four ground balls and three or four at-bats during a two-to-three hour game. In the pre-game warm up where the coach hits infield and outfield to the team, I might get 10 or 12 warm up ground balls and maybe 20 swings while at bat. This meant that over a course of a season I actually got a lot more practice or, if you will, a bigger chance to get better, in the pre-game than I did in the actual game. Once I figured this out in baseball, I've applied it to all other sports. A split end in football may only get 4 or 5 catches a game; but we can get him 20 to 50 catches in pre-game warm up, and that's going to be what continually makes our players better.

As an athlete I've always told kids that "you are your most important coach." I can't tell you how many basketball programs I've seen where the coach comes out for pre-game warm up, hands balls to the kids and then sits on the bench with legs crossed watching the players stand around and shoot warm up shots. The kind of warm up I want for a basketball team is one that involves dribbling against a defender under pressure, making the most difficult lay-ups, working on the three point shot, driving up for the short jumper, going through all the gyrations and motions that you might get in a game, and most importantly, improving, not just for this game, but for the one ten games out. I've always felt if the talent level was close, the coach that makes the most of the pre-game warm ups and gets extra practices will eventually beat the coach who doesn't. And, the player who takes this time seriously and does not use it for a social hour or to go through the motions will, over time, become a better player than the one who does not.

Remember, make the most of every session you have on the court because in the end every time you walk on the court should be an opportunity to improve, whether it is a practice session or a game.

## Questions/Discussion

1. Do you use your warm-ups to get better and improve or just to get loose?

CHAPTER

# 38

# Be the Fittest

I've never seen a coach who couldn't find a spot for Charlie Hustle who is in shape. The kids I coach and my friends who are coaches all know that the player who is the fittest on any of my teams is sure to be a starter. How do you know if you are the fittest? If you can win all the wind sprints and lead all the laps around the field, then you know you are at least as fit as any other player out there. Whatever the sport: football, basketball, baseball, soccer, wrestling, or swimming, if you can beat the other players in the sprints and laps, and if your body is at maximum fitness, you'll be good enough to start.

If you're a starter and you're not the fittest member of your team, then you can become a more outstanding player by improving your fitness to the point where you can win the sprints and laps. I find that fitness is more about attitude and hard work than it is about natural God given-ability. When I was a wrestler on my college wrestling team my freshman year I was the weakest of the ten starters in the lineup, yet I won every single wind sprint in every practice for the entire year. I was determined to win those fitness drills and not let anybody beat me. It wasn't that I was that much faster than anybody else; it was an attitude and I wanted to show them I could compete. The fact that I wasn't the best wrestler on that very talented team may have made me even more hungry, but it also gave me an edge when I wrestled because I always knew I could go longer and harder than anyone I ever went up against. As I continued to improve in my later years I kept my fitness up and coupled that with improved wrestling ability to become very successful.

Put in the extra laps, run the extra wind sprints and be the most fit; and not only will you find yourself in the starting lineup and improving as a player, but you'll also likely be the captain of your team because everybody respects the people that run the hardest and give the most during practice.

## Questions/Discussion

1. Where do your rank fitness-wise on your team?
2. Are you eating properly?

CHAPTER

# 39

# Who Was the Best Player Today

The soccer coach with whom I coach the Mighty Bluebirds is Chris Owen. Chris grew up playing soccer in Europe, and, at the age of 15 signed a professional contract. In Europe, they identify the great soccer players, and these players leave school and get their schooling done while they are playing professional soccer. Chris was coached by his father for many years, and throughout his pro career, his father would be at all the games watching him. One of the common denominators that made Chris great is that after every practice or game his father would ask him, "Who was the best player on the field today?" He wanted Chris to be able to answer that he was the best and that he had done such a good job during the course of the practice or the game that it would be clear to everyone who the best player on the field was.

Certainly to be the best player on the field each day would require a lot of talent and some of you reading this may not ever be able to be the best player on the field on any given day. However, what you can ask yourself is, "Who was the best at shooting free throws today? Who was the best at running sprints today? Who was the best hustler today? Who was the best leader today?" If you are a player that has great talent, then you should be asking yourself each day, "Was I the best player on the court today?" "Did I make it clear to anyone who was watching that I was the best?" The great ones such as Michael Jordan, Tiger Woods, and Barry Bonds know that every day they go out to play a game thousands of fans are watching. The fans are watching and evaluating them on maybe that one pro game in their lifetime in which they will get to see that player. These professional athletes learn to perform everyday and to give their best because that fan may never see them play again.

If you are a young player in Junior High, High School, or College, you are being evaluated by coaches every day. Some may come and scout you for a college scholarship and they have to make their decision in just one game. Get used to performing and practicing with the attitude that you want to leave no doubt that you are the best player on the field. When the time comes that someone is looking at you where it really matters, it will come naturally to you how to be the best player when you walk off the field. After hearing Chris's success and his father's question, I often ask my kids at the end of a practice, "Who was the best player on the field today?" Sometimes they can give me their name, and sometimes it is someone else's, but it is a good question and a test of how well you competed on that particular day, and a question that every player should ask himself or herself.

## Questions/Discussion

1. Do you ask yourself this question after practice or a game?

# Attitude

# Sweat the Small Stuff

There is a book out that I really enjoy entitled "Don't Sweat the Small Stuff". It focuses on all kinds of categories one should not worry about. This book may apply well to quality of life issues, and it works well in business and family matters; but it does not work when it comes to winning championships. When you look at the great coaches, you see that they sweat the small stuff; they sweat the big stuff; they sweat everything! In other words they take care of and try to control as many details in the contest as they can.

Becoming a champion and maintaining championship status can be done in so many different ways. For example, just before I wrote this chapter I dropped my daughter off for Olympic development soccer training. The shin guards she had were not quite long enough to cover the full part of her shin; she was about to go out with short shin guards. As we get older and have more experiences we get wiser because we've made all those little bitty tiny mistakes. I told her, "If you wear that short shin guard and you get kicked, your basketball season may be over. You could fracture your leg or get a bruise that would keep you out for a couple of games." So she put on two shin guards to protect her leg.

This may sound like a silly little thing, but I always insist that my players wear their warm ups into practice and out of practice. I've been around long enough to know that a little cold might cost them a chance to play in the championship game, and that bruised leg may keep them out of a couple of basketball games. It can go deeper than that. Sometimes the slightest little injury gets you behind and somebody gets your position and you can't ever get it back.

I am reminded of a girl who was playing college basketball and was in a car wreck about a month before the season started. It took her about two months to recover, so when she got to her first basketball practice as a college freshman she had already missed the first month. The coach had already settled on her rotation, and this very talented basketball player who might have had a chance to be a starter found herself at the end of the bench. If you don't think little details like wearing your seatbelt, driving safely, getting enough sleep, making sure that you have the proper equipment and hundreds of other things make a difference, think again. THEY DO!

I can remember as a kid not going to a couple of summer baseball games because I was in a summer camp for three weeks and had fallen in love in the summer of my ninth grade year. I wanted to be at the camp and not miss the dance and the play that this girl was in during our summer camp. I thought it was just summer baseball games and wouldn't be a big deal to miss. The high school coach wasn't coaching this summer team, but the summer coach told him I missed the games. The high school coach decided not to move me up to the varsity as a sophomore because of that lack of commitment. This small detail didn't seem significant at the time, but it became very significant. You need to understand that everybody is watching, and every little detail can make a difference to somebody. Some little details have a domino effect and can lead to another action and another action and another action that most young people can't see.

You want to be the best? Worry about what you're eating; make sure you get to practice fifteen minutes early; make sure you have your game jerseys on game day; make sure you have your practice jerseys with you if the coach requires; get your homework done so you can practice; get good grades so you'll be eligible; don't hang around with the wrong crowd where you may get into trouble and miss games; and honor the vow, which means that you don't do anything that is against team policy or against the law. If you don't think the small stuff makes a difference, pick up the sports page on any day and you will find an article about an athlete that didn't take care of the little details and is injured, or is not able to play for some disciplinary reason. Sweat the small stuff if you want to be a great athlete. And, when you become a coach, sweating the small stuff becomes even more important.

## Questions/Discussion

1. Is there anything important enough to you that you sweat the small stuff? What is it?

CHAPTER

# 41

# Sweat the Big Stuff

In Rick Pitino's book, Success is a Choice, he says sweat the big stuff; sweat the small stuff; sweat it all, as it all makes a difference between winning and losing. For an athlete, sweating the big stuff and the small stuff is just as important as it is in coaching. The big stuff in athletics is doing the obvious. If you're a basketball player, it's being able to make your jump shot and your free throws, being able to make good passes and to play defense, etc. In soccer it's being fit, being a good passer, being able to make some fancy moves to get the defender off of you, and being able to shoot the ball accurately and hard. For the distance runner it's getting your miles in, being able to run with pain, having the courage to persevere, and training at a fast pace.

Sweating the big stuff means that when you're training and practicing in all these areas you don't let anybody tell you that it's okay that you just missed those two free throws; it's no big deal. Don't let them tell you that it's okay that your soccer shot was 3 or 4 feet wide on the penalty kick. Don't let them tell you it's okay that you take a couple of days off from running, and that it won't make that much difference on race day. Sweating the big stuff means that you understand the importance of the basics in your sport or whatever it is in life you're trying to accomplish. Sweating the big stuff means working for perfection on the key elements of your game that will make a difference.

Success is not an accident. It truly is a choice, and that choice is made by coming to practice every day and working diligently to get perfection on the key points of your game. It is true that the higher the level you play in any sport the more simple that sport becomes. In other words, against the very best opponent fancy moves don't work as well as fundamentals. You win the basketball game with the basic pass and the jump shot, not with the behind-the-back passes that may be good for a play or two; but the basics, the big stuff, are used over and over throughout the game. Sweating the big stuff and perfecting those things that are going to be used most often in a game are what make champions. Consistency and being able to execute the fundamentals at the key times are what win championships.

Wrestlers know there are thousands and thousands of wrestling moves and counters to stop other people's moves. I find it interesting when I watch the National Championships and they get down to the two best wrestlers in the world, that the match is almost always decided by a simple single or double leg takedown, one of the two most basic moves ever taught in wrestling. Everybody knows it's coming, and it just gets down to who can execute and who can stop the other opponent from getting the basic takedown that will win these very, very close matches. They generally get down to a point or two, and most of the scoring comes from one wrestler escaping and the other taking him down. Thousands of other moves that they have worked on for years become peripheral, and the big stuff is the execution of the basics they learned long ago at their first wrestling practice.

Sweat the big stuff; practice; perfect the fundamentals; and you'll become a champion.

## Questions/Discussion

1. What is the difference between Big Stuff and Small Stuff?

If you're going to be the leader of the pack, there will be many times when you're running out there all by yourself.

# Moderation in All Things Makes You Mediocre

I say this not to be funny, as I respect my father a whole lot. But one of his sayings is "Moderation in all things." My father is right if you want to live a long healthy life. Moderation in all things can be good. It keeps your stress level down and keeps you well rounded. But, I also tell my father that moderation in all things makes you mediocre. I say that with tongue in cheek, but at the same time I believe it to some degree. I've never known anybody who is the best at what they do that was moderate.

Was Walter Peyton moderate when he was the greatest rusher in NFL history? I don't think so. His off-season workouts involved running up a mountain until he puked each day. There's nothing moderate about that. Haven Moses, who won over 100 hurdling races without a loss and ran well into his thirties, used to submerge his body from the neck down in an ice bucket after his workouts to prolong his athletic career. Nothing moderate about that. The top salesmen, the top businessmen, and the best coaches are anything but moderate; in fact I would call them almost psychotic. They have a desire to be the best; they work as hard to put forward whatever effort it takes to be the best; and they are all a little bit out of balance in some way. You have to be a little fanatical to be the best.

It gets back to the same old thing. If you want one thing you're going to have to give up something else in order to get it. I can tell you this from my own experiences as well as what I know about other people who are extremely successful: there is a huge price to pay to be the best at something. But I will also tell you that it's generally worth it.

### Questions/Discussion

1. Is there anything that you're passionate enough about that people think you're a little crazy?

CHAPTER

# 43

# The Crying Game

I always tell the girls on my teams "Don't cry." When you start crying, you let the other team know that you're beaten, that they've gotten under your skin, that you can't do it, that you've given up, and that you're feeling sorry for yourself. Kids tend to cry at different times—after missing a key shot, when they are running sprints and they're tired, or when they are just really frustrated from not doing as well as they wanted to. Crying doesn't help anybody. It makes everybody feel sorry for you, but most importantly it makes you feel sorry for yourself. When Coach Kevin Kelley coaches for Pulaski Academy and it's 20 degrees out and his players are worried about the cold, he wears a short-sleeved golf shirt. He tells his players that it's not cold out there unless he decides it is. He says he can go out in the 20-degree cold and he can make himself sweat, or he can go out in 90 degree heat and make his arms have goose bumps. He simply imagines himself in the weather environment he wants to be in. And it works. Certainly this won't work if we drop him in a freezing cold bucket of ice, but it's amazing how he can survive in almost any temperature and still be comfortable just by using his mind.

When I was a runner or when I had to run wind sprints at practice, I used to imagine something wonderful or something pleasant to help pass the time as I went through my sprints. Many times I had a smile on my face as I was running, but I learned to block out the pain; and I certainly never got anywhere near crying. In fact I am to the point that pain doesn't make me cry anymore. Only frustration can make me cry.

When I first started coaching soccer we played a game one day against a team that was a year older than we were. My team was probably five years old, and the other girls' team was six years old. It was a very hard fought game and our team ended up winning 1-0. There was a lot of commotion in the stands, and a lot of parents on the two teams got upset with each other. The reason for this was that there are a lot of collisions on the field in five and six year old soccer, and in just about every collision when two girls went down, the girls on our team got up, and the girls on the other team started crying. Each time they fell down and cried either one of their parents would run out on the field and help them off, or the coach would take them off the field and put them on the bench where their parents would hug them and nurture them as they continued to cry. By the end of the game the other team thought that our team was playing dirty and was a mean and unsportsmanlike team.

This was kind of amusing since our team was a year younger than theirs, and they were all physically bigger than us. What it all boiled down to was that the other team had their bench on the side of the field where the parents were and we had our player's bench on the other side of the field away from the parents. Each time a kid would get hurt on the other team they'd come over to the bench, and the parents would sit there and hug them and the kids would continue to cry, getting more sympathy. As we all know, for five and six year olds, getting a lot of sympathy creates more crying. After the game one of the parents from the other team called me and asked me what my take was on the game and if I thought our kids were as dirty as she thought they were. Our conversation went on for two hours, but in the end I told her what made the difference. The reason there was so much crying on their team was that they had placed their bench near the parents and allowed the parents to run on the field and hug the kids every time they got hurt. This parent understood, and a couple of years later her daughter joined the Mighty Bluebirds soccer team. Her daughter is probably the toughest kid mentally that we have on our team. She would never even think about crying if she got bumped or bruised all because of the way she is trained and looks at things today. In one of the games this season she bit her tongue very badly. There was a lot of blood, and it was near the end of the game. She ran over to the sidelines and had me look at it. I told her maybe she should come out. She said she wasn't coming out. I told her to spit the blood out, which she did; and she finished the game, and then gave her mouth a good rinse. We expect this from a college player, but this was one determined 11 year old girl.

Just recently at a fourth grade basketball game that I coached, one of our players got bumped underneath the basket and started crying. We took her out of the game and put her on the bench where she continued to cry. Several minutes later she was still sitting there and sniffling and I went to her and said, "You did a good job in there; but as long as you're crying, no coach will ever put you back in the game because you let the other team know that they've gotten to you. You just can't be ready to battle out there if you're sniffling and crying." The other coach I was coaching with watched her and she continued to sob. He told her, "If you want to play any more, stop that. Get up and go tell Coach Hatcher that you're ready to play." A few minutes later I got a tug on my arm and she said, "Coach, I'm ready to go back in." I put her back in the game and she did well.

Can you imagine going into a business appointment and not getting what you want, and starting to cry? It sounds ridiculous. Well, it's just as ridiculous to start crying when you're having a tough practice. Once you do that you've given up and you've let the coach and all the players know that you're not one that can be counted on when the going gets tough. Even if you're throwing up at practice, try not to let the tears come out, not because it will make you a sissy, but because it won't help you in your performance. I've cried and we've all cried, and I'll probably cry again. My point here is that crying doesn't help you get through whatever it is you're trying to get through. And it won't help you gain the respect of your teammates. Most importantly, it won't help your performance.

When you get bumps and bruises during ballgames you'll be a lot better off if you can handle it without crying. There are certainly some situations where it just can't be helped, but most of the time we just get a little bump and feel sorry for ourselves. If you want to play as you get to the higher levels, you have to let the coaches know that you're ready to stay in or go back in. Your temperament and your determined attitude make this possible. I am writing this the day after one of my soccer players ran into our own goalie in a game and split her lip badly enough that it was debatable for stitches. She came off the field with blood flying everywhere, and we took her to the bathroom and got her cleaned up and called her parents over and told her that she might need to go get stitches in her lip. We had some doctors look at it, and they said it was a 50/50 call. As we got toward the end of the game, her parents said, "Let's go to the hospital and take a look at it." She said, "No. I want to stay and watch the end of the game." When the game ended, we did some of our after game warm downs and running, and I looked out and there she was running right with the rest of them. She said that the doctors on the sideline said it wouldn't make any difference whether she got there in 15 minutes so she was going to stay and participate with the team.

It's really no surprise that this player, Caty McMains, who is the smallest on my team, is also the toughest. She'll battle anybody, any size, any time, and anywhere because she's got a great, tough mind and character. When the competition gets tough and the players are all fairly similar—for example, in a college situation where you're competing for playing time—it's the intangibles that will separate one player from another. Mental toughness is at the top of the list of those intangibles. I have learned from coaching that if you promote toughness, your players and your team will be tough. If you don't develop a tough mindset they won't be tough, and many times that's the difference between playing and sitting and winning and losing.

Make no mistake about it, there's a huge difference between injury and pain. A player with an injury should not play any more because they could do more damage to that injury. Pain is where something hurts, but you're not going to injure your body by continuing to play. Players have to learn the difference between the two and work through the pain but get off the field when there's an injury. I would never let one of my tough players play if they would endanger themselves or another player, but I do try to help my players be tough guys mentally.

One final funny example is one that my old coach used to tell me. He would say, "Isn't it amazing how people can sit in a movie theater and be laughing one minute and crying the next? The temperature hasn't changed; nobody's touching them or doing anything to them; they are simply watching a film with emotion; and it's that emotion in their mind that makes them laugh, cry, or get scared." When you learn to control your mind in sports, it can help your body overcome a lot of obstacles. Try to reserve your crying for happiness over a championship won because of the blood, sweat, and tears you have put in that season. Don't cry tears of frustration over an obstacle you might face. Some of your parents may say that I'm too tough or that this crying chapter is ridiculous, but I can assure you of one thing… a person with a strong mind that understands what I'm saying will regularly beat someone who does not.

## Questions/Discussion

1. When things get tough, how do you react?
2. Can you think of a sporting event in which your crying helped?

CHAPTER
# 44

# No Discipline, No Success

I dictated this chapter while in Las Vegas at the Venetian Hotel riding a stationary bike at about 8:30 in the morning. I was in Las Vegas for a basketball tournament with my eleven year old twins and had gotten up to get in my workout. It would be tempting to sleep in, have a big breakfast, and just enjoy the day in Las Vegas. After all, I could justify that I deserve a break, don't need to work out, and don't need to spend time writing this book during my time off. The truth is, almost this entire book has been dictated or written on airplanes or while on vacation because it's hard to squeeze it in during the normal hectic day to day workdays I have.

One thing I've learned over the years is "No Discipline, No Success." It doesn't matter whether you're trying to stay fit as you get older or make that sale for your company or become the great high school athlete or college athlete that you want to be. You have to prime the pump; in other words, you've got to put a little something in in order to get something out. Success is a very simple formula: if you pay the price, odds are you can be very successful. The beauty is that once you get started and you show discipline it's actually kind of fun. I would rather be dictating this book while riding a bike than lying in my bed then getting up and knowing that I'm not going to feel as good today or be as fit, and that I may have trouble getting those pants buttoned up as my waist line continues to grow.

The difference between being extraordinary and average is just a few percentage points. Say, for example, that you are a soccer player, and you're pretty even with the other top soccer players in the state. On your off day on Sunday, you go run a three-mile jog to help get yourself more fit, and you stay after practice 15 minutes each day to work on your penalty kicks, your direct kicks, and some special moves. It won't be long before you'll be outperforming your competitors that were at your ability level in every game. It just takes the discipline to do a little extra that makes the difference. One of my favorite lines was in the movie, Million Dollar Baby. There was a quote on the wall that read, "Winners are Simply Willing to Do What Losers Won't."

The longer I live, and the more I watch people in sports, business, and just in their personal lives, the more I realize that the race we're running is a marathon. It's not a race that's determined most often by who has the most talent because people do have different levels of talent. The game is determined most of all by who is going to have the discipline to put in the time and the effort to do the right things and improve and work towards their goals. "The race is not to the swift, but to those who keep on running." I can't even count how many times I've seen a kid be a better athlete in the sixth or seventh grade only to watch the athlete with less talent continue to work through the junior high years and the high school years and be a far superior performer on the field by their junior or senior year simply because the other more talented athlete stopped putting in the time, started going to parties, to the lake, and generally just wanting to have more fun than the other one.

I certainly am all about fun as much as anybody, but it's after I put in my time and my work on the things that are important to me; then it's time to celebrate and have fun. And you know, that fun is a lot better when you know you've accomplished something first.

## Questions/Discussion

1. What are you really disciplined about? Are you successful in this area?
2. What are you not disciplined about? Are you successful in this area?

CHAPTER

# 45

# Passion

When I look back at the sports heroes I had when I was a kid, they all had a common denominator. I didn't realize it at the time, but I realize it now. That common denominator was passion. One of my three heroes was Pete Rose, who played baseball harder than any baseball player of any era. He would sprint out a walk to first base, dive head first when stealing a base or trying to take an extra base, and smash into the catcher if there was a close play at home plate.

In basketball my hero was John Havlicek about whom I've written a chapter later in the book. Havlicek worked so hard that he visited his doctor to ask if he could die of a heart attack from putting forth so much effort. When the doctor told him that he would pass out first in giving such an effort, Havlicek smiled because knew he would be able to continue playing the game with his relentless style.

In football, it was quarterback Roger Staubach of the Dallas Cowboys who led his team to comeback victories in the fourth quarter more than any other quarterback before him. He never quit competing and always believed there was a way his team could win.

As the father of five children that I coach, and after watching hundreds of other kids that I coach as well, I have no doubt that some kids are born with more great talent for the game than others. If you ever get a great athlete who has passion to go with the talent, then you have the full package; and they will go as far as they want to go. If you have great talent without passion, or passion without great talent, you don't have a chance to be the best. But when the two are intertwined, it's a lethal combination.

If you're an athlete that doesn't have great talent, but you have passion you will beat many people in your lifetime who are more talented than you. If I had to choose for my kids whether I would want them to have just talent or just passion, I would always choose passion. There will come a time and place (for example, in the business world) when you don't have to have athletic talent to be successful. Then passion will take you straight to the top. God gave me, as a player, as much passion as Pete Rose had; and he gave me some talent. It is hard to ever know exactly how much talent he gave me because every coach I ever played for would have said that I was an overachiever, which I guess means I didn't have much talent. I'd also like to think that when you're that passionate it's hard for a coach truly to know how much is talent and how much is the effort you put out on the field. One of the reasons I wrote this book is because of my passion for sports and because I believe had I known a lot of the things outlined in this book as a young athlete and combined it with the passion and whatever athletic talent I had, I simply could have done a lot more. And those of you who are wise and are willing to learn from those who came before you will have a chance to improve your athletic career without having to learn it all yourselves.

As I said, I have five kids and they all have different natural talent levels. I and the coaches that I coach with can take any loss; we just can't take it when the passion isn't there or the players are not giving maximum effort. Are you a player who is willing to dive on the floor for the loose basketball? Are you vocal? Do you lead your team, help communicate, and be the coach on the field? Do you have your game face on, and do you mentally prepare before ballgames? Does it take you 30 minutes to unwind after a game because you're replaying the game in your mind and trying to figure out what you did well and what you could do better?

If you're not doing these things, you don't have the passion that the very best players have.

If you've ever dealt with someone passionate about their game you'll know that you can ask them a question a few minutes before game time and they may not even hear you. They may be a little tense or even irritable because they're so focused on their mission. Probably the best example I can give for a sport where you need to have passion is boxing. When I was in high school one of my friends, Michael Saldana, was boxing for the State Golden Gloves Championship. I had never seen him box but had played baseball with him and we were friends, and Michael was always a funny guy and a lot of fun to play with. I decided I would go see that State Championship fight. About 15 minutes prior to when he would enter the ring they came out. They had him in a warm up area, and I wanted to go over and talk to him. I walked over and was two feet away and said, "Hey, good luck, Michael." His eyes were focused, staring straight ahead; he had Vaseline all over his face; he never blinked; he never nodded; he never acknowledged me; and he was completely in a zone.

As a high school and collegiate wrestler I knew what it was like to be focused before a match, but I'd never been that focused. I guess if a loss in my sport could mean getting a black eye, a broken nose, a cut up face, or even death I would be as focused and passionate as the boxer. I'm convinced that there is no sport where you risk more than boxing. Can you imagine participating and not being passionate about it? You'd literally be risking your life. Why not be just as passionate about your sport…you'll certainly be more successful.

## Questions/Discussion

1. Are you a passionate player?
2. Are you focused before every competition, or just some of them?

> The very best have to brave uncharted waters.
> That's part of what makes them the best.

# Obsessive Discipline

It has been said that one of the keys to success is trying to take the good traits from your parents and friends and leave the bad traits alone. My mother and father are certainly an interesting combination. My father is one of the most disciplined, organized men I've ever known and my mother is one of the most obsessive. It's not that my mother doesn't have discipline; it's just that she only has discipline for the things she wants to have discipline for. My father is disciplined in things he enjoys and is also disciplined about things that are just plain no fun. The perfect combination, however, for over the top success is obsessive discipline. My father has certainly been successful in life because of his broad forms of discipline and the fact that he is organized and does what he says he's going to do when he says he's going to do it.

People who know me and know how I love competition can see that a lot of that competitiveness came from my mother. Throughout her life she's had many different hobbies and things she was interested in. Those hobbies got her full attention, and she became the very best at what she did. When she was a grade school teacher she was always the teacher that the school system raved about, as she was extremely creative and had a lot of ingenuity. Then she went through years and years of different little projects, many of which were art related. Finally, in her late forties or early fifties, she decided to take up quilting. Now I know this is a sports book; and I don't want you to think that Greg is falling off his rocker and now goes to quilting shows, but I do have respect for my mother's quilting art. You see, my mother works eight hours a day quilting, and she'll work for approximately one year to complete one quilt. Her quilts are masterpieces. She has become one of the best in the world, if not the best in the world for one particular era of quilting. One of her quilts is on the cover of a book that features the top 100 quilts of the 20th century. She has three quilts in Paducah, Kentucky in the Quilters Hall of Fame. When I think about obsessive discipline I think of my mother, along with many of the great athletes. Obsessive discipline means being disciplined in a given area and being completely outside the box of being a normal person when it comes to that particular activity. It's impossible to be the best any other way.

We've joked before in the book that my father says moderation in all things is good. I always say moderation in all things will make you a little bit better than mediocre. When you become obsessive about something, you're going to get really, really good at that one thing. When that happens, you may develop some weaknesses in other areas. However, it's impossible to ever be the best at anything without being obsessive. Was Tiger Woods a little obsessive about golf when he was growing up? Was Michael Jordan a little obsessive about basketball? Was Lance Armstrong obsessive about his bike riding? Was Larry Bird a little obsessive about shooting a thousand shots every day? Are Siegfried and Roy a little obsessive about magic shows and tigers? Show me anybody that's the best, and I'll show you somebody whom a whole lot of people consider absolutely nuts for spending so much time on that particular activity.

It is also true, however, that the same people who talk negatively about them while they are putting in all that time begin to see things differently when the "obsessives" achieve the pinnacle of success. Once they become the best in their field, the public has great respect and admiration for them. They may even begin to ask themselves why they were not willing to pay such a price.

Remember, to be the best you have to be the leader of the pack; and the leader of the pack runs many times and many miles all alone. In the end, however, it feels really good to be the best. Obsessive discipline about something that's good for you and something you love can be a wonderful thing and is very likely to put you at the top of your field.

## Questions/Discussion

1. Can you think of something you know more about than anyone in the world?
2. Can you think of something you are more obsessed with than anyone in the world?
3. Are you good at or with those things you have listed above?

# CHAPTER 7

# John Havlicek, Boston Celtics

When I was growing up I had several boyhood heroes that I always loved to watch play professional sports. In football, it was Roger Staubach, quarterback of the Dallas Cowboys; in baseball it was Pete Rose of the Cincinnati Reds; and in basketball, it was John Havlicek of the Boston Celtics.

John Havlicek was a gritty player and a unique professional athlete in that he got drafted to play professionally in football, basketball, and baseball; but he decided to go with basketball. Havlicek made his reputation early with the Boston Celtics as the sixth man, which means he wasn't even a starter. He would come off the bench and provide energy, and he scored a lot of points for the Celtics—more than most of the starters. What I admired about Havlicek was that he was the hardest worker, the smartest player, and the gutsiest player on the court. When Havlicek was playing he played harder than anybody that ever played the game both in practice and in games.

I later learned that Havlicek had come up with a theory on how he could play so hard. He went to the doctor and asked if it was possible for him to play so hard that he could have a heart attack and die or if he could do damage to his body if he ran too many sprints, ran them too hard or just worked out too hard. The doctor told him," John, your body will shut down and you'll just pass out before you push yourself to the point where you could actually die." That was all John needed to know to give him the assurance that he could lay it all on the line each and every game, and the worst thing that could happen would be, in his mind, that he would just pass out. Armed with this information, Havlicek gave it all he had throughout his career.

All-time sports lovers will never forget many of his memorable plays. One of the most famous was in the playoffs when Havlicek stole the inbounds pass from the opponent when they were getting ready to have a chance to score the game-winning basket. The announcer went crazy and yelled, "Havlicek stole the ball! Havlicek stole the ball! Johnny Havlicek stole the ball!"

At the end of the game a lot of players are tired, but Havlicek was always the best in the clutch when the game was on the line. I'm convinced that was because Havlicek was physically fit, his mind was strong, and he knew he had paid the price in practice and throughout the game so he deserved to win. It's amazing how often you win when you think you deserve to. There are no short cuts to deserving anything... it has to be earned, and John Havlicek earned his success everyday when he went out to play or to practice.

## Questions/Discussion

1. What is your definition of a person who has good luck?
2. Do you believe people can be consistently lucky?

> A bump in the road is either an obstacle to be fought or an opportunity to be involved to you.

# Second Chances

One thing I love about sports is that so often they give you a second chance in life.

Michael Jordan had a commercial once that said, "I've taken the game-winning shot for my team 82 times, but it's the 36 times I made the shot for which I'm remembered." In sports we learn to count our victories and not our losses. We learn not to lie around and wallow in our failures because another chance is coming up to redeem ourselves. This is the way God intended life to be. I believe God wants us to have a world of second chances. None of you is perfect, nor am I. We will continue to make mistakes, and I hope that all of us will get a second chance to redeem ourselves on some of our screw-ups in life.

People who have played sports, I believe, are better managers, better Presidents, better CEOs, and just better people to deal with in general. They gain some things from sports that are hard to gain anywhere else. A true athlete knows not to get too cocky in victory because every dog has his day, and there will come a time when they will be on the losing end. At the same time an athlete knows when things aren't so good to put an arm around a friend and stick with them when times are tough and give them that second chance.

When I was younger my father warned me about drugs, driving too fast, alcohol, gambling, sex, stealing, and dishonesty in financial matters. I thought my dad was a worry wart, and a little bit hypersensitive on these subjects. I am now 43 years old, and I can tell you that I've had a teammate, friend, or business acquaintance or client in trouble for every one of those situations. My father's advice to me on those issues at an early age has kept me clear of trouble, but I can see how good people can fall into any of those traps, and I have a healthy respect for all of these issues and realize that anyone can be vulnerable — including you and me. When some of the people I knew got into these situations, I didn't turn my back and run. I've had the courage to talk to them, write them a note, stand beside them, and even help them in their time of need. They always say when the crap hits the fan you'll find out who your real friends are. I can tell you these individuals didn't have a lot of people sticking around.

One of the things I learned in sports is when the team loses, we all lose; and we all stick together. We don't start pointing the finger and running for cover. Sports helped me hold my head up high and help people when they needed me most. And you know what? When times have been tough for me, I've always had plenty of friends around. The best way to have a lot of friends is to be a friend yourself.

In business, I have given several employees second chances. Most of the time things turned out for the best. Even the couple of times when things didn't work out, I'm glad that I gave them the second chance. I just feel like everybody deserves a second chance and then they and I can move forward feeling that at least we tried. I've seen some businesses make horrible moves by not giving somebody a second chance. Sometimes the result was that it has hurt or ruined their business in addition to failing to help an individual get a new start in life. Generally, the decision makers who won't give people second chances aren't secure enough with themselves to lead and take the heat if things don't work out.

I am a movie lover. I think I love movies because I'm allowed to dream, and because the writers of these movies are artists who are trying to communicate messages that are very important to all of us and are not so easily communicated in everyday life. There are many father and son relationships out there where the father and son don't speak to each other. In the movie, Dad, which starred Jack Lemmon and Ted Danson, there was a situation where Lemmon, who played the father of Danson, was dying. Danson had been a busy son, making millions of dollars on Wall Street and never taking much time for his family. When his dad went into a coma, Ted left Wall Street and slept in his father's hospital room for months. This catastrophe brought father and son back together. The son said he had to be there just in case his father woke up. During the hospital stay Danson's son came to visit his grandfather and told Ted what a horrible father he was. This grandfather, his son, and grandson all re-bonded. At one point in the movie the grandson asked his father, "What's the most important lesson you've learned in life?" Danson's character responded, "To be forgiving." That line has stuck with me ever since.

There will be many people that cross you in your life; there will be times when things are unfair; but if someone says they're sorry, be forgiving, go forward, and never hold it against them again. Give people a second chance in life; you'll feel better about yourself; and someday when your life's done and you arrive at the pearly gates, you'll be praying for your own second chance. Thank goodness we have a God who gives them.

## Questions/Discussion

1. Can you remember a situation in your life where you needed a second chance?
2. Were others forgiving?
3. Are things always fair in sports? Why?

In major league baseball they spend a lot of time reporting how many home runs somebody hits in a season, but they spend hardly any time reporting how many times a player strikes out.

# Swing for the Fences

When I was in my senior year at Alma College in Michigan, Hall of Famer Willie Stargel came to speak to our Fellowship of Christian Athletes. Stargel was the captain and Most Valuable Player for the Pittsburgh Pirates who won the 1979 World Series. Willie gave an hour talk, and I will never forget the way he ended his speech.

He said he had been asked many times what was the greatest thing he learned during his career as a professional baseball player. Willie said the answer was very clear. "In the early years of my major league career when I came up to the plate with the bases loaded and two outs, I would say to myself, "Please Lord, don't let me strike out. Let me make contact with the ball because the last thing I want to do is strike out with the bases loaded." Willie said he did not strike out much early in his career. He often hit a ground ball to the second baseman or a fly ball to the right fielder that ended the inning with no runs scored, but he didn't strike out.

Later in his career, when Willie came up to bat with the bases loaded and two outs, he learned to swing to hit the ball as hard as he could and knock it out of the ballpark. He said he struck out a heck of a lot more than he did early in his career. However, he also hit quite a few grand slams and a whole lot of doubles and singles as well. He became the hero for the Pittsburgh Pirates many times by swinging as hard as he could in a critical situation.

He finally realized that whether he struck out trying to hit the ball out of the park or hit a ground ball to the second baseman, the result was an out. Early in his career, Willie spent his at-bat trying not to fail. Later in his career, when he was no longer afraid to strike out, he came to the plate and swung as hard as he could to help his team win. When you go out on the court or field to practice or play a game, there will be times when you feel like Willie Stargel coming to bat with the bases loaded and two outs. When you get in the batter's box and you feel that fear, step out of the box for a second; adjust your attitude; step back in the box; and swing for the fences. When you do, you will feel better about yourself, and you will often be a hero like Willie Stargel. You can never be the hero if you don't take a big swing. Good luck, and swing for the fences!

## Questions/Discussion

1. What do you do to keep track of your failures or successes?
2. Who holds the major league record for home runs?
3. Who holds the record for strikeouts?
4. Who's the NFL's all-time leading passer?
5. Who's thrown the most interceptions?
6. Who's the NBA's all-time leading scorer?
7. Who's had the most turnovers?

# 50

> Obstacles are those frightful things you see
> when you take your eyes off your goals.

# Focus

One of the things I have learned from watching my players over the years is that the great ones have the ability to focus in important situations or when things are not going well. Some players will be out shooting the basketball during the drills and just start missing, and they can't ever adjust their shot or seem to get it going right. Sometimes it takes the coach talking to these players and correcting something before they can get their shot adjusted. Other players have the ability to focus on the fundamentals and correct their shot quickly. I have watched players come and get ready for a game when there is very little time to warm up, and they can be ready to play immediately because they have great focus. The ability to get prepared mentally and to be able to focus in key situations may be the difference between a great player and an average one.

Focus is all about mental attitude; it's the ability to be positive when something around you is negative, such as a hostile environment. Focus can keep you on target even when you are tired or perhaps injured during a ballgame. Focus can come into play after you have had a bad breakup with a boyfriend or girlfriend; and you can still walk out onto the court and concentrate on the job at hand, putting any personal problems behind you to do your very best.

Recently Brett Favre, of the Green Bay Packers, lost his father. The day after his father's death he went out and played one of his best football games ever. This shows his ability to focus even at the most trying times. He hadn't had time to practice; he had been through a horrible situation; but he was able to flip the switch of focus on and perform at his best. When asked why he played, he said his Dad would have wanted him to. He made the best of a difficult situation by having a positive mental attitude. Neither he nor his Dad would have wanted Brett to let his teammates down. Each athlete needs to learn this unique ability to focus in order to bring out their very best in game situations.

## Questions/Discussion

1. We've all had games in which we were really on and those in which we were really off. Do you think focus has something to do with that?
2. When it's game time, can you block out all your troubles or distractions and play?

> "Leadership is doing what's right
> when no one is watching."
> —GEORGE VAN VALKENBURG

# Corner Cutters

The world is made up of corner cutters. It could be your spouse, your coworkers, your boss, your friends, your family, and yes, yourself. We all have been corner cutters at times, trying to make things a little easier on ourselves. Whether it's not making up your bed right or studying just to pass the test and not to ace it, or running eight laps around the gym and cutting the corners, being a corner cutter is no way to get through life.

When we run laps at Mighty Bluebird Field, if I catch one person cutting a corner even by a step I make the whole team redo the laps. When we're running line drills, I require each athlete to touch the line on the turn and on the starting line. If anybody misses touching that line even by one inch I make the whole team start over and rerun the line drills. Why do I make such a big deal out of inches and cutting corners? I do so because in sports that's often the difference between winning and losing. Hopefully it teaches the kids a more important lesson in life.

In business being a corner cutter can be even more serious than in athletics. Can you imagine corner cutting if you were an airline pilot, an airline mechanic, a sky diver, a taxi cab driver, a neurosurgeon, a heart surgeon, or had any other job that might involve someone's life? Certainly we don't want corner cutters when it comes to those professions. Even if you're working in the financial world—let's say you're an investment broker, an insurance agent, or a bank loan officer—if you cut a corner you could end up with a commitment unfulfilled and a lawsuit soon to follow. I can tell you that as the employer of 30 employees at The Hatcher Agency I know who my corner cutters are, and I know the ones who will absolutely never cut corners. When I have a huge prospect or client that I want to make sure is taken care of, you can be sure I don't give that case to the corner cutters. In fact, corner cutters don't last very long at The Hatcher Agency. If you've ever cut the corner on me just one time, it causes me not to trust you for a long, long time with my most prized clients. All clients want to know that they can count on you to do it right when nobody's watching, to execute, and to not cut any corners when taking care of their client.

This next sentence may be the most important sentence in the book if you could remember it the rest of your life. If you will agree not to cut corners and to do whatever you're doing to the best of your ability, and if you'll agree to take on whatever project you're doing and try to do it better than anybody else in the world then you will be a millionaire someday. I don't care what it is you're doing, if you become the best in the world at it, you'll become a millionaire. I don't care if you want to be a cook; I don't care if you want to be an aerobics instructor, a physician, a painter, a builder, a coach, an architect…if you absolutely refuse to cut corners and work to be the best in the world at your profession, you will be paid handsomely for it. Think about it…think of the best person in any possible industry and you'll find yourself a millionaire. Find that millionaire and you'll find someone who is not a corner cutter.

I teach my kids when we're in practice that it actually feels good to know you're not cutting corners, that you're running a little further than the other guy, that you're doing a little extra, and most importantly, that you're not cheating yourself. In the end, corner cutters will never be as satisfied with their life. Those who don't cut corners have the satisfaction of doing a job right, and that satisfaction stays with you for the rest of your life.

After reading this chapter I hope that as you go through your day you will notice the corner cutters in life. A building that hasn't been built to top notch standards, a person who is wearing a wrinkled shirt and hasn't taken the time to iron it, a limousine driver who doesn't take the time to roll out the red carpet, a man who doesn't take the time to open the door for a girl, you'll see corner cutters everywhere everyday. Just make sure you're not one of them and again, we'll see you at the top.

## Questions/Discussion

1. Name a time in which you were a corner cutter. Why did you cut corners?
2. Can you think of something on which you'll never cut corners? Why not?

CHAPTER

# 52

# Don't Be Afraid to Fail

I am amazed by the number of people who will not try something new because they are afraid they will fail. It happens to all of us at a very early age. I have a 15-year-old daughter, eleven-year-old twin girls, a six-year-old son, and a four-year-old daughter. I spend a lot of time at the lake teaching my kids and their friends to ski. It always surprises me that many of these kids are afraid to even try to learn to water ski. This is especially true if there are other children present who have tried and succeeded at getting up on the skis. These children won't try because they are afraid they will fail. We are born to win; but as soon as we get out of the womb, society conditions us to fail. By age five many children are already learning the fear of failure. Their parents have not encouraged them to try new things because the parents have their own fears, and they don't want to see the children fail. When my children say, "I can't," I tell them those words are simply not acceptable. The only words I will ever accept are, "I'll try." I want to instill in my children at a very early age that failure is okay, but refusing to try is unacceptable.

One of my all time favorite poems is called, "The Race." The first time I read the poem I almost cried. It is a poem about a young child with courage and the will to continue and try and a father in the stands who rewards him for his ability to get up and try again. We all need to realize that there is nothing to lose by trying. If we try and fail, we are no worse off than if we had not tried to begin with. Actually, if we do not try, we may be worse off because we may begin a practice that could become a habit and a way of life. More than anything else, attitude determines the success a person will have in life. Top athletes must have a wonderful attitude. You simply cannot be at the top year in and year out with a poor attitude. You have to be willing to try new things, to continue to learn, to implement new concepts and to be open to new ideas. If you are not willing to try new things, you will simply be passed by.

The older we get, the more we tend to be afraid of failure. The reason is that we add to our list of failures each year. As those failures add up, we become more resistant to trying new things, as we almost would rather not succeed than to take the chance of trying and failing one more time.

If you study the lives of the greatest people in this world, you will be amazed at all the failures they have had. The common denominator for all these people who have had so many failures is that they have gotten out there and tried again. We all know that Michael Jordan was cut from his high school basketball team but went on to become the greatest basketball player of all time. Many other people in sports have failed miserably many times before they became a huge success.

One of the most amazing records of failure is the one listed below.

Failed in business . . . . . . . . . . . . . . . . . . . . . . . . age 22

Ran for legislature (defeated) . . . . . . . . . . . . . . age 23

Failed in business . . . . . . . . . . . . . . . . . . . . . . . . age 24

Elected to legislature . . . . . . . . . . . . . . . . . . . . . age 25

Sweetheart died . . . . . . . . . . . . . . . . . . . . . . . . age 26

Had a nervous breakdown . . . . . . . . . . . . . . . . age 27

Defeated for speaker. . . . . . . . . . . . . . . . . . . . age 29

Defeated for elector . . . . . . . . . . . . . . . . . . . age 31

Defeated for Congress. . . . . . . . . . . . . . . . . . age 34

Elected to Congress . . . . . . . . . . . . . . . . . . . age 37

Defeated for Congress. . . . . . . . . . . . . . . . . . age 39

Defeated for Senate . . . . . . . . . . . . . . . . . . . age 46

Defeated for Vice President . . . . . . . . . . . . . . age 47

Defeated for Senate . . . . . . . . . . . . . . . . . . . age 49

Elected President of the United States . . . . . . . . age 51

That is the record of Abraham Lincoln. Obviously, Abraham Lincoln had a heck of a lot more failures than successes; but overall he was a huge success because of his courage, persistence, and perseverance.

My father has always kidded me that I have one of the most selective memories of any person he has ever known. He says I always seem to remember only the accomplishments of my high school and college sports careers and in my business dealings and forget many of the difficult times I had over the years. He says when I recall the past all I remember is the good.

I am not sure that my having a selective memory is so bad. Who knows? This "selective memory" may be what gives me the ability to go forward and try virtually any new challenge. Because I remember my successes and focus on them I have the confidence to believe that I can do just about anything. I have successfully tried many things just for the sake of knowing that I have attempted and completed them. When I accomplish a new task it gives me more confidence to take on the next challenge.

Some examples of challenges that I have attempted and accomplished include: running a marathon, completing a triathlon, completing a 150-mile bike race, sky diving, parasailing, scuba diving, barefoot skiing, taking over 2,000 hours in continuing education at insurance schools and passing more than 40 insurance exams, writing two books, starting my own business, and making the starting lineup on three different college sports teams. I have called back to insurance companies who rejected me earlier to develop a better relationship; and I have gone back to try to mend fences with vendors, friends, and competitors with whom I had differences.

I get along with all types of people and have friends from all walks of life, but my very best friends are people who are willing to try new things and are not afraid to fail. I want to spend my time with people who continue to grow, and to grow you must be willing to try new things.

Following you will find some of my favorite motivational poems. I hope they inspire you and you like them as much as I do.

## Questions/Discussion

1. Can you think of something at which you've been afraid to fail?
2. Have you ever failed at something simply because you were afraid to fail? If so, what?

# Motivational Poems and Stories

# The Guy in the Glass

When you get what you want in your struggle for self,

And the world makes you King for a day,

Then you go to the mirror and look at yourself,

And see what that guy has to say.

For it isn't your Father or Mother or Wife

Whose judgment upon you must pass.

He's the feller to please, never mind all the rest

For he's with you clear up to the end,

And you've passed your most dangerous, difficult test

If the guy in the glass is your friend.

You may be like Jack Horner and "chisel" a plum

And think you're a wonderful guy,

But the man in the glass says you're only a bum

If you can't look him straight in the eye.

You can fool the whole world down the pathway of years,

And get pats on your back as you pass.

But your final reward will be heartaches and tears

If you've cheated the guy in the glass.

—DALE WIMBROW

# It's All in a State of Mind

If you think you are beaten, you are;
If you think you dare not, you won't.
If you like to win, but don't think you can,
It's almost a cinch you won't.

If you think you'll lose, you've lost;
For out in the world you'll find
Success begins with a fellow's will;
It's all in a state of mind.

For many a game is lost
Before even a play is run,
And many a coward fails
Before even his work has begun.

Think big and your deeds will grow,
Think small and you'll fall behind,
Think that you can and you will;
It's all in a state of mind.

If you think you are outclassed you are;
You've got to think high to rise;
You've got to be sure of yourself before
You can ever take home the prize.

Life's battles don't always go
To the stronger or faster man,
More often than not, the man who wins
Is the fellow who thinks he can.

—OFTEN QUOTED BY NICK MOUROUZIS
HEAD FOOTBALL COACH, DEPAUW UNIVERSITY, 1981-2003
(Winningest coach in school history)

# Attitude
By Charles Swindoll

"The longer I live, the more I realize the impact of attitude on life.

Attitude, to me, is more important than facts.

It is more important than the past, than education, than money, than circumstances, than failures, than successes, than what others think or say or do.

It is more important than appearance, giftedness or skill.

It will make or break a company... a church... a home.

The remarkable thing is we have a choice everyday regarding the attitude we will embrace for that day.

We cannot change our past...we cannot change the fact that people will act in a certain way.

We cannot change the inevitable.

The only thing we can do is play on the one string we have, and that is our attitude... I am convinced that life is 10% what happens to me and 90% how I react to it.

And so it is with you... we are in charge of our attitudes."

# Rise Each Time You Fall

They all lined up so full of hope, each thought to win the race

Or tie for first or if not that at least take a second place.

And parents watched from off the side, each cheering for their child

Each one hoped to show his folks that he would be the one.

The whistle blew and off they went, young hearts and hopes afire

To win and be the hero there was each runner's desire.

And one runner in particular whose dad was in the crowd

Was running near the lead and thought, "my dad will be so proud!"

But as they speeded down the field across the shallow dip

The runner who thought to win lost his step and slipped

Trying hard to catch himself his hands flew out to brace

And mid the laughter of the crowd he fell flat on his face.

So down he fell and with him hope – he could not win it now.

Embarrassed, sad he only wished to disappear somehow;

But as he fell his dad stood up and showed his anxious face

Which to the boy so clearly said "Get up and win the race."

He quickly rose no damage done – to catch up and to win –

His mind went faster than his legs; he slipped and fell again

I'm hopeless as a runner now, I shouldn't try to race."

But in the laughing crowd he searched and found his father's face

That steady look which said again. "Get up and win the race."

So up he jumped to try again – ten yards behind the last.

"If I'm trying to gain those yards", he thought, "I've got to move real fast!"

Exerting everything he had he regained eight of ten,

But trying so hard to catch the lead, he slipped and fell again.

Defeat! He laid there silently – a tear dropped from his eye

There's no sense running anymore, three strikes I'm out. Why Try?

The will to rise had disappeared; all hope had fled away.

So far behind, so error prone, a loser all the way.

"I've lost so what's the use?" he thought, "I'll have to live with my disgrace"

But then he thought about his dad, who soon he'd have to face.

"Get up!" an echo sounded low. "Get up and take your place."

"With borrowed will get up" he said. " You haven't lost at all.

For winning is no more than this: to rise each time you fall."

So up he rose to run once more and now with new commit

He resolved that win or lose, at least he would not quit.

So far behind the others now, the most he'd ever been

Still he gave it all he had and ran as through to win.

Three times he'd fallen, stumbling; three times he rose again

Too far behind to hope to win, he still ran to the end.

They cheered the winning runner as he crossed the line first place

Head high and proud and happy – no falling, no disgrace,

But when the fallen youngster crossed the line last place,

The crowd gave him a greater cheer for finishing the race.

And even though he came in last, with head bowed low – unproud

You would have thought he'd won the race, to listen to the crowd.

And to his dad he sadly said, "I didn't do so well."

"To me, you won," his father said, "you rose each time you fell."

So when your life seems dark and hard, things difficult to face

May the memory of that little boy help you in your race.

For all of life is like a race, with ups and downs and all,

And all you have to do to win is rise each time you fall.

—FROM "THE RACE" BY DEE GROBERG

# Don't Quit
## by Edgar A. Guest

When things go wrong, as they sometimes will,
when the road you're trudging seems all uphill,
when the funds are low and the debts are high,
and you want to smile but you have to sigh,
when care is pressing you down a bit—
rest if you must, but don't you quit.

Life is queer with its twists and turns.
As every one of us sometimes learns.
And many a fellow turns about
when he might have won had he stuck it out.
Don't give up though the pace seems slow—
you may succeed with another blow.

Often the goal is nearer than it seems
to a faint and faltering man;
often the struggler has given up
when he might have captured the victor's cup;
and he learned too late when the night came down,
how close he was to the golden crown.

Success is failure turned inside out—
the silver tint of the clouds of doubt,
and when you never can tell how close you are,
it may be near when it seems afar;
so stick to the fight when you're hardest hit—
it's when things seem worst, you must not quit.

# The Only Way to Win

It takes a little courage
And a little self-control,
And some grim determination,
If you want to reach your goal.
It takes a deal of striving,
And a firm and stern-set chin,
No matter what the battle,
If you really want to win.

There's no easy path to glory,
There's no rosy road to fame.
Life, however we may view it,
Is no simple parlor game;
But its prizes call for fighting,
For endurance and for grit;
For a rugged disposition
And a don't-know-when-to-quit.

You must take a blow or give one,
you must risk and you must lose,
And expect that in the struggle,
You will suffer from the bruise.
But you mustn't wince or falter,
If a fight you once begin;
Be a man and face the battle—
That's the only way to win.

—NAVY SEAL MASTERCHIEF

# Another Way to Win

Kay Poe and Esther Kim have been best friends since they were seven years old. Among other things they have in common, the two young ladies from Houston both compete at the highest levels in taekwondo. How good are they? Esther and Kay advanced to the finals in the Women's Olympic Flyweight division at the 2000 U.S. Olympic Team Trials on May 20 in Colorado Springs.

"I don't think of her as just a friend. I think of her more as a sister," Kay says. "We've grown up together, and we always push each other and help each other out the best we can training wise." What a story was unfolding! Reporters and photographers were poised to record the outcome of so intense a competition between two girls who have been close for so long. But a sports story would soon be overshadowed by a far more important friendship story.

Kay had dislocated her left kneecap in her semi-final match of the round robin tournament. Though ranked number one in the world at her sport, it was questionable that she could compete against her best friend. She could barely stand, so it was a foregone conclusion that Esther would win, travel to the 2000 Olympic Games in Sydney, and represent the United States in the International competition these two had trained and worked toward for so long.

On the day of the match, Esther Kim shocked the crowd by forfeiting rather than defeat her friend in an unfair competition. In allowing the better taekwondo fighter to represent the United States in Sydney, she won a personal battle over ego and selfishness. Amidst frequent stories of cheating and taking unfair advantage in order to win at any price, Esther showed how to win by losing.

"Even though I didn't have the gold medal around me," said Esther, "for the first time in my life, I felt like a real champion." Her generosity of spirit was honored with the Citizenship

Through Sports Award and with an all-expenses-paid trip to the 2000 Olympic Games from the International Olympic Committee.

In the Bible, Paul wrote about giving up certain "rights" for the sake of people he loved (see 1 Corinthians 9:1-15). Parents do it all the time for their children. And occasionally friends make magnanimous gestures like Esther's.

The next time you are inclined to bemoan the selfishness of the masses, recall this story of a twenty-year-old athlete's largess. The next time you have the chance show magnanimity let it inspire you to rise to the level of her example.

BY: <u>RUBEL SHELLY</u>, SOURCE UNKNOWN

# If the Shoe Fits

Please don't curse that boy down there;
He is my son, you see:
He's only just a boy you know,
He means the world to me.

I did not raise my son, dear fan,
For you to call him names:
He may not be a super-star
And these are high school games.

So, please don't knock those boys down there,
They do the best they can;
They've never tried to lose a game,
They're boys, and you're a man.

This game belongs to them, you see,
You're really just a guest;
They do not need a fan that gripes,
They need the very best.

If you have nothing nice to say,
Please leave the boys alone,
And, if you've forgot your manners,
Why don't you stay at home!

So, please don't curse those boys down there,
Each one's his parents' son,
And win or lose or tie, you see,
To us, they're number one!!!

—MARY BRITT, EPHRATA, PA

# A Pioneer in Taking One for the Team

Montreal, 1976 — After severely breaking his knee during the floor exercise, Japan's Shun Fujimoto ignored his injury as long as possible, knowing such news could shatter the confidence of his teammates. The injured gymnast continued to the pommel horse routine, miraculously scoring a 9.5 out of 10. He then faced the rings, which would be his final event of the day. Shun performed extraordinarily, ignoring the inevitable consequences of dismounting from eight feet off the ground. Upon completion of his routine, he hurled himself into a beautifully executed, triple-somersault dismount. When his feet hit the floor, the pain sliced through him like a knife, but he kept his balance. Gritting his teeth, he raised his arms in a perfect finish before collapsing in agony. He was awarded a 9.7, the highest score he had ever recorded on the rings. After winning the closest gymnastics team competition in Olympic history, Shun received his gold medal, but only after insisting that he could make his own way to the podium.

# Let Go...

To "let go" does not mean to stop caring, it means I can't do it for someone else.

To "let go" is not a cut myself off; it's the realization that I can't control another.

To "let go" is not to enable, but to allow learning from natural consequences.

To "let go" is to admit powerlessness, which means the outcome is not in my hands.

To "let go" is not to try to change or blame another; it is to make the most of myself.

To "let go" is not to care for, but to care about.

To "let go" is not to fix, but to be supportive.

To "let go" is not to judge, but to allow another to be a human being.

To "let go" is not to be in the middle arranging all the outcomes but to allow others to affect their destinies.

To "let go" is not to be protective; it is to permit another to face reality.

To "let go" is not to deny, but to accept.

To "let go" is not to nag, scold or argue, but instead to search out my own shortcomings and correct them.

To "let go" is not to adjust everything to my desires, but to take each day as it comes, and cherish myself in it.

To "let go" is not to criticize and regulate anybody, but to try to become what I dream I can be.

To "let go" is not to regret the past, but to grow and live for the future.

To "let go" is to fear less, and love more.

—AUTHOR UNKNOWN

# His Name was Fleming

His name was Fleming, and he was a poor Scottish farmer. One day, while trying to make a living for his family, he heard a cry for help coming from a nearby bog. He dropped his tools and ran to the bog.

There, mired to his waist in black muck, was a terrified boy, screaming and struggling to free himself. Farmer Fleming saved the lad from what could have been a slow and terrifying death.

The next day, a fancy carriage pulled up to the Scotsman's sparse surroundings. An elegantly dressed nobleman stepped out and introduced himself as the father of the boy Farmer Fleming had saved.

"I want to repay you," said the nobleman. "You saved my son's life."

"No, I can't accept payment for what I did," the Scottish farmer replied waving off the offer. At that moment, the farmer's own son came to the door of the family hovel.

"Is that your son?" the nobleman asked.

"Yes," the farmer replied proudly.

"I'll make you a deal. Let me provide him with the level of education my own son will enjoy. If the lad is anything like his father, he'll no doubt grow to be a man we both will be proud of." And that he did.

Farmer Fleming's son attended the very best schools and in time, graduated from St. Mary's Hospital Medical School in London, and went on to become known throughout the world as the noted Sir Alexander Fleming, the discoverer of Penicillin.

Years afterward, the same nobleman's son who was saved from the bog was stricken with pneumonia.

What saved his life this time? Penicillin.

The name of the nobleman? Lord Randolph Churchill. His son's name? Sir Winston Churchill.

—ANONYMOUS

# Big Rocks First!

One day, an expert in time management was speaking to a group of business students and, to drive home a point, used an illustration those students will never forget.

As he stood in front of the group of high-powered overachievers, he said, "Okay, time for a quiz." He then pulled out a one-gallon, wide mouth Mason jar and set it on the table in front of him. The he produced about a dozen fist-sized rocks and carefully placed them, one by one, into the jar. When the jar was filled to the top and no more rocks would fit inside, he asked, "Is this jar full?"

Everyone in the class said, "Yes."

Then he said, "Really?" He reached under the table and pulled out a bucket of gravel. He dumped some gravel in and shook the jar, causing pieces of gravel to work themselves down into the space between the big rocks.

Then he asked the group once more, "Is this jar full?" By this time the class was on to him. "Probably not," one of them answered.

"Good!" he replied. He reached under the table and brought out a bucket of sand. He started dumping the sand in the jar and it went into all the spaces left between the rocks and the gravel.

Once more he asked the question, "Is this jar full?" "No!" the class shouted. Once again, he said, "Good!" Then he grabbed a pitcher of water and began to pour it in until the jar was filled to the brim.

Then the expert in time management looked at the class and asked, "What is the point of this illustration?" One eager beaver raised his hand and said, "The point is, no matter how full your schedule is, if you try really hard you can always fit some more things in it."

"No," the speaker replied, "that's not the point. The truth this illustration teaches us is this: If you don't put the big rocks in first, you will never get them in at all. What are the big rocks in your life? God, your children, your spouse, your loved ones, your friendships, your education, your dreams, a worthy cause, teaching or mentoring others, doing things that you love, time for yourself, or your health?"

Remember to put these BIG ROCKS in first, or you will never get them in at all. If you sweat the little stuff (i.e. the gravel, the sand) then you will fill your life with little things you worry about that don't really matter and you will never have the real quality time you need to spend on the big important stuff (the big rocks).

So, tonight, or in the morning, when you are reflecting on this short story, ask yourself this question: "What are the 'big rocks' in my life?" Then put those in your jar first.

—AUTHOR UNKNOWN

# How Do You Spend Your Dash?

I read of a man who stood to speak
At the funeral of a friend.
He referred to the dates on her tombstone
From the beginning... to the end.

He noted that first came her date of birth
And spoke the following date with tears,
But he said what mattered most of all
Was the dash between those years. (1934-1998)

For that dash represents all the time
That she spent alive on earth...
And now only those who loved her
Know what that little line is worth.

For it matters not, how much we own;
The cars... the house... the cash,
What matters is how we live and love
And how we spend our dash.

So think about this long and hard...
Are there things you'd like to change?
For you never know how much time is left,
Than can still be rearranged.

If we could just slow down enough

To consider what's true and real,

And always try to understand

The way other people feel.

And be less quick to anger,

And show appreciation more

And love the people in our lives

Like we've never loved before.

If we treat each other with respect,

And more often wear a smile...

Remembering that this special dash

Might only last a little while.

So, when your eulogy's being read

With your life's actions to rehash...

Would you be proud of the things they say

About how you spent your dash?

—LINDA ELLIS

# Quotes of Bear Bryant

FOOTBALL COACH, UNIVERSITY OF ALABAMA, FROM THE JUNCTION BOYS

If you believe in yourself and have dedication and pride—and never quit—you will be a winner. The price of victory is high, but so are the rewards.

In a crisis, don't hide behind anything or anybody. They're going to find you anyway.

In life, you'll have your back up against the wall many times. You might as well get used to it.

You never know how a horse will pull until you hook him to a heavy load.

Sacrifice. Work. Self-discipline. I teach these things, and my boys don't forget them when they leave.

I can reach a kid who doesn't have any ability as long as he doesn't know it.

I don't care how much talent a team has—if the boys don't think tough, practice tough, and live tough, how can they play tough on Saturday?

The first time you quit, it's hard. The second time, it gets easier. The third time, you don't even have to think about it.

When you win, there's glory enough for everybody. When you lose, there's glory for none.

Winning isn't imperative, but getting tougher in the fourth quarter is.

I'm just a simple plow hand from Arkansas, but I have learned over the years how to hold a team together. How to lift some men up, how to calm others down, until finally they've got one heartbeat, together, a team.

You have to be willing to out-condition your opponents.

Football changes and so do people.

The first thing a football coach needs when he's starting out is a wife who's willing to put up with a whole lot of neglect. The second thing is a five-year contract.

When you make a mistake, admit it; learn from it and don't repeat it.

What matters…is not the size of the dog in the fight, but the size of the fight in the dog.

I'm known as a recruiter. Well, you've got to have chicken to make chicken salad.

When we have a good team, I know it's because we have boys that come from good mamas and papas.

One man doesn't make a team. It takes eleven.

If anything goes bad, I did it. If anything goes semi-good, we did it. If anything goes real good, you did it. That's all it takes to get people to win football games.

Every time a player goes out there, at least twenty people have some amount of influence on him. His mother has more influence than anyone. I know because I played, and I loved my mama.

No coach has ever won a game by what he knows; it's what his players know that counts.

I left Texas A&M because my school called me. Mama called, and when Mama calls, then you just have to come running.

Someone once said: What goes around comes around.

Work like you don't need the money.

Love like you've never been hurt.

Dance like nobody's watching.

Sing like nobody's listening. Live like it's Heaven on Earth.

# Helping Others Win

A few years ago, at the Seattle Special Olympics, nine contestants, all physically or mentally disabled, assembled at the starting line for the 100-yard dash. At the gun, they all started out, not exactly in a dash, but with a relish to run the race to the finish and win. All, that is, except one little boy who stumbled on the asphalt, tumbled over a couple of times, and began to cry.

The other eight heard the boy cry. They slowed down and looked back. Then they all turned around and went back—every one of them. One girl with Down's Syndrome bent down and kissed him and said, "This will make it better." Then all nine linked arms and walked together across the finish line.

Everyone in the stadium stood, and the cheering went on for several minutes. People who were there are still telling the story.

Why? Because deep down we know this one thing: What matters in this life is more than winning for ourselves. What matters in this life is helping others win, even if it means slowing down and changing our course.

—AUTHOR UNKNOWN

# Who Makes a Difference in Your Life?
### COURTESY OF CADILLAC JACK INTERNATIONAL

Name the five wealthiest people in the world.

Name the last five Heisman trophy winners.

Name the last five winners of the Miss America contest.

Name ten people who have won the Nobel or Pulitzer prize.

Name the last half dozen Academy Award winners for best actor and actress.

Name the last decade's worth of World Series winners.

How did you do?

The point is, none of us remember the headliners of yesterday. These are no second-rate achievers. They are the best in their fields. But the applause dies. Awards tarnish. Achievements are forgotten. Accolades and certificates are buried with their owners.

Here's another quiz. See how you do on this one:

List a few teachers who aided your journey through school.

Name three friends who have helped you through a difficult time.

Name five people who have taught you something worthwhile.

Think of a few people who have made you feel appreciated and special.

Think of five people you enjoy spending time with.

Name half a dozen heroes who stories have inspired you.

Easier? The lesson?

The people who make a difference in your life are not the ones with the most credentials, the most money, or the most awards. They are the ones that care.

Pass this on to those people who have made a difference in your life...

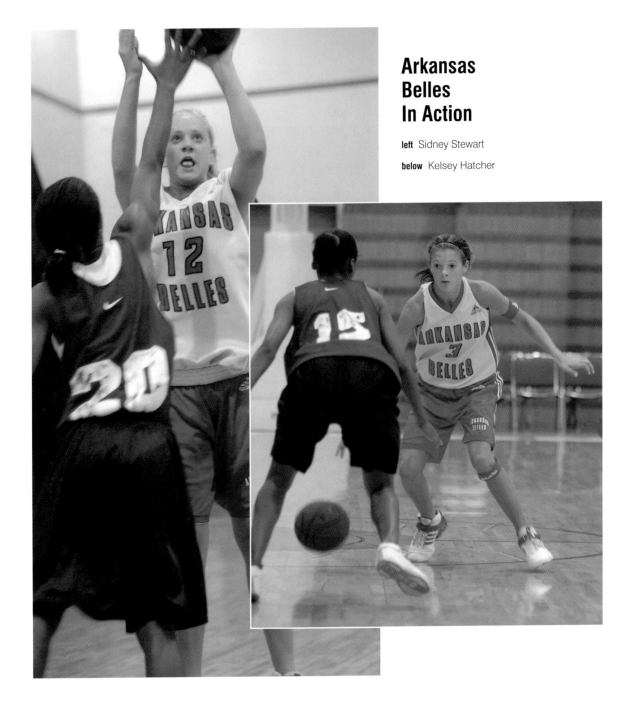

# Arkansas
# Belles
# In Action

**left** Sidney Stewart

**below** Kelsey Hatcher

# Arkansas Belles at Duke

**below** The Belles tip it off at Cameron Indoor Stadium.

**left** The Belles five starters will play Division I Basketball. (L-R) Chelsea Jones (Ft. Smith Southside), Kelsey Hatcher (Central Arkansas Christian), Mahogonny Williams (J.A. Fair), Julie Inman (Carlisle), Sidney Stewart (Greenbrier).

**below** Julie Inman shows her shooting range.

**right** The Belles outside Duke. Front row (L-R) Maddie Helms, Maddie McIntyre, Antonia Jones. Back row (L-R) Julie Inman, Kelsey Hatcher, Mahogonny Williams, Sidney Stewart, Chelsea Jones, and Michelle Hedgecock.

**below** The Belles celebrate a victory at Macaroni Grill.

## Arkansas Belles

Three future Division I players— Kelsey Hatcher, Julie Inman and Sidney Stewart at the Arkansas Prep Hoops banquet.

# Four-Sport Athlete

It was a pretty good freshman year of high school for Kelsey Hatcher.

**below** As a freshman Kelsey led her team to the final four in basketball leading the team in scoring while being named the team's Outstanding Offensive Player, 1st Team All-District, and to the 1st Team Future Starzz Team.

**far left** Kelsey is named All-State in cross country and track. Here she is with Coach Kevin Kelley after winning three individual State Titles in track in the 800, 1600, and 3200 meters. She broke the all time AAA State Record in the 1600.

**left** Kelsey played an instrumental part in leading Pulaski Academy to the State Championship in soccer her freshman year. She led the team in goals and assists, and the team didn't lose a game once she joined the team following basketball season. She was named to the State All-Tournament team.

# No Sophomore Slump

after transferring to Central Arkansas Christian to play for the Mustangs.

**right** Kelsey celebrates after hitting the game's final penalty kick as CAC wins the state soccer title in a sudden death shootout. She was named the tournament MVP.

**left to right**

Kelsey finishes as runner-up in the State Cross Country Meet.

Taking a corner kick in the State Finals.

Kelsey helps CAC win back-to-back state titles, including the #1 ranking in Arkansas for all classifications.

All my best friends I either always played sports with or went to battle with. Here are me and some of my buddies attending Jermain Taylor's Championship fight in Las Vegas when he upset Bernard Hopkins to claim the Middle Weight Championship and make Arkansas proud. From left to right, Chris Owen soccer coach Mighty Bluebirds, Scott Allison former softball teammate, Lennie Segal former softball teammate, Coach Hatcher, Aaron Lubin baseball player and the Membership Chairman during my Rotary Presidency, Bruce Dickey my college soccer, wrestling, and assistant baseball coach. Back row, Coach Scott Loucks Head Coach of the Arkansas Belles.

# Three Things You Can Do to Keep Your Kids Off Drugs

1. Attend church together as a family.

2. Have your child participate in sports.

3. Sit down for dinner at least three times a week as a family.

# On Being A Team Player

I've played in the NFL for a long time and in all that time

I have learned one thing: There is no "I" in the word Team.

—WALTER PAYTON HALL OF FAME INDUCTION CEREMONY

# Negative Wizards

CHAPTER

# 53

# Negative Wizards

In almost every organization and on almost every team there's probably at least one negative wizard. A negative wizard is someone who seems to always find the worst instead of the best in people. There are people who criticize the coach, criticize other players, and generally run around talking badly about other people. If you don't have a good leader on the team who can keep the negative wizards in check, these wizards can take your championship from you. It only takes one negative person to completely mess up a team. I've played on numerous championship teams, but I've never played on one where a negative wizard was a leader. In fact on all of these championship teams, the leaders of the team would be sure to squash any negative wizard quickly because they cause too much commotion.

Most of the time negative wizards aren't happy with themselves and are jealous of other teammates' playing time or accolades. Or, they may have parents who are out of balance and who want the team to be centered more on their child, and who pass this attitude on to the child who is playing. If you hear a teammate talking badly about your coach or other players, help them see the other side of the equation. Whatever you do, don't jump on the bandwagon to support them. No team that's got a lot of infighting can ever win because there's always a competitor; and a team that gels together will find a way to beat the one who has infighting.

Sometimes we think the coach isn't giving us a fair shake, or that a particular player is coach's favorite. Life's not always fair on sports teams; coaches do have particular players that they may appreciate a little more for one reason or the other. What you have to do when you're in that situation is focus on your attitude, your work ethic, the things that you can control, and make yourself the best you can be. Leave no doubt in the coaches' minds and the players' minds that you're needed in the lineup and you'll find yourself there sooner or later. Negative energy never helps you, nor does whining and complaining. Buckle down, work hard, and have a great attitude. Don't become a negative wizard, and don't let negative wizards affect you or your team.

## Questions/Discussion

1. Have you ever had any players on your teams that were negative wizards? If yes, were you able to still win a championship?
2. Have you ever been a negative wizard? If yes, did you feel good about it?

# The Champion Killers

Every great champion is surrounded by champion killers.

There will always be people saying, "Why do you want to get up and work out like that; I enjoy my pillow."

They'll say things like:

"Come on, you don't want to eat all of that healthy stuff; have another piece of pie."

"Come on, have a beer or a margarita or a cigarette, or even a puff of this joint.'

They're the ones who tell you that you work too hard, you need a break, you need to take a day off, and that winning isn't everything. They're the ones who tell you that you are pushing too hard, you ought to skip a practice, that it is the holidays. Why practice on holidays? In other words, they want you to be like them and everybody else.

The champion killers don't know what it is like to be the best, to pay the ultimate price to get to the top. Because they have never gotten to the top they can't understand, they don't know how sweet it feels to have discipline and sacrifice and to be the very best. They also don't know how badly the champion wants to stay at the top. These champion killers may be your very closest relationships, and sometimes they don't even realize that they are a little bit jealous of you. They may not want you to be your best because it makes them feel badly that they aren't doing as well.

You will know who these champion killers are because when you are most successful they don't show up. I have watched my friends' kids and even myself have fantastic games and fantastic years, on the sports field and in business. When the company or salesman wins awards or accolades, their closest friends don't congratulate them because they're jealous that they didn't win the awards and pay the price for success. They just can't bring themselves to congratulate someone who did what they were not willing to do. In fact, a group will stick together and talk about the person and say, "Oh, they don't have a life or they work too hard at basketball (or work or whatever it might be)" to put the winners down.

At this point the champion stands all alone, but you should know that you stand alone only because of envy, and this soon will pass. Champions will find if you continue on your road to success and continue your discipline the very people who are huddling and saying bad things about you will change. Their jealousy will take a new form. They begin to have respect for you, and that respect turns into admiration. Before long, those people will decide that they can't compete with you any more; and once they put you in that separate league where they can't compete with you, they actually look at you as somewhat of a hero.

Hang in there, Champion, for dear life. Don't succumb to mediocrity. Don't succumb to the pressures of anyone else who is not willing to pay the price. At the end of the rainbow, there will be admiration from others; but more importantly, you will have the satisfaction of knowing that you had the discipline, the work ethic, and the sacrifice to do your best and be the best. There is nothing that feels better than that.

## Questions/Discussion

1. How do you deal with champion killers?
2. Do you know one who is close to you?

# Don't Hang Around Naysayers – Warriors Need Warriors

"Hey, that's not the crowd you want to hang around with."

"Don't be in the wrong place at the wrong time or you'll get yourself in trouble."

We've all heard these warnings from our parents or some responsible adult. As an employer at The Hatcher Agency I am amazed at how many people are what I call just loser magnets. They attract other losers and these losers take them to places they shouldn't be. Maybe it's that they drink too much, they do drugs, they go to places they shouldn't be going to and they do things they shouldn't do. It's amazing how these people that are negative wizards, naysayers, and losers love to bring other people into their pity party.

You have to decide what you're going to be in life and what you'll accept and what you won't accept. For example, I enjoy going to parties and meeting with friends, but if I went to a party and people were doing cocaine I would walk out instantly. I know that being around a situation like that can only bring trouble. The police might show up at the party and arrest everybody there, whether you're involved in the cocaine or not. Somebody could get so high on the cocaine that they end up stabbing somebody or getting in a fight, possibly even killing you. You may think this sounds a little extreme, and Coach Hatcher's hyperventilating. I remember my father always giving me all these warnings and I thought, "Gosh he's going a little overboard." But I learned as I got older that everything my father warned me about eventually came true.

I've had friends who drove too fast and killed themselves by running into a bridge at 110 mph. I've known people who died from a drug overdose. I know several people who drank and drove and died in an auto accident. I know people who cheated on their taxes and went to jail. I know people who became enraged in a relationship with a boyfriend or a girlfriend and got in a fight and are now in jail for manslaughter or assault and battery. You have to draw the line for acceptable behavior; and when someone crosses that line, you end the relationship and have nothing more to do with them.

In sports it's no different. I simply don't want to be around people who don't obey the rules of the team, that do drugs, or even that are negative wizards or naysayers. Warriors need Warriors to hang around with. The Bible says "Iron sharpens iron as one man sharpens another." If you want to be the best, practice with the best; hang out with people that are a good influence, and simply do not tolerate anything less. I have a lot of close friends, but the common denominator of most of my best friends is that they are either professional coaches at a school or a university, or they are dads that coach other teams. I enjoy people that are competitive enough, intense enough, and driven enough to get out there and coach. I have a great respect for them, and hanging out with them helps me do my everyday job and all the other things I need to do. I would even go so far as to say that I consider any friend I have a Warrior, a hard worker who is disciplined and does good things. It's simply impossible for you to be a good friend of mine if you don't have discipline, and if you're not a hard worker.

I have a lot of acquaintances whose company I enjoy; but if I am going to spend a lot of time with someone, I need them to be Warriors as well. You are sure to adopt many of your habits from the people you spend a lot of time with, and that's how your reputation is built. So pick your friends carefully because you want to make sure the habits you pick up are good ones.

## Questions/Discussion

1. Do you have friends who are naysayers? Why do you still hang around them?

CHAPTER

# 56

# May God Bless You
# with Foolishness So You
# Can Make a Difference

"Bless us all with enough foolishness so that we can make a difference."

When a friend of mine prayed this prayer last Thanksgiving, it really hit home. Sometimes it's a blessing to be a little naïve or to be young and optimistic. I've always said that as people get older their failures in life all add up to the point that sometimes they remember the pains a lot more than the successes they've had in life. One of the keys in life is not to count your failures, but to learn from them and to count up all your successes and remember them. Doing this will give you the courage to try new things and to continue to try to make a difference in this world.

I was talking to a good friend of mine who is a little sarcastic about my writing this new book, and she said, "Why do you want to write a book? Nobody wants to hear all your opinions. Why don't you just keep them to yourself?" She was ribbing me a little bit, but at the same time she really couldn't imagine why anybody would want to spend a lot of time writing a book, as she just wouldn't be motivated to do that. Our conversation took place shortly before I heard this prayer: "May God bless you with foolishness so that you can make a difference." I can assure each and every one of you that the day you give up on the idea that you can make a difference will be the day you give up and lose a lot of your zest for life.

The theme of this book is that all kinds of little details make a difference, those details could be the difference between success and failure. For me, getting up every day and trying to make a difference to help someone else or to better myself is what it's all about. I encourage each of you to challenge yourself to help someone every day and to make yourself a little bit better in all the things you do. If you do this, you'll live a life that's not wasted, one that you can be proud of and one that you can let go of with no regrets when your time comes.

## Questions/Discussion

1. Can you think of something or someone where you were a difference maker?

# 57

"Sometimes you have to take a step
back to throw your best punch."
—FROM THE MOVIE "MILLION DOLLAR BABY"

# We Won Without Them

Over my playing career in high school, college, and after college in competitive softball and tennis leagues, I played with many great players who were negative wizards. Negative wizards are people who just create negativity on the team, cause problems, set bad examples, don't come on time, may break team rules, may think they're too cool to wear the uniform, or in general, have to bring special attention to themselves that's detrimental to the team. If a player who has these tendencies is not any good, it is not a problem, because a coach will get rid of them immediately. A poor player with a poor attitude never lasts very long on any team. There are, however, situations that arise where you have a player who is particularly good, maybe even the best player on the team, but they have a negative attitude. Coaches sometimes feel like they have to work with these kids because they are so good, and many times the team would be much better off without them. Generally a player this good has to do something so bad that the coach has no choice before he will suspend them or kick them off the team, or the players on the team may get to the point that they would rather lose than have to deal with this prima donna.

When I think back over all the years of playing, there are three players who come to mind—prima donnas that didn't obey the team rules and just were basically negative for our team. Coincidently, all three of these players were baseball or softball players. All three were arguably either the best player on the team or one of the two or three best players. In all three situations these players got booted from the team either by the coach or by the players themselves, and in all three cases the team went on to do much, much better without them.

I can remember one year we had a shortstop that was arguably one of the best softball players, not only on our team, but also in the whole state of Arkansas. He was a shortstop who came late for games or simply did not attend a game, didn't run out his fly balls, got upset if he didn't hit a homerun and walked to first base; when he made an error, he didn't chase the ball down, and he just basically had a bad attitude when playing on our team. He would only play hard if it was a super big tournament, but not in our league games. Eventually, after he missed one of our games without calling in and caused our team to play one player short, we decided not to call him back anymore. Our team was four and four at the time. We put in players with good attitudes and won our next 22 games consecutively to finish the season 26-4 and to win the overall city title.

Another situation occurred in high school on our spring trip to Florida, and our shortstop was out smoking marijuana and breaking team rules. The captain of our team really thought this player was good but decided that was it, and he went to the coach and told on him and another player. The two were sent home and were kicked off the baseball team. Our team went on to have its best baseball season in the high school's history after losing one of our two or three best players because we put in a new kid that was a sophomore who was eager to play and had a great attitude.

The third player always had something negative to say to players when they made mistakes, would never come in the appropriate team uniform and complained about where he batted in the order and everything else. After a while everybody just got tired of listening to the negativity, and we played without him as well. Again, our team did better and everybody was happier.

Anybody who plays sports long enough will run across a prima donna or negative wizard that is a detriment to the team. In the early stages you have to ignore them and you have to try to be a good influence and see if you can turn them around. If you can't, and they break a team rule don't be afraid to stand up to them. Just because they are a great player doesn't mean that your team is better off with them. If you can't turn them around, hopefully either the team or the coach will take care of business so your team can have a great season. Be sure that you're always setting the type of example that will help your team get better because in the end all coaches and all players know which players have a positive effect on the team and help them win and which ones don't.

Special Note: As I've coached over the years, I've learned that not only a player with a poor attitude, but a coach or a parent can ruin a team as well. I've never seen a team win a championship with a negative wizard destroying chemistry.

## Questions/Discussion

1. Can you think of a teammate or former teammate that, even though talented, you were better off without? If yes, why?

# Pre-Game

CHAPTER

# 58

# Pre-Game Preparation

There's an old saying that my good friend, Curtis Bailey, and I used to say before we played softball our many years together. The saying went, "The game is not won in the game; the game is won before the game." What this saying meant was that when you actually got to the game you were going to play the horses were in the barn and now the fun begins. In other words, once it was tip-off time or the opening kick was taken, you had already done or not done all the things that would make you successful or unsuccessful in that game.

Pre-game preparation is so important to success. Being successful on the sports field is not just about executing during the game, it's doing all the right things before the game as well. Many of these items will be outlined for you in more detail item by item throughout the Book. Pre-game preparation includes getting a good nights sleep, not going to a sleepover and staying up all night before a game, and setting your alarm clock early enough so you won't be rushed as you get ready for your big game. Rising early will provide the ease and peace you need to focus on what you have to do that day for the game. Pre-game preparation includes eating right, especially the night before or even two nights before, an athletic contest. It includes writing down on a sheet of paper the things you need to focus on during that game. This can be done on your way to the game, or even better yet the night before so that you can sleep on it and even possibly dream about those items. Pre-game preparation includes two or three minutes of quiet time just minutes before you go out to play, allowing you to visualize yourself making the right moves and decisions to be successful during the game. Pre-game preparation includes packing all the things you'll need for that game—warm-ups, hats, gloves, energy bars, drinks, chapstick, and any possible item that might help you be more comfortable and ready to go at game time with very few worries or last second emergencies that might come up.

Failure to execute on any of these pre-game items hurts your chance for success. I've always been a detail man; show me a person that forgets one or two key details and I'll show you a person I can beat because I'm not going to forget the little details that are nothing other than mental parts of the game. You can always control the mental parts of the game each and every game; you can't control the physical parts. Make sure you control these items in your pre-game preparation and remember, "The game is not won in the game; the game is won before the game."

## Questions/Discussion

1. What do you do to get ready before a contest?
2. Can you break down what you do physically and mentally to get ready?

CHAPTER

# 59

# Visualization

Serious high school athletes, college athletes, and pro athletes learn very quickly that visualization can be a powerful tool in sports. Visualization involves mind work. You visualize yourself driving down the lane against the defender, making a good move, and finishing with a left handed lay-up. Or you may visualize yourself out there on the football field catching a punt and not being intimidated by the defender that's coming right at you.

Most young kids don't understand visualization in sports. When you are young, you simply don't think much about your games; you just show up and play. As you get a little older you start thinking about your games in the car on the way, concentrating on some of the things you need to do in the game. As you get older yet you learn to take two or three minutes of quiet time maybe in the locker room right before you go out on the court to give your very best. As you continue to progress and become a mature player, you visualize the moves you're going to make in a game situation, the time on the clock, and even the actual defender you're playing against—seeing their facial expressions, their intensity—and even the crowd that you are playing in front of.

Visualization allows you to get better while lying in bed, riding in a car, or simply taking a walk. It allows you to see the game more clearly, and those who use their visualization skills will beat an equal opponent who does not. Professional athletes may seek counselors and seek sports psychologists to help them get better. Many times it's nothing more than the sports psychologist helping that athlete visualize being successful over and over and over again in certain situations. Sure enough, when that situation comes up in the game the mind is trained to be successful and the athlete just reacts, making the big hit or scoring the huge basket.

Have you ever played in a game and made a great play and you don't know why you did it; you just reacted? That comes from muscle memory, from practicing over and over a physical skill. Visualization works the same way. If you visualize enough being successful or reacting in a certain game situation a certain way, then when you get in that situation you'll make the right decisions.

To summarize, an athlete goes to practice and practices over and over throwing a baseball or shooting a basket or perfecting a crossover dribble or catching a football. Any athlete and any coach knows you must do this over and over and over to become great. The truth is this is just the physical part of the game, which makes up about 50 percent of your success. Great athletes learn to prepare themselves for the mental part of the game in the same way by practicing over and over in their minds, by visualizing certain situations and being successful in them. No athlete will be great just by being able to do all the physical things required of the game. You must be mentally prepared as well, and visualization is the key.

## Questions/Discussion

1. Do you believe that you have to think you can do it before you actually get it done?
2. Can you think of an example in your life where you dreamed it and then got it done?

# Take Enough Practice Before the Game That on Your First Shot or Swing You're Ready to Play

I've played baseball since I was five years old. Every summer from age 5 to 42, I played baseball or softball. Baseball is an interesting sport in that you get out there and play for two hours, and in that two hours it all comes down to four at bats and at best four or five balls hit to you, depending on what position you play. Those four at bats and those four or five balls hit to you total less than two minutes of actual play. The rest of the time you are really standing around or sitting in the dugout. Those two minutes of play, however, are played at the highest speed and intensity. One of the reasons more injuries occur in softball than any other sport is that the body is sitting there lethargic one second, and in the next second you're either swinging that bat as hard as you can, throwing the ball as hard as you can, or running to first base as hard as you can. This sudden dramatic change causes a lot of injuries.

Since your entire success offensively comes down to those four at bats you've got to be ready for the first pitch thrown to you and be at your optimal level to hit the ball. When I played, if I could get to a batting cage I took at least 100 cuts prior to the game and got to the point that I was in a full sweat. Most players don't do this. They come to the game, swing the bat a few times in the on deck circle, and get in there to bat. There's no way they can possibly be ready to hit the ball as well as if they've taken 100 cuts and practiced hitting the ball to all areas of the field and actually feel the contact of the bat hitting the ball. Baseball is even more difficult because the speed that the pitcher throws in a game is hard to duplicate in practice. But I can assure you that walking up there without getting your cuts in is going to put you nowhere near being your best. In situations when I got to games and couldn't get in live batting practice, I would have a person get down on a knee and toss me 100 balls where I would swing and hit the ball into the fence. This exercise is called toss and hit. Most people thought that was a little psychotic or a little intense, but it helped me to get ready, so I did it anyway.

When it came to fielding the ball I warmed up and practiced every kind of throw I could possibly make in a game—an overhand throw, a side arm throw, a three quarters throw, a throw moving to my right, a throw moving to my left, and a throw as if I was turning a double play, which includes a hop step after the throw to avoid the runner trying to take my legs out. I practiced throws where I had to field it backhanded and had to plant my foot like a quarterback and throw over the top. All of these different throws I probably practiced 10 different times getting in easily 150 to 200 throws just to be ready for those four or five chances I would get in a game. When it came to base running I warmed up by jogging around the field and then building up to full speed on the sprints, by running the distance to first base first slowly and then speeding up until I got to maximum speed. By doing these warm-ups I prepared myself to play on the first pitch of the ballgame and also helped prevent injury by having already built up to those explosive motions and actions prior to the game.

In baseball I generally batted lead off, which is the first hitter to bat in the game. The best pitch I always thought to hit was the very first one. You see the pitcher has decided that he needs to get in the groove, and most of them aren't as warmed up as they should be so they throw the first pitch right down the middle of the plate to kind of get the game going. I always wanted to be ready to hit that first pitch if it was right down the middle and start my team off with a base hit and me standing on first base. So many missed opportunities go by if you're not ready for that first pitch.

In a sport like basketball it's no different. You need to warm up with every type of dribble and every type of shot that you could possibly do in the game, so that when you get the opportunity you're practiced and ready. If you're a basketball player and they bring the ball down the court for the first time and throw it to you on the wing and you're open for a wide open three, there should be no hesitation about taking that shot five seconds into the game because you are warmed up and ready to play. I can sit in the stands and tell what players were not ready to play on the first second by the opportunities they pass up.

Remember, the beginning of the game is just as important as the ending of the game and you need to be ready to play both.

## Questions/Discussion

1. Are you always ready physically and mentally for the first second of the game?
2. What is your warm up ritual?

CHAPTER

# 61

# Quiet Time Before Games

I wrote many of my chapters for this book after dealing with a frustrating experience. In fact that's how I came up with many of the chapters. Today my fourth grade basketball team all had dinner together. It was time to get ready for the game, and . I got a phone call that was urgent. When I got off the phone, my players were running around without their basketball shoes on, playing tag in the gymnasium. Although this is an extreme situation it's hard to believe 25 minutes prior to the game that this is going to be the best way to get them ready to play for the game.

As players mature and get older they learn that a few minutes of quiet time sitting in a corner, sitting in a locker room, visualizing the game that they are about to play and getting their thoughts focused on what's going to be required of them in that particular game makes all the difference between a very successful game and an average one. Take some time whether it's on the bus ride to the game, the ride in the car with your parents, in the locker room or a corner of the field to help get yourself mentally ready to play.

Football teams understand this better than any other sport. Coaches take their players out; they get them warmed up; they bring them back in the locker room; the players sit in the locker room quietly, each thinking about their duties; then the coach comes in and gives them a final pep talk, and off they go out to play. Football may be one of the more complex games because 11 players all have to work together to help each other, and there may be more mental aspects required of the game as they all depend on each other. However, I can assure you that the diver, the swimmer, the wrestler, and the boxer all need their private times before they go out and play as well.

I guess the ultimate experience of quiet time before a fight was when I was in high school, and I went to see one of my friends fight in the Golden Gloves State Championship Boxing Tournament. I went to see him fight for his second consecutive State Championship, and he was over in a corner with his manager with Vaseline all over his face to help the blows slide off when he got in the ring. I walked by just two feet away and waved to him and said, "Hi, Michael good luck". He was in a daze and so focused on the fight at hand he did not even acknowledge me. I said hi to him again. He never blinked, and his manager waved me off and said, "Michael's getting ready for his fight; he doesn't talk to anyone before a fight."

The focus of a Warrior, and a Warrior he truly was…he was going out there literally to fight. Many coaches refer to your sporting events as battles or wars or even a fight, but it takes a real fighter to know just how important quiet time is before a game.

## Questions/Discussion

1. Do you spend quiet time before games? Where? Do you write out a game plan?

# Game Time

> "I expect you to give 100% whether the score
> is 100 to 0 or 0 to 100. If you can score 100,
> put it on the scoreboard."
> —MORLEY FRASER, ALBION COLLEGE FOOTBALL COACH

# Playing Against
# the Weak Opponent

For years, I have coached players who play their best games when we play against the toughest opponent, and then they don't play very well when we play a weak opponent. This type of player plays to the level of the competition. I've also coached players who are fantastic against a poor opponent and don't play very well in the big games because they get nervous. These players only play well when they know they're better.

Michael Jordan scored the most points per game of his NBA career against the New Jersey Nets. This may sound unimpressive since the New Jersey Nets were one of the worst basketball teams in the NBA for years. Jordan scored the most points of his career against the weakest team he ever played.

The point is that Michael Jordan went out and played hard every single night. He played well in the big games, and he played well in the weaker games because he was focused just as much against the horrible opponent as he was against the great opponent.

As a young player, playing against a much weaker opponent is an opportunity to challenge yourself. Work on the behind-the-back pass and the between-the-legs dribble in basketball. Work on your special move in soccer. In football or whatever sport it might be, try some different plays to see how they work. If you're a runner or a swimmer, compete to break your personal best or to break the course record. Being prepared to play against a weak opponent is just as important as being prepared against the strong one because you want to do your best each and every day you go out to play.

I've heard many pro athletes say they want to perform their best every day they come to play. They understand that there may be people in the stands who will only see them play this one time, and they will make their judgment as to how good the player is based on that one game. If you're going to be out there, you might as well be doing your best. In my opinion, what causes people to perform less well against a weak opponent is their mental preparation for that opponent. They know they are playing someone weak that day, so they may not warm up as well, they may not eat as well and most importantly they may not prepare themselves as well mentally. This is why every now and then you have major upsets because the weak opponent who knows they're playing someone strong gets mentally prepared for battle and does all the right things to get ready for that opponent while the strong opponent takes the game lightly, doesn't get mentally prepared, and thus we have a huge upset.

You've heard many people say it was impossible for that team to beat them; they didn't have near the athletes; it was a fluke; I don't know how they lost. What people fail to realize is that the game is about 50 percent physical and about 50 percent mental. If you go out there and don't take care of the mental aspects, you reduce your game from 100 percent to 50 percent of your potential, and the opponent who is much weaker but prepares mentally and physically can win easily. It's not an upset at all. It's a preparation loss. Prepare yourself mentally and physically for all games regardless of the opponent, and you'll have more victories.

A side note: When you're playing high school and collegiate sports and your goals are to make All Conference, All State, or All American, those statistics in the games against the weaker opponents count just as much as the ones against the stronger opponents. Many times coaches also are evaluating players, and coaches may put somebody in the starting lineup based on how they performed in one of those games. So if you're looking for a starting spot or trying to keep the one you have, there's one more reason to prepare yourselves just as much for the weak opponent as for the strong one.

## Questions/Discussion

1. Do you play all-out against every opponent, or give the effort that is needed at the time?
2. Have you ever taken an opponent lightly and then not performed very well? Why?

CHAPTER

# 63

# Are You More Concerned about Somebody's Feelings than about Winning the Game?

This question was a difficult one for me as a young player. When I first started competing, I didn't want to hurt people's feelings; but I wanted to win the game. As I got older and had more experience in sports I decided that I'd rather win the game then spend my time worrying about hurting somebody's feelings. As a coach, I really learned to understand this principle. At first I had all the kids take the same number of shots and rotated them at all the different positions. That didn't hurt anybody's feelings, but I was risking losing the game. Finally I learned that I wasn't doing anybody any favors as a coach trying to make everything equal because things are not equal in sports.

You have the superstars that need to take the most shots, the role players that need to set the screens or do the blocking, and the solid players that need to perform when the opportunity comes their way. The key to winning as a coach is to get players to buy into their roles and do their job to help the team win. This is what they teach in the Army, Navy, Air Force and Marines.

A funny example occurred just recently when I was playing a little 3-on-3 basketball. My team had won the first two games by 10 and our team was playing well. We were playing unselfishly, making the right passes, and setting screens. I learned a long time ago that the best way to help my team win in a 3-on-3 basketball game is by setting screens and getting rebounds because nobody else wants to do that; they all want to just get their shots in. The quickest way for me help my team win time and time again is to set screens, rebound and play defense because I'm not a great basketball player, but I am a solid shooter if left wide open.

Anyway, we were playing this 3-on-3 basketball team and a couple of new guys decided to join in so we decided to play 4-on-4. Before we knew it our team was down about 4-2. The new player on the opposing team, whom I didn't know at the time, had played basketball for the University of Georgia. He made two wide-open jumpers in a row to put them up 4-2.

The game went on, and he made six consecutive jumpers without a miss. I yelled out to my teammates, "Who's guarding him?" The big guy, new to our team and more athletic than me, raised his hand. I said, "We can't let him take the open jump shots. Stay on him." Sure enough, the newcomer got the ball again; he wasn't guarded; and he hit his seventh in a row. At that time I said, "Let's switch, I'll take him." This was a pick-up basketball game, and I didn't even know the guy I was talking to prior to that day, nor did I know the guy I was about to guard. I knew this, however; we weren't keeping a hand in his face, and he had made seven in a row. I wasn't rude, but I wasn't scared to make the change with two people I didn't know because I was trying to win the game. I did stop him from taking the outside jumpers, but he made one more inside on me. At least we made him change what he was doing.

We lost the game anyway as we were too far behind to catch up, but as I went to the car afterwards I thought to myself: "This is a lesson that I hope my kids are willing to learn, and that is to take the leadership or make decisions if necessary to help your team win. You can't be afraid to hurt people's feelings."

The next day another one of my friends who knew the great shooter said that he had heard I was playing basketball and had switched defenders because I wanted a piece of him. I said, "No. I switched defenders because he hit seven shots in a row, and it was time for a change." My good friend who played sports with me for years simply laughed and said, "Once a competitor, always a competitor."

My goal is that each of you at age 80 will be willing to say "let me guard him" in whatever game you're playing if you think it will help your team to win.

## Questions/Discussion

1. Are you willing to be very intense in order to win?
2. Have you ever caught yourself worrying more about someone's feelings than winning the game?
3. How can you balance the two?

> The standards we set
> determine how high we go.

# Playing Hard

A coach will notice within a couple of minutes those who play hard in practice; and without any question, if two players are close in ability the player who plays hard will be the one that gets the nod for the starting job. Not playing hard exasperates a coach quicker than anything, and playing hard makes a coach love a player more than anything. Players who play hard will get the MVP awards, the coaches' awards, and the most improved awards; and they will be most respected by their teammates. What's wonderful about playing hard is that you don't have to be born with any God-given ability to play hard because playing hard is an attitude.

I won't deny that it's genetic that some of us were born with more intense chromosomes than others. But I will tell you this: if you want to be the best you can be and always be one of the ones that the coaches love and the players respect, then play hard, dive on the floor, play with injuries, give a second and a third effort, play great defense, have the eye of the tiger, be fired up, be the most fit, and give it everything you have.

There is no substitute for playing hard, and once you develop that characteristic as a player it will carry over in your business life, and you'll be a hard worker. And folks, being a hard worker in the business world will reap you the same rewards…the promotions, the respect of your peers, and most importantly respect in yourself.

## Questions/Discussion

1. How hard do you play?

2. Do you leave it all out on the field some of the time, most of the time, or all of the time?

> Unless you try to do something beyond what you have already mastered, you'll never grow.

# Play the Best; You'll Rise to the Competition Level

As the head coach for the Mighty Bluebird soccer team I am always amazed at how many games we have canceled each year because coaches and parents don't want to play our teams. At the time I write this book, the Mighty Bluebirds have two U-16 girls soccer teams, two U-12 girls soccer teams and a U-8 boys soccer team. Over the years our oldest team, the U-16, has won six State Championships and has currently proven itself the best team in the state. In the early years when we were playing recreational soccer, and even when we moved to the Classic soccer division there were teams that would schedule games with us every year at the scheduling meeting and then cancel them. The best team in the state, other than us, canceled at least ten consecutive games with us, and we finally just quit scheduling them. Other teams would cancel games if they had an injured player or if somebody had another commitment that day, and it got to the point that this team just had to go to tournaments where people could not cancel games in order to get the games in that we needed. We also started playing boys teams, as they would show up and play.

What was happening was that some coaches, because they knew our team was good, didn't want to play and risk losing and hurting their kids' confidence. Literally, we'd have coaches call and say, "Well, we're going to cancel the game this week because we're going to see you in this upcoming tournament; and I don't want to get the kids' confidence down before we play. We think we'd have a better chance of beating you if we just played you once."

I would ask myself, "What in the world are you teaching your kids? And how in the world is your team going to get better?" If you want to be the best that you can be, play the best competition you can get. In fact, you should actually try to play teams that can beat you. That's why we schedule as many games against boys as we can. That's why we play teams two and three years older than us to get the best competition possible. If anyone gets the short end of the stick in these games, it is the better team because when they play teams that aren't as strong as they are, they're not challenged and pushed to their absolute limits.

When I was in college my wrestling coach understood this better than anyone. When we had our non-conference schedule we would wrestle Division I and Division II schools exclusively, even though we were a Division III college. We lost a lot of those matches, probably even most of them; but when we got to our Division III wrestling conference we did not lose a match my last three years at the college. We were from Michigan, but when it came time to go to wrestling tournaments prior to our conference meet, our coach took us to Florida, Illinois, and many other out-of-state tournaments; and we wrestled against Division I teams. It was a thrill to know that we were wrestling the best; and we won matches against the likes of Ohio State, Syracuse, Illinois, Michigan, Michigan State, and Notre Dame, just to name a few. When we got back in our own conference after wrestling that tough competition, it seemed like a breeze. Our coach wasn't trying to pad his won-loss record in non-conference; he was trying to make us the best that we could be.

There are a lot of people out there who, if Michael Jordan were here to play one on one, wouldn't want to play him because they know that they would lose. I would be the exact opposite. I would love to play Michael Jordan and get pummeled, and I would learn some things from the person that plays the game better than anyone else. If you're a tennis player you want to play the best tennis players; it will make your game better. Each year in the national championship race for the college football crown there are teams that play a very easy non-conference schedule, and then they have trouble when they get to their conference games. In fact, the Bowl Championship Series, or BCS, has recognized the fact that strength of the schedule is important. Today it's hard to win the national championship without playing some tough non-conference games because a computer ranks the teams based on the strength of the opponents they beat and how the opponents fared against other competition. Finally, someone has recognized strength of schedule for those who don't understand how important it is to play the best to begin with. If you want to be the best at your job, if you want to be the best at your sport, don't run from the best competition. Embrace it, learn from it, and you'll get better.

## Questions/Discussion

1. Do you like to play the best even if it means that you get beat?
2. Do you practice with someone regularly who is better than you? Why is this important?

CHAPTER

# 66

# Shaking Hands

Coaches are always looking for players who are leaders. You can tell a leader by the way they walk into the room, whether or not they look you in the eye, and how they shake your hand. Many times players are put into the lineup just because of their confidence and their leadership ability. The next time you go to a basketball game, take a look at the visiting team and watch the players warm up. See if you can pick the five starters without knowing anything about them based on the way they conduct their warm-ups, their swagger, their confidence, and just the way they conduct themselves in general. It's really not that hard to get four out of five right. When the team breaks the huddle to start the game and the players come out, the really good ones come out and shake hands with the other players and they'll act like a player. You should be able to pick out your top two or three players on the court just by the way they carry themselves in those pre game handshakes. It's so important to come out and shake hands with the other players, shake hands with the referees, and show respect to the other coaches, as all of these things determine what type of player you're going to be.

One coaching friend of mine says it's important to always go over and shake hands with the other coach before the game, and after the game to say, "Yes sir," or "No, sir," or "Yes ma'am," or "No, ma'am". The way you conduct yourself may be the difference between making All Conference and not making All Conference at the end of the year because a coach will remember a kid who had respect for authority. In that close vote where they just can't decide who to choose, almost any coach will choose the leader who has respect for the other team. The same goes with referees as well. When you get fouled, hand the ball to the referees. If a ball goes out of bounds go get it for them. Show the referees that respect, and it's amazing how they'll show you the respect when you get fouled as you drive in for that key lay-up at the end of the game. That referee is not going to let you go down as the goat when you've treated them properly and show that you have the proper respect for the officials, the other coaches, and the game. Yes, all these are little tiny details; but they could make the difference between All Conference and Honorable Mention. It's the difference between getting the foul shot and not getting the foul shot; it's the difference between being a captain and being just another player.

Showing good manners on and off the court will help you feel better about yourself, develop your confidence, and make you a better player.

## Questions/Discussion

Can you shake hands before the game, go to war during the game, and then shake hands and be friends afterwards?

# 67

> The Protestant work ethic does not guarantee success for giving your best and working the hardest, but it does allow you to live with yourself knowing that you gave it your all.

# Puke or Place

My senior year in high school, I was a cross-country runner. Although I played other sports and never ran until that senior season, cross country ended up being a sport I was a natural at. I wasn't the best runner on my team my senior year; I was second best and my good friend, John Turnbull, was the best runner we had. He went on to be an All-State performer and then an All-American runner at DePaul University. When it came time to go to college I was a good enough runner to run in college, but I decided to play soccer instead as I thought it would be more fun to run around and kick a ball than to just run around. I did, however, fall in love with running following my college years. With no more super competitive sports to play after college I ran the Dallas White Rock Marathon six months after college graduation. Then I began to get on the road racing circuit, running about 30 road races a year. I even had some sporting goods stores sponsor me and ran for them. Although I wasn't the type runner who would win every race, you could count on my being in the top five or top ten in almost any race.

One of the things I learned during my post college running career was that I could psyche myself out to either Puke or Place. What this meant was that if anybody was running next to me by the time we got to the last quarter mile, especially the last 300 yards or so, I could simply will myself to win. After all, if they were that much better runner than me they would have beaten me by now; so if we were that close after three miles or six miles, certainly the ability level was there for either one of us to win. What I learned to do was to be able to look at that finish line and zero in on it with my eyeballs and to make my body run as hard as I possibly could towards that finish line with no regard to the pain I felt. I convinced myself that for 30 or 45 seconds, even a minute, I could push my body harder than it felt like going. In my mind I knew that the worst thing that could happen would be that I would run so hard I would puke. I called this "puke or place." In those situations where I had a runner close to me I would simply look at the finish line from 400 yards out or so and take off on a dead sprint. The other runner either had to try to keep up with me or quit. If he quit and I was able to win I didn't push myself to the point where I threw up; however, if the runner stayed with me I would run full speed, many times throwing up while pushing myself to this limit. When these runners heard me throw up it certainly was a distraction, but it also meant that considering the good shape I was in, they would also be throwing up soon if they kept up with me. When I would throw up and keep on running at the same speed, in almost every situation the other runner gave up and quit within 10 seconds or so, letting me cruise to the finish line. I remember only one race where I threw up multiple times and the runner stayed right with me; and still, in the last 50 yards or so it got to him. Most runners were not willing to pay that price in order to win.

My daughter Kelsey is a cross-country runner today and a much better one than her father. She's won almost every race she's ever run and she, too, at times has had the courage to run to the point where she puked trying to win. "Puke or place" probably seems too intense for most, but not for your real Warriors. You'll recover from puking within 30 minutes after the race, but you'll never recover from running a race or participating in a sporting event where you know you didn't give it your absolute best and lost. In my mind, if I push myself hard enough to puke and I don't win, I can live with that. But to not push myself hard enough to puke and lose is something I can't live with. Get your mind mentally tough enough to puke or place and you won't lose any more close matches that you had an opportunity to win.

## Questions/Discussion

1. How do you know for sure you have given the best effort?
2. Have you ever tried to be sure that you are working harder than anyone else at a particular sport or project?
3. Can you live with losing if you know you have given your best?
4. How does it feel to lose when you know you didn't give your best or you didn't prepare properly?

CHAPTER

# 68

# Five Situations that Will Determine Whether You Win or Lose in the Close Game

No matter what the sport, whether it is tennis, basketball, football, golf, baseball, soccer, wrestling, swimming, or just about any other sport, there are five situations that will come up in any close contest that will determine the outcome of a game. The five situations we're talking about are situations where a hustle play one way or the other, doing the fundamentals the way you've been taught, a mental mistake, or a hustle play or an assignment on offense or defense that you're supposed to do each time will come up and will determine the ballgame.

Some good examples of these possible five situations that you can identify with might include the following:

Your teammate has stolen the ball and has a breakaway contested lay-up. You have the choice of watching him or her take the lay-up or you can follow at full speed down the floor from two foot back and prepare for your teammate to miss the lay-up so that you can be there for the rebound and put it back in. Nine times out of ten your teammate will make the lay-up. Are you willing to run down there all ten times so you will be ready for the one he misses? It could determine the outcome of the game.

You're a baseball player and you play right field. The ball is hit to the third baseman for a routine play at first. Your job is to back up the first baseman should there be an errant throw. It's a lot of work to sprint down there each time you see this play develop; your third baseman is a great fielder and 95 out of 100 times he makes an accurate throw. Are you willing to run over there 100 times to catch the five errant balls that he'll throw away each year?

You're a soccer player. The best player has a breakaway shot against the goalkeeper. He'll be shooting from the right side. You're the left forward. Are you willing to run to the far post to be there just in case he misses the shot wide a foot or two left so that you can kick it in? Your friend on the team will make 9 out of these 10 shots. Are you there all 10 times to knock in the one that he or she is due to miss?

Your team is playing in the national championship football game. It's third and one from the goal line. The snap count is three. Are you mentally focused day in and day out in practice to make sure you don't jump off sides at this critical point that will move your team back five yards and cost them a touchdown?

In the national championship football game between LSU and Oklahoma in 2004, LSU was up 21-7 and had the ball on the 10 yard line poised to score a TD or certainly get a field goal. On the next play one of the LSU players got called for holding and got a 10-yard penalty which moved the ball back from the 10 yard line to the 20. But another player got a personal foul for unsportsmanlike conduct for arguing with the referee on the play, and that moved it back another 15 yards to the 35. This was all on third down. This 25 yards worth of penalties, which was due to a player just mentally losing his composure, moved the ball back to the 35 yard line, which means the field goal kicker has to spot the ball 7 yards back in order to kick it, putting the ball at the 42 yard line for a 52 yard field goal. These penalties cost LSU an almost certain field goal that would have put the game out of reach. Instead they came away with no points, and Oklahoma almost came back to win the national championship. How big would those penalties have been had Oklahoma scored when they were inside the

20 in the last few minutes with the game on the line? Nothing would have been talked about more than the ridiculous penalty that moved them out of field goal range.

Great athletes prepare themselves for those five situations that may come up. There is no way to know if they're going to come up on the first play or the 70$^{th}$ play or any play in between in a football game, but the only way to capitalize when these situations occur is to be at your best and be prepared for all 70 plays. The person who always does the fundamentals, is always hustling, and always knows his or her assignments will perform when it really counts.

We all hear about players who perform at crunch time. This player is at his best when the pressure is on. The truth is, these players are always performing on each and every play. But when that big situation comes and they capitalize on it, people think they just have focused in on those big plays and that they're big time and big game players. You can't just get lucky consistently by knowing that you have to be ready for play eight of this game or play fifteen of that game. The players that perform well at crunch time are the players who have discipline and are prepared for those five key plays of the game by playing every play as if it might just be the one. Be mentally focused, make hustling a habit, and understand the parts of your job in whatever sport it might be. If you'll play all out on every play, you'll find that you, too, will be looked at as Mr. Clutch. The situations will come to you, and you will be a hero. There's an old saying, "the harder you work the luckier you get." There's nothing lucky at all about being in the right place at the right time because to be there you had to be doing your job on the other 69 plays of the game.

## Questions/Discussion

1. How good are you in the clutch?
2. Do you believe the more you practice the better you'll be in the clutch?
3. Have you ever hustled to do a little detail for your team that ended up winning the game?

"Never let the fear of
striking out get in your way."
—BABE RUTH

# Are You Hungry?

I'll never forget the article I read in the paper one day about Wade Boggs. The title of the article was, "Boggs is a hungry hitter." For those of you who don't know, Wade Boggs is a Hall of Fame baseball player who played for the Boston Red Sox and the New York Yankees. Over his career he won eight batting titles as the game's best hitter for average. Citing the difference between Boggs and other major leaguers, the writer of this article said if Boggs came up to bat and got hits the first two times up, he would say, 'Today is going to be the day I go 4 for 4" while most players would say "Wow, even if I don't get hits the last two times, I still am two for four and that's a great day."

Boggs would look at his 2 for 2 start as, "Wow, I'm seeing the ball well today." In other words, he was never satisfied with a good day..... if he could have a great day he was always hungry for more.

Isn't that the way most of us are? We're satisfied with a win; we're satisfied with doing better than most. The bottom line is that's not good enough if it's not your best. John Wooden, the great basketball coach for UCLA never used the word "WIN" in any of his practices or games. It was not that he wasn't concerned with winning; he was more concerned with his team doing its best. After all, UCLA could beat almost everybody anyway; but one of the reasons they got to that point was that they were always focused on improving and doing the best that they could do. Winning was not enough; he wanted his team to execute and do their best. If they did their best he figured the wins would come.

If you are capable of scoring 40 points in a basketball game and you score 30, you're not very hungry. If you are the best player on your team, but you're not hungry enough to be the best player in the state, you're not very hungry. If you're a salesman that goes out and makes a sales quota the first week of the month, but doesn't strive to break the record for that month during the last three weeks since you're off to a good start, you're not very hungry. The bottom line is that great players are always hungry.

Be hungry, strive to be the best and you'll find yourself among the very elite.

## Questions/Discussion

1. Are you afraid to swing for the home run, to take the winning shot, or have to make the game-saving tackle?

CHAPTER

# 70

# Time, Score, Momentum

Anybody who has played baseball knows that if you play shortstop you have to know before the ball is pitched what you're going to do if it's hit to you. If there's a man on first only, you're going to throw the ball to second and try to get the force play at second and hopefully a double play. If a slow roller is hit to you and there's no way you can get the force out at second, you have to go to first. If there's a pop fly hit to you at shortstop and the man on first is assuming you've caught it and is not running to second base, then you know to intentionally drop the ball, step on second, and get the double play at first. All of these situations you determine in your mind before the pitcher even throws the pitch. The nice thing about baseball is that technically you get a little timeout between every pitch to reevaluate what you want to do based on the situation.

In other sports like basketball or football or soccer you need to know the time, the score, and the momentum. These three important factors influence how you play the game. For example, in basketball if there's five seconds left in the game and you're down by two points, you know that the momentum is in the other team's favor; you know that you're down by two, and you know you have five seconds to score a two pointer to tie it and a three pointer to win. This will determine whether you take a shot a little earlier, or you may take a shot you wouldn't normally take, based on the situation. This past summer in AAU basketball, we were up by two points with about 30 seconds left, and we were on defense. The other team shot the ball and missed, and we got the rebound. Based on time, score, and momentum a player would know that all we want to do is bring the ball down and hold it, making them foul us and shoot free throws to put the game away. Our player who rebounded the ball was not paying attention to the time, the score, or the momentum; and as soon as she got the rebound, she threw a one-handed long pass down the court, trying to hit an open person for a lay-up. Instead she threw it away; the other team got the ball, came down, and because they understood time, score, and momentum, hit a three pointer to win the game.

Young kids really have trouble keeping track of time, score, and momentum, but it's an important part of being a smart player and a successful player in any game. If your team is up, you've just scored, and you have the momentum it's a great time to press the other team in basketball. Go ahead and put the pressure on them while they're not feeling good about themselves and make them make some more mistakes. In football, after you've just intercepted a pass from the other team, how often do you see the coach call for the bomb or a long pass play afterwards? The reason they do that is the momentum has swung their way. The defense comes out on the field reluctantly, upset that they just had a turnover, and the offense is fired up that they now have the ball. So many times right after a turnover a team scores immediately, or at least, very quickly. This is because of a huge momentum shift. Players who are able to score and swing the momentum back their team's way after another team has had the momentum are invaluable. Players who understand time, score, and momentum know exactly what they have to do in a given situation to give their team an advantage.

I often ask my players, "What would you do in a particular situation?" to test their knowledge of the game. Most of the time when I ask them that question I leave out a few facts that are important to know in order to give the right answer. Most of the time kids will just blurt out answers, when in fact they need to say, "Hey Coach, I need to know this, this, and this before I answer." This is exactly how you must play the game. The answer is, "It depends on the situation." And often, that situation is what's the time, the score, and the momentum?

## Questions/Discussion

1. Do you believe most games are lost, not won? Why?
2. Do you believe most games could be won "Between the Ears?"

# Anyone, Any Place, Any Time

As a youth coach I have learned a lot about how other coaches and parents think. Over the years we have had numerous soccer teams and basketball teams cancel games or not even want to play our teams. The reason that they cancel the game often is because they don't want to lose their momentum or lose their confidence by playing a tough team. They even go as far as to say that directly to me or my other coaches on the phone. I find that utterly amazing, but realize that that's the way the majority of the world is. Most people want to feel good about what they're doing, play people they can beat, and feel good about themselves.

What I've learned over the years is if you really want to get better you have to play some people that are better than you on a regular basis. Sure, you need to play some teams that you can beat from time to time to develop confidence and to work on building on your strengths. What we try to do in the Mighty Bluebird Organization is play a lot of games against teams that we have very little chance of winning against, play some teams that we can win against and constantly move up and down the cycle so that we're developing our players' confidence one day and humbling them the next. Playing an opponent that can beat you will show you your weaknesses and what you need to work on quicker than anything else. Also, playing a great opponent will challenge your best players and make them better because they have to rise to the level of the competition.

We've entered many a soccer and basketball tournament only to hear the tournament director say, "Hey, we don't have enough teams in your age group, will you play up?" Our response is, "Anyone, Any Place, Any Time." We are a girl's team, but we'll play against girls or boys, and generally up to a couple of years older than us on a regular basis. As long as the kids are not physically in danger of getting hurt due to the huge size differential, we go ahead and play. It's no wonder that our kids are a little tougher than the average kids.

After all, if you're truly trying to develop the kids you coach or your own kids to be able to compete at the high school or the college level when they're a freshman they're going to have to play kids three years older, when they're a sophomore two years older, and a junior one year older. Protecting your kids by always having them play kids their own age is no protection at all. In fact, it's almost a guarantee that your kids won't compete as well as they could have when they get to high school and college because they're not used to playing against kids older than them. Don't be an excuse maker; be a person who works on getting better not just on counting your victories. Play Anyone, Any Place, and Any Time and you'll get better.

## Questions/Discussion

1. Do you like challenges?
2. Do you put yourself in situations intentionally that will give you a great challenge?

> "Don't bunt. Aim out of the ballpark."
> —DAVID OGILVY

# 72

# Feeling Loose – In the Zone

We take our Arkansas Belles team across the country from Atlanta to New Orleans, to Las Vegas and other cities throughout the United States. We play before college coaches who are looking at AAU prospects, players they will give scholarships to attend their university one day. The key to these kids doing well under this intense pressure with college coaches taking notes on them is to feel loose and to play to win, not paying any attention to those coaches in the crowd. The key to getting a scholarship is to be in the zone when the coaches are watching. Being "in the zone" just means having one of those wonderful days where you're shooting well, you're playing great defense and you don't feel the least bit tired. A good way to say it is you're feeling just a little frisky, a little wired.

How do you get yourself in that zone? Certainly if I could give you a formula for that I'd be counseling all of the professional players in all of the sports because playing in the zone doesn't come along every day. It's maybe a feeling you get once a month. I will tell you some things you can do, however, that give you a better chance of being in the zone. They include getting a good nights sleep, eating properly the night before and the day of the contest, getting to your athletic event a little early so you don't feel rushed and you have time to use the bathroom, stretch out, get accustomed to the surroundings, and evaluate your competition. It involves taking enough warm up, whether it's shooting or taking a few extra swings in baseball; its feeling prepared and ready to play. Like Wade Boggs from one of our previous chapters, if you're having a good day and you're seeing the ball well, why not go ahead and have a magnificent day? A lot of being in the zone is not being satisfied with just having a good day, but wanting to have a great day. When you get in that zone, let it go; take the open shot every time when you're feeling it and put your foot on your opponent's throat and finish them off. Having killer instinct can contribute to being a player who is good in the zone. Don't settle for the success you've had until you have finished your opponent off to the point that there's no way they can come back and win.

If you are fortunate enough to be "in the zone" when the coaches are watching, you have an opportunity to cinch a place for yourself in college athletics. Don't miss it. Do your homework, be prepared, and then move into it as if your life depended on it. The coaches will notice.

## Questions/Discussion

1. If you are in the zone, do you thirst for even more, or do you wonder how long it will last?

CHAPTER

# 73

# Finish Your Masterpiece

A good friend of mine, Coach Kelley at Pulaski Academy, came in the locker room at halftime after his team had played a great first half and started yelling at them: "Finish Your Masterpiece, Finish Your Masterpiece!" What he was saying was that they'd played a wonderful game the first half and that they had to finish it. Just as it doesn't do any good to paint half a painting, it doesn't do any good to play great for half a game.

For young athletes this can often be a problem. I remember my daughter as a high school freshman going out and scoring 15 points in the first half of a basketball game only to come out the second half and only take two shots. Can you imagine being a freshman and having that kind of half and thinking, "Hey, today I'm having a great first half; I've got a lot of rope. I'm not going to get pulled if I make a couple mistakes after that kind of half. Let's go ahead and go for 30 today," and you feel like you have the freedom to shoot the ball. Young people, and even adults, often are satisfied if they get off to a good start and say to themselves, "Boy, I've had a good day already", and they lose that killer instinct. Great players go out and finish off the competition playing hard for every minute; and experienced athletes have learned if you don't do this, occasionally somebody will come back and beat you when you don't finish them off.

Boxers and wrestlers understand that being way ahead is not good enough; your opponent can throw a knockout blow at any time or flip you on your back for a pin. It doesn't do any good to paint half a masterpiece; you must finish it. Even a good salesman, who makes a couple sales in the first couple hours of the work day, if he's a true champion, will say, "Boy, I'm having a good day today. I'm going to break the all-time record."

What kind of player are you? Are you a player that looks to achieve new goals every day to break through the glass ceilings and shatter records? Are you the kind of player that has learned to play every second of the game and finish it off? I hope so. Far too often games are lost, and competition for a starting job is lost simply because when you get up you don't finish your opponent off. You have to have the mentality of a boxer, and when you get somebody down make sure they don't get back up again to win the fight. The next time you go out and have a great first half of a game or a great first half of a season or a great morning in sales, or a great start to anything, Finish Your Masterpiece. You'll be glad you did.

## Questions/Discussion

1. Have you ever played a great first half and then not played a great second half to finish it off? If yes, why do you think you had a bad second half?

CHAPTER
# 74

# Know the Playbook

Of all the reasons not to be in the starting lineup, not knowing the playbook is about as dumb as any I can think of. You would be surprised at how many times coaches have to put good players on the bench or simply don't put certain players in at critical situations because they don't trust them with the knowledge to run the system that the coach is running. In football a playbook can be quite thick, intense, and extensive. It's so important that all eleven players on the field know exactly what each and every offensive play is. If anybody is out of sync, it can destroy the whole play for the team. In basketball there are only five players that have to get it right; but still, one snafu and the whole play is messed up. At the end of games, especially in basketball and football, if the coach can't be absolutely sure that a player knows the plays and can be trusted to execute them, that player has to be on the bench.

I can't tell you how many times I've had to pull kids that I coach and say, "If you just knew the plays, I'd have you in right now; you're going to go back and learn them." A person who has just joined a team may be a great player, but the coach may not trust him completely until he is comfortable that the player knows his system. Study your playbook thoroughly. Show your coaches that you can always execute and are intelligent during practice, and they will trust you in the games. Before you go to bed at night, on your way to school, or just during some down time while you're watching TV, get out a scratch piece of paper and draw out each and every play and study them and visualize the play actually occurring in the game. As you're studying the playbook, be creative and imagine a few things going wrong or different defenses playing against your team on that set play. If you can figure out every possible alternative and how you'll react to the situation, your coach will appreciate this extra book time; you'll be rewarded with more playing time, and the coach will know you're a player they can depend on at crunch time.

Remember, when the chips are on the line and a game is down to the final few plays, athletes are tired and they tend to react in a way in which they were programmed. There's no time to think and say, "I need to rethink through my play." It will be a reaction, and if you've spent time over learning your plays, you'll react correctly. Know the playbook, and you'll be appreciated by your coach and your teammates.

## Questions/Discussion

1. Do you know your team's plays inside and out?
2. What is your role on your team?

section 9

# Leadership – Parenting

CHAPTER

# 75

# Be a Leader
# on the Court

You can always tell who the leaders are in any sporting event. Many of them walk differently as they walk with confidence; they encourage their teammates; and they even yell instructions to their teammates when needed. They are the ones who say, "Give me the ball," when the game's on the line; and they're the ones that make the great defensive plays because they're intense and ready to go when they are needed. There are many other subtleties that leaders do that an experienced coach or fan will notice immediately. Little actions like shaking hands with the referees before a game or shaking hands with other players in a confident way show that they are comfortable on the court and ready to play. The player that calls out the defense that they're going to run, constantly encouraging other players and even communicating with a coach, shows good leadership.

The hard part about leadership is you can't just tell a player to go out there and do it. They have to earn the confidence to do it. They earn this by being prepared for the game, by going through the proper warm-up, by being on time and setting an example that other players look up to. They do it by being confident in their own game through a lot of hard practices and knowing that they can perform in this game. Most of all, they do it by being so prepared mentally and physically that they feel they are the best person to lead the team, and that's why they're leading the team. We've all been in situations where we've looked around and said to ourselves, "Gosh, nobody's more qualified than me; therefore, if it's going to get done I better take control of this situation." Work hard enough; prepare well enough; and be ready and intense enough to assume the role of the leader of your team. It's a right that's earned, not given. The coach can make you captain; but only hard work and the respect of your teammates that you've earned can make you a leader.

One final note: Leaders are not limited to one per team. They are limited to the number of leaders that have earned the right to be a leader on that team.

## Questions/Discussion

1. Have you ever led your team to victory by simply carrying almost all of the burden yourself?
2. Are you a leader on your team? Why or why not?

# Making Others
# around You Better

What kind of player are you? Are you the kind of player that's a cancer on a team that brings a team down and nobody likes? Or are you the kind of player that makes everybody else around you better? Some players do this by staying after practice and working out extra. Before they know it other players are staying and working too. Some players make others better by giving them a pat on the back when they need it or a kick in the butt when they need it. Others make the players around them better by being unselfish, always finding them for the open pass. They communicate on the field to make everybody more aware of what's going on, and give other players the confidence that they can get the job done by letting them know they are being counted on.

I can tell you this as an athlete and coach: you know when you're around somebody that makes you better, and you always want that person on your team. That person may not be your best friend. It may be someone you don't even like, but you sure do respect them. There are famous players in pro sports that had the ability to make others around them better. Some names that come to mind include Magic Johnson, Roger Staubach, Michael Jordan, Larry Bird, and Joe Montana. There are a lot of players who aren't necessarily superstars who make their teams better such as Derrick Fisher for the Los Angeles Lakers and Brian Piccolo for the Chicago Bears.

If you want to be a champion, find ways to make the players around you better, and you'll have a lot more championship teams.

## Questions/Discussion

1. Do you make other players on your team better?
2. What are some ways you can make other players around you better?

# Help Your Team Win
# Any Way You Can

Warriors help their teams win – period. There are many times over the years in sports when I've gone out to play a basketball game, a soccer game, or a football game, when what was needed from me was totally different from one game to another. Sometimes I would be one of the best players on the field or the court and I needed to be counted on to score. At other times I was perhaps the weakest player on the team, and I needed to be counted on to block or to screen or to play fantastic defense to help stop a key player. Sometimes when I played I wasn't anywhere near the best player, but we didn't have any leadership on the team and our team needed someone to help keep people organized and to communicate. It was my job to help the team win that way.

I have played in, say a 4-on-4 basketball game where I was clearly the worst shooter, and we had three great shooters on our team. In those games I realized my role would be to take only a wide-open easy shot and to get the ball to these other three to take as many shots as possible. I also figured out that the way to help my team win was to be scrappy and get a couple extra rebounds per game to give those guys a couple extra shots that the players on the other team weren't willing to fight for. A Warrior will analyze the game they are playing in and figure out what role they need to take and then do everything possible to help their team win. In close games it's always the little things, the loose ball, the turnover, the extra rebound, the screen, or tough and gritty defense that can make the difference.

In the end it's not how many points you scored, how many rebounds you got, or the number of touchdowns you ran for. It's whether your team wins. And Warriors find a way to make their team win a lot more often than anybody else.

## Questions/Discussion

1. What are you willing to do to help your team win?
2. Do you take responsibility after a game for your team's win or loss?

> You've got to stand for something
> or you'll fall for anything.

# Why We Wear
# #3 and #1

When I was in high school I started off wearing #22 and #11. I loved the double numbers; I thought they looked cool. In the summer, going into my junior year in high school my summer boss and former coach, Morley Fraser, paid for me to go to the Fellowship of Christian Athletes summer camp. Though I'd been to church for years I really didn't have a deep faith. It was at the Fellowship of Christian Athletes Camp that I became a Christian and realized where my priorities ought to be in life and what kind of example I wanted to set for others and what I wanted my life to be about. I read the book, <u>I Am Third</u>, by Gayle Sayers and from that point on I wore the #3. In the book, <u>I Am Third</u>, Gayle Sayers says the Lord is first, my friends and family are second, and I am third. A lot of things changed after that. Every night when I did my push ups before I went to bed, I did my 50 push ups and then finished with three extra saying, "I'm third, my friends and family are second, and God is #1." I can even remember in summer baseball wearing the #3, and instead of having Hatcher across the back of my jersey I just had the words; "I AM" with the #3 below it.

When you're not worrying about drawing all the attention to yourself and living your life just for yourself it's amazing how much more wonderful life can be. First of all things don't seem as important; the pressure comes off in sports; and you become a lot kinder person, developing much better friendships and relationships with your family and friends. When you do get in a battle, refocusing on your priorities makes it a lot easier to say "I'm sorry," and "I love you," and to help work things out. I don't know if I'll live to be 100, but I know my life is not being shortened any by worrying or holding grudges because it's simply not in me. My nature is to spit it all out. Even if I get mad and scream it, I get it off my chest; and generally after an outburst I'll be the first one there to say "I'm sorry" and try to work things out.

I know that I was born intense, but with a good heart. Get to know your nature and your priorities, and get together a strategy to live the life you want to live. Wearing #3 in all the sporting events I've played always helped me every time I put on the jersey to remember what was truly important. If for some reason #3 was already taken, then I like to wear the #1 to remind me that The Man Upstairs is really #1 in this world. Anyone that's ever watched my kids play will see that all my kid's wear #3, and since I have twin daughters who play on the same team, one wears #3 and one wears #1. When we assigned them numbers when they were little bitty they had no idea why they were wearing these numbers, but today as my daughter plays high school sports she understands exactly why she wears #3, not because her father wore it, but because that's where her priorities are.

## Questions/Discussion

1. What do you stand for?
2. How would others describe you as a teammate?

# As the Kids Get Older Solicit Someone Other Than a Parent to Help

As I've coached my kids and they continue to get older one thing that I've always incorporated was getting another coach or mentor to help them. It doesn't matter how good a coach you are or how good a parent or what your qualifications are, when kids get to a certain age they just listen better to anybody but their parent. I have a friend who played professional basketball and his kid just simply won't listen to him when it comes to basketball advice. He brings his kid to the gym to work with Coach Loucks and myself and his child will listen better to us than his more qualified father. Our kids also will listen to him more than they will to us. It's an interesting phenomenon, but one that is certainly true and should not be taken personally.

I always have to tell myself don't give up, be there to support your child, be there to help them with tips as they are still listening, but not with the same respect and admiration they may have had when they were younger. As we all look back at our high school years we will have a significant mentor in our life that we may actually give all the credit to and not our parents. It was certainly true for me, but years later when you come back those parents are still the single greatest influence in your life. It just takes you until you're about 25 to 30 to realize that. So as a parent, hang in there; but solicit outside help as that will be best for your child. I will tell you that when it comes to athletics or success in any endeavor I have rarely ever seen a kid get to the top without a good strong parent influence to help them. Certainly you can say, "Well, Mike Tyson (or other pro athletes with great ability) got to the top without that," but I think for the ones that have a solid base and are well rounded individuals, it takes a parent being there all along the way to provide that stability.

## Questions/Discussion

1. Do you have problems listening to your parents or did you at one time? What age did this start approximately?
2. Who do you get advice from? Why?

CHAPTER

# 80

# Get in a Good Program

When your kids are growing up finding them a great program to participate in is so important. A great school administrator, a great coach, or a great leader in any organization is so important. It always starts at the top. My oldest daughter, Kelsey, is enrolled at Central Arkansas Christian School. The President of the school is Dr. Carter Lambert, and he is a fantastic leader for the kids and a great administrator. She plays for Coach Quattlebaum in basketball, Coach Shackleford in cross country and soccer, and Coach Sullivan in track. All are outstanding coaches, but more importantly outstanding people. Dr. Lambert believes in getting the absolute best coaches and paying them well and then leaving them alone and giving them the ability to run their programs. He doesn't allow parents to go into the coaches' offices and complain about playing time. If they have any of those issues they have to come see him. Because of this leadership his sports programs are very successful with very few problems.

I can't think of anyone more important in the high school years than a kid's coach on developing great character, leadership, confidence, etc. in your child. If you don't get your kid in the right program, even if they have far superior talent, I believe they will eventually fall behind kids that get in a great program, not as much from the physical side, but from the mental side. Anybody that's ever been in a winning program versus a losing program knows the losing program can develop in players that loser's limp, and a winning program can develop that winner's confidence. I'm so thankful for the great programs my daughter has been able to be involved in during her high school years and the qualities and enjoyment that she gets from these programs. When it's time to pick a high school, or a summer program, or your college you'll have the choice of picking your coaches: pick a great program. It's not a fluke that Pat Summit at Tennessee has a great women's program in basketball every year and it's not a surprise that Coach K at Duke has a great program on the boys' side. Year in year out no matter who they have in the system they produce winners both on and off the court.

## Questions/Discussion

1. What's the best program in your area? Why?

# Your Parents
# Know You Best

Isn't it amazing that a child is born and in the early years loves their parents more than anyone else? A five year old child will want to spend all the time they can with their parents. They want to play with them; they want to eat with them; and they even want to sleep in their bed at night if they can. As a child gets older they start enjoying being with their friends more than anyone else, and by the time they hit fifteen or sixteen years old they want to be as far away from their parents as they can possibly be. The reason for this is that children need to develop their own identity, and they have to separate from their parents for a period of time before they come back.

As an athlete some of your most important years will be age fifteen, sixteen, and seventeen as you start entering varsity sports at the high school level. What a shame it is that these, the most critical years, may be the very years when a child rebels from their parents and does not want to listen to their advice anymore.

Certainly an athlete should always listen to their coach and do whatever their coach wants them to do on the particular team they play for. Nobody believes in this more than I as I am a coach that often has to deal with kids getting different instructions from their parents than from me. If my kids are playing for someone else and I'm the parent it's just as important that they listen to that coach and that I not give instructions. You will, however, be better as an athlete if you're still willing to listen to your parents when they talk to you about things you can do better on as they may have had experiences that will help you in life and in sports.

Remember, there's nobody that watches your every move more than your parents, and there's nobody that cares more. Your parents will know your strengths and your weaknesses better than anyone. Having that support system that you can go to and trust can be a real difference maker in your long term career not only in athletics but in life. So while it's natural to break away from your parents and do some things on your own it doesn't hurt to still listen a little bit as you're going out the door. It's the little edge that may be the difference.

## Questions/Discussion

1. Do you find it hard to listen to your parents at times? Why?
2. Can you think of anyone who cares more about you than your parents? If so, who?

# Listen to the
# Wise Old Man

Many times people have asked me for some secrets to success. One of the things I've told them often is that I've always felt I had the ability to listen to the wise old man. I'm constantly making friends with people 20 years, 30 years older than I. One of my very best friends was Horace McKenzie, whom I met when I was 25 years old and he was 82. We became great friends and I used to spend the night at his house any time I went to Prescott, Arkansas on business. We remained great friends until his death at 92. I learned a lot from Horace, and you can learn a lot from anybody who has already been down the road that you are now traveling. The wise old men love to help and mentor young pups, and young pups need the wise old man.

Many times these friendships will come from somebody other than a parent, someone who is not quite as emotional or attached to the situation that can help give you wisdom and advice that will save you years of hardship and prevent many major mistakes. If you want to be the best in life, find yourself a personal coach or a mentor or just a wise old man to help you out. You'll have a lot of fun along the way, and you'll be a lot wiser and a lot more successful. The neat thing is the wise old man loves the energy he receives from helping a young pup. We all get great satisfaction from helping others. Young and old is a great combination for a partnership as each brings something to the table the other doesn't have. The movie Scent of a Woman starring Al Pacino is one of my favorites because it's a story about a young man and an old blind man helping each other and forming a lasting friendship.

## Questions/Discussion

1. Do you have a mentor or a wise old man or woman in your life?
2. Would you consider yourself open to learning from someone with more experience? Why, or why not?

# Coaching and Mentoring

CHAPTER

# 83

# People Will Say, "Let Them Learn From Their Own Mistakes."

I'll be out working with my kids after ballgames or before ballgames to try to help them get ready for every situation. Every now and then someone will say, "Why don't you just let them learn from their own mistakes!"

I have to remind myself and want to remind all of you that a coach's job is to prevent them from making the mistakes that we made before them. My job is to educate them and train them so that when we get in certain situations they will make the right decision.

I love talking with older men because I'm wise enough to try to learn from their mistakes so I can get way ahead in the game and not have to make them all on my own. Can you imagine where this country would be today if we started all over and everybody had to bang their heads against the wall and learn from their own mistakes instead of learning from those who came before them? Basically, if we weren't going to learn from those ahead of us, we would still be a country without running water and electricity.

Any coach will tell you that any player who is truly a student of the game spends a lot of time watching and learning from others. One of the things you'll find about great players is that they love to watch their particular sport on TV. The reason is that they can learn so much about playing the game from watching other players. They can see a super star handle a difficult situation that may come up in one of their own games; and when it does, they will have learned from the expert how to handle it or how not to handle it. They can learn from someone else's mistakes instead of making their own.

As a parent and as a coach your job is to make your kids and your players much better than you ever were. After all, they should be better, at least mentally, if you teach them all the things you've learned and prevent them from making the same mistakes.

## Questions/Discussion

1. Are you willing to learn from someone else's mistakes so you don't have to make them all yourself?
2. Can you think of a mistake someone else made that you learned from?

> A brilliant man is wise enough to learn
> from someone else's mistakes and not
> have to make the mistakes himself.

# A Father's Job

Sometimes my kids ask, "Why can't we learn from our own mistakes?" Other people say, "Let them learn from their mistakes. Don't try to help them too much. Let them fall flat on their faces and they'll learn some good, tough lessons."

I can see the truth in a lot of those statements because I certainly learned some lessons in the most painful of ways. But, I must tell you that I have watched a lot of people learn some lessons in some tough ways that hurt them very badly; and it simply wasn't necessary.

I remember a friend who, when he enrolled in college as a freshman, wanted to get off to a real good start, so he took the most difficult classes he could possibly take his first semester. He took algebra and calculus and chemistry and biology before he really even learned how to get adjusted to college life and the college workload. When he finished that semester with barely above a 1.0 grade average, he had learned a lesson the hard way. He would spend the rest of his college years trying to improve that GPA. He certainly could have benefited from a wise person telling him to take the easier classes the first semester while he was getting acclimated to college life. Since you're going to have to take them sooner or later, you might as well take the easy courses first and build up to some college studying experience.

I've also seen a situation where someone took a person who had never skied to the top of the mountain and tried to teach them to ski from up there only to have them be carried down on a stretcher.

I think a father's job is to educate his kids on every possible thing he can so they can make the best decisions. What I try to do is teach my kids and educate them on all the mistakes I've made in the past so that they don't have to make the same ones. My ultimate goal is to have my kids be much, much better than I am by gaining education from the mistakes I've made. Of course they will make new mistakes on their own that I'm not wise enough to see, and I hope the new mistakes will be at a much higher level than the ones I made. I want all my kids and all the kids I coach to know that my ultimate goal is to make them much better than I am by taking the combined knowledge that I've gained over the years from coaches and from the mistakes I've made. When they become coaches someday I hope they can then take all the experiences they learned from me and the ones they learned on their own and make that next set of kids even better. History has a way of making us all smarter, and to me the most brilliant person of all is one who can learn from other people's mistakes without being so hard-headed that he or she has to make their own mistakes in order to learn something. Some of my favorite people in life are what I would call wise old men. They are mentors that can provide me with insight into mistakes that they have seen over the years and that I need to avoid. I try to be smart enough to listen to them and not have to test the waters for myself.

To all my kids (my own and the ones I coach) my hope for you is that you will far surpass "Old Dad" or "Old Coach" and become a much greater success than I am.

## Questions/Discussion

1. Do you make the same mistakes over and over or do you only make them once?
2. Are you a very coachable athlete?

# You Are Your Most Important Coach

In your playing career you will play for a number of different coaches. Some will be very good coaches, some not so good. The most important coach, however, is <u>you</u>. The coach of a basketball team is watching 15 different players; a head football coach may be watching 60 players, and a soccer coach maybe 16 players in their hour and a half of practice. In the end the coach will give instructions to the players and then ask each of you to go off and work on the skill or drill. One of the most important things to developing as a player is to be able to listen to that coach, analyze every little detail and every little fundamental, and go off and work on that fundamental to perfection. Some players simply become better than others because they are better listeners and they're more coachable. When they go off to work on the fundamental the coach has demonstrated, they understand what needs to be done, and they make sure they learn it properly.

Remember, the coach doesn't have time to watch you; you have to make yourself better. You have to know how to do the fundamental correctly, and you have to do it with the proper intensity, constantly trying to make yourself better than any other player. The way you do this is to watch yourself and know yourself as you're going through the different fundamentals in practice.

I've never considered myself one of the most premier athletes ever to play, but I wouldn't trade places with anybody when it comes to understanding a game or analyzing what a coach is trying to say and then going off and working on it myself. I think one of the things that helped me move past many players was the fact that a coach could show me something one time and I could go off and work on it and figure out what it took to get that fundamental down properly. I was willing to take notes, and I was intense enough to figure out the little details that would make me better.

Some athletes are just born with God-given ability that makes them faster, quicker, and able to do a particular skill quicker. That part you can't control, but the part you can control is coaching yourself, being a good listener, and making yourself better every day.

Finally, there are all kinds of things you can do that the coach doesn't ask you to do to help make yourself better. For example, let's say you're playing basketball and the coach has you doing lay-up drills. Everybody gets in a line and they drive to the basket to do the lay-ups, but you add a special little move, maybe a behind-the-back or a between-the-legs move as you get started on your lay-ups each time. By the end of the season you'll be so much better at the moves than anyone else because you added that little twist before every one of those fundamental drills, making it a little bit harder; and therefore, making you better. No matter what the sport, continually raising the bar and adding extra work to the practice routine that the coach gives you will make you even better.

Remember, nobody is watching you as much as you watch yourself; and nobody cares as much about your development as you do. The saying, "If it is to be, it's up to me," is so true. Be a good example, push yourself, and most importantly coach yourself to be the best that you can be. If you do it, you'll make yourself a lot better.

## Questions/Discussion

1. Why are you your most important coach?
2. Do you read the sports page every day? Why is this important?
3. Do you watch ESPN Sportscenter every day? Why is this important?

CHAPTER
# 86

# Know Yourself, Trust Yourself

I've spent a lot of time coaching, and I guess you could say experimenting with, my oldest daughter. I've tried all kinds of different ways to motivate and to prepare her before games. Some of the things I and other coaches have taught her have worked, and some have failed miserably. Probably the worst mistake I've made with her was giving her Aleve to take for a sore back 30 minutes before a cross-country race. She ended up throwing up about five times in the first half mile, as her 95-pound body wasn't ready for Aleve on an empty stomach. My body would have been fine with it, but it just wasn't the right formula for her.

Sometimes I've given athletes so much information before a game that they have more than they can deal with, and they are so focused on remembering the checklist that they just can't play. Sometimes when a coach calls a particular play on offense in basketball, kids will concentrate so much on running the play, whether it is open or not, that they throw the ball away instead of just playing basketball.

It is essential that you listen to your coach, but you also need to know and trust yourself. You need to know what kind of warm-up works best for you and what kind of food gives you the best results the night before or the day of a contest. You need to know whether you need lots of quiet time before a game, or if you need to listen to rock music. You need to know

277

if you should put pressure on yourself or just go out and be loose and play. You have to learn how to respond to the different coaches you play for. In the end, you play the game for yourself and nobody else. Know what's enjoyable to you, what makes you tick. Trust yourself, and be aware of the trials and errors you've had over the years in sports. Come up with the right formula for you. The previous chapter in this book says you're the most important coach you'll ever have, and that really is true. Nobody will ever care more or know more about what works for you than you know about yourself; so learn from everybody else, tinker and experiment, and then fine tune it to develop the best engine for you.

Knowing yourself and trusting yourself in big game situations is what develops confidence. Confidence then produces a great performance.

## Questions/Discussion

1. Do you want the ball at the end of the game?
2. Do you know what your strengths and weaknesses are?

You will look back on your high school
and college years for the rest of your
life...to waste them will be very painful.

CHAPTER

**87**

# Four Years

Four Years is all we get in high school. No other time defines a young person more than High School. We all tend to fall into stereotypes. Were we the athlete, the burnout, the brain, a nerd, or just some combination of the above? How you perform in high school has a lot to do with the confidence you will carry with you the rest of your life. A lot of people have become very successful later on in life even though their high school years weren't very good. If you ask those successful people how they feel when they look back at High School there will still be complaints, comments, regrets or other feelings that they carry with them. Nobody can simply say they didn't care about their high school years.

Since you only have four years, make the best of them. You will look back on those four years for the rest of your life. You will look back on those four years as you raise your own children. You will look back on them when you come back for a high school reunion and everybody you went to school with will first remember you the way you were then. Everyone that you met, teachers, friends, or other students, will remember you that way first and then possibly change their opinion after seeing you in your new role. How you behave in high school may affect where you get to go to college and what kind of job you get later on in life. The same applies to your next four years of college.

My point is that each chapter of your life is important. At every stage you meet people and form relationships that may or may not last a lifetime, but they are still significant for that period of time. If you make a point of always conducting yourself honorably and giving your all, you can look back at that chapter and feel good about your four years of high school and your four years of college. You only get to do it once. These will be some of your best years in life, and you sure don't want to look back and feel like you wasted them.

## Questions/Discussion

1. What percentage of people do you think graduate from High School with no regrets?
2. Have you given your best?

CHAPTER

# 88

# Stay Out of Trouble

As you get older, if you stay in competitive athletics, you will find there are a lot of rewards. The other kids in school will look up to you for being an athlete, and the newspapers will start covering your accomplishments. By the time you are in high school it will be reported whether you had a good game or a bad game. You may see your name in headlines many times if you are particularly successful. With all this glory and publicity comes the chance for exposure if you do something you're not supposed to do. An athlete who gets in trouble will make the headlines in a hurry for things he or she does off the field. If you truly love your sport and want to be playing all the games for your team this season, then stay away from mischief and other things that can get you in trouble.

Over the years I've known athletes who were severely embarrassed, had their names in the headlines, or were permanently in the dog house with the coach for doing something that would not have had serious consequences for non-athletes. Some of these actions were as minor as obnoxious horseplay, such as snowballing cars. Other cases involved more serious behavior such as cheating on a test, getting in a fight at a bar or at school, destruction of property, getting a ticket for DWI, being in a car wreck, driving irresponsibly, being at a party that was busted while drugs were present, or drinking alcohol when under age. When non-athletes skip classes or fail to make passing grades, nobody notices. But for an outstanding athlete, these actions can make headlines in addition to making a permanent dent in their reputation.

You shouldn't do any of these things to begin with, but I'm not naïve enough to believe that all kids aren't exposed to every single one of these things in high school and college. Sometimes athletes are afraid they will look like a nerd or a square if they make a big deal or refuse to participate in "what everybody is doing." As an athlete, you have an easy out. You can simply tell everyone that you're not going to participate in any activity that will run you the risk of missing the big game or put your team in jeopardy. In a way, being an athlete kind of gives you a cool way out of something you probably didn't want to be involved in to begin with. It's a legitimate excuse because any coach who catches you doing any of that stuff is going to punish you, which is going to punish your team. I always felt that playing sports gave me an excuse to be dedicated, to stay out of trouble, and to be a little square when it came to passing on those things that we shouldn't be doing anyway.

It's also true that I didn't want to risk anything that would keep me out of the ballgame because I love the game that much.

## Questions/Discussion

1. What is the worst trouble you have ever gotten into?
2. Can being an athlete be a good excuse to keep you out of trouble? If yes, explain how.

# A Prophet is Not Known in His Own Town

One of the things I have constantly had to teach my kids and my athletes and even remind some of my own friends who are in the coaching profession is that a prophet is not know in his own town. April Heinrichs, the great soccer player for the University of North Carolina and Player of the Year, was despised by her own soccer teams growing up because she was a female athlete and better than everyone on her team, outworked them and then stayed afterwards to put in extra hours. Her teammates became so jealous of her success that she was not well liked. Jesus himself came to the world to save the world, yet his own people turned their backs on him out of fear and jealousy.

If you are a great athlete putting forward extraordinary effort, you may find the same thing happening to you. When you raise the bar high for excellence and you put forth an extra effort, some people will find it easier to tear you down than to simply admire you for it. Sometimes great coaches are not appreciated for the work they do every day in their own town but have unbelievable respect by outside communities.

When these things happen it's your inner core, your character, and the foundation you have built your success on that will be very important. Stick to your guns and someday when the smoke clears, the very people that have caused you grief will recognize how good they had it and that maybe the prophet was indeed right there among them.

## Questions/Discussion

1. What does "a prophet is not known in his own town" mean?

2. Where does it stem from?

> It's amazing how much you can get done
> when nobody cares who gets the credit.

# Jealousy Has Killed More Championships than any Other Disease

Whether it's a sports team, a business, or just about anything else where there is competition involved, jealousy can kill more championships than any other disease. Today the coach's primary role is to get a group of young men or young women working together in a common cause without focus on self. They say there is no 'I' in team. I heard a professional coach say the other day that the key is to have a whole bunch of 'I' players who are talented and great at what they do. The tough part is getting each of those players to still be the man and get things done for their team while all bonding together. You have to have superstars on a team to win; the key is to channel their energies in the proper form.

As I've coached and observed, the younger the team is the worse this disease is. When kids are five years old and playing soccer their parents don't really care who wins; it's how many goals little Johnny scored. They may give incentives such as ice cream after the game if Johnny scores a goal, or a bigger prize if he scores two. There are no incentives for passing, defense, and other skills that help the team win. Very little focus is paid to becoming a complete player. As kids get older parents will vie for whether their kid is the best on the team. They want their little Johnny or Julie to be the best, and jealousy often occurs with the kids who really are. During the high school years when kids mature and the gaps start to widen, most parents begin to accept that their little Johnny or Julie is not maybe as talented as another kid. Many times when they give up, these jealousies get remanufactured into "the coach has so-and-so as a favorite" or "so-and-so is only good because they have no life," or some other excuse is attached. Very rarely do we hear a parent, or for that matter, a child who is envious come to the conclusion that "hey, so-and-so is just better" or that they've worked harder and they deserve it. These undercurrents can get very strong to the point that you'll have some of your best players isolated and even picked on by others due to jealousy.

It's no different in sports than in anything else. Most people competing for things do not like their competitor. I deal with people in business who strictly hate their competition, and they're both just out doing the same thing: trying to make a living. You can pick up the newspaper everyday and read about a person who has killed his girlfriend's new lover because the new lover was a threat. Jealousy is a dangerous emotion because it is based on fear.

If you become successful at anything, there will be people who are jealous who will try to tear you down and who truly may not be your friend at the time, or maybe ever, because of your success. You'll have to accept this as part of being successful.

I have never seen a team with a whole lot of jealousy win a championship because jealousy will destroy a team. A great coach spots this disease on his team and works very hard to tear it down and get people to buy into their roles. The more talent a team has, the harder it is because more people want the credit. The great coaches know how to turn this competitiveness and jealousy into championships.

## Questions/Discussion

1. Have you ever been on a team where jealousy was a problem?
2. If yes, how did you handle it?
3. Is jealousy and envy likely to be a problem throughout your life?

> Do not let what you cannot do
> interfere with what you can do.

# Familiarity Breeds Contempt

One of the things I've learned from coaching a lot of kids over the years is that if you put the same kids together for an extended period of time, say more than the four years of high school or four years in college that eventually familiarity breeds contempt. Anyone who has brothers and sisters knows that you know every fault of your brother or sister and there will be certain things about them that may irritate you. Every mother and daughter knows that though they love each other, they can get in more arguments than any two people you'll know. The same applies to sports and competition. It's healthy sometimes to play on a club team or an AAU team with one group of players and play on your high school team with another group. Too much time spent together with the same players set in the starring roles and the others in the supplemental roles can wear on players. It can lead to jealousy and contempt for the other person.

I've also learned as a coach that coaching the same player for too many years can lead to a stale relationship as well. I must say it can also lead to one of the most rewarding relationships that you'll ever have, but there is certainly some risk that goes with it. We all like a fresh start and new things. Be sure to evaluate the situation and if it starts to become stale don't be afraid to recycle or at least have breaks so that familiarity does not breed contempt.

Many have been great friends until they became roommates. An even better example is two college friends who go into business together where they were once inseparable end up hating each other by the time they have worked together for a few years and then had to split the company apart. These business owners have spouses that have to be kept happy and the constant evaluation of who is working harder tends to tear people apart.

Coach Loucks who I coach with always says take a look at any great rock band and they almost all break up based on jealousy and contempt at the star singer getting all the recognition or too much of the money. The star singer feels like they would do even better on their own and if these others don't appreciate them they'll break off on their own. Only the great ones with a leader with unbelievable charisma and a view for the big picture can hold them all together. Bands like the Rolling Stones are truly amazing because they have survived all these years together. Though I obviously don't know any of the band members well, I'm smart enough to know that there is a strong leader among them. If you are to be a great leader on your team and help your team win many championships you will have to learn how to lead through this type of human nature.

## Questions/Discussion

1. Is it good to do everything together with your best friend or family?
2. Why do doctors not operate on their own family members?
3. Have you ever had one of your best friends, teammates, or family members become the enemy? If so, why?

**clockwise from top right:**

Six future college basketball players. Amanda Morris, Julie Inman, and Kelsey Hatcher for the Arkansas Belles and Breanna Gordon, Haley Hatcher, and Larkin Hatcher for the Mighty Bluebirds.

Three Warriors (L-R) Amanda Janton, Annie DeCoursey, and Jonie Block have been mainstays for the Bluebirds for years.

Breanna Gordon shows her size with Haley and Larkin all members of the Mighty Bluebirds BCI State Champion and Arkansas Slam-N-Jam National Championship teams.

Bluebird Soccer Ball – The Mighty Bluebird imprinted on the soccer ball has become a symbol of excellence in Arkansas soccer. The Bluebirds have won 13 State Championships in 14 tries.

**clockwise from top right**

Two future Division I football players for Pulaski Academy. Stefan Loucks who is the son of Coach Loucks and Stephen Newell, who worked for me at The Hatcher Agency during the summers.

It's hard to find three prettier guards than Julie Inman, Kelsey Hatcher, and Amanda Morris.

Six-year-old All-Star second baseman, Max Mendelsohn and All Star shortstop, Layne Hatcher.

Super seven year old
soccer players, Michael
Pugh and Will Stafford.

A couple of the toughest
players on our Broncos
Football Team, Justin
Charette and Zack Kelley.

**above**

A picture of the Bluebird Championship
Ring for the U15 team

**right**

The Bluebirds first boys team. Justin
Charette, Layne Hatcher, Will Stafford with
Coach Chris Owen and Coach Hatcher.

The Bluebirds at North Carolina Soccer Camp.

Close friendships are developed.

The Bluebirds and their families spend a lot of time collecting trophies after tournaments.

# Kids and Running

Kids enjoying running today are very rare. I've always gotten my kids involved in running at an early age and taught them that it was fun before they knew any different. You'll see photos of the kids running the Little Rock Marathon and having fun doing it. Getting your kids involved by running a 5K with them at an early age can give them a lot of confidence and have them associate running with fun.

**clockwise from top right**

Bluebird players with their medals after running the Little Rock Marathon

Mattie (the little one) finishes the race with some support from big sisters, Kelsey and Haley and big brother, Layne.

Only a 6th grader Haley Hatcher is all alone at the finish and wins the junior high cross country meet (7th, 8th, and 9th graders) at Ouachita Baptist University with no training other than Bluebird soccer practice, Haley also won the Little Rocker's Kids Marathon with over 1,200 runners two years in a row.

**clockwise from above left**

Layne Hatcher shows its fun to run.

Haley and Kelsey share a hug after the Ouachita Baptist race. There will be many running state titles by these two before they graduate.

Four of the five Hatcher kids after a 5K. (L-R) Kelsey, Haley, Mattie, and Layne. Running is a way of life. Larkin was at a sleepover.

Kelsey Hatcher was an All-State cross country runner as a freshman and sophomore, and won the Little Rock Marathon 5K.

## Championship Hill

One of the keys to the Mighty Bluebirds
13 State Championships to date is running
The Hill. The Hill is a small mountain out
at Bluebird Field that the kids run up and
down four times to equal one sprint. These
kids age six to fifteen will run The Hill
ten to twelve times when at peak fitness.
Recently a high school football team came
out to run The Hill and by the time they
had run four they had players throwing up.
We teach the kids that running The Hill
separates them from the competition and
will help them win the close games because
they know they deserve to win. You will
also notice the girls carrying a couple of
the younger boys back like they are a log
following the run. This is to promote team-
work and have a little fun after running
The Hill. As you can tell from the kids
faces they don't view running The Hill
as punishment, but simply as work that's
required to be a champion.

**clockwise from top right**

The Bluebirds visit Magic Springs Amusement Park

Coach Hatcher reads a chapter from the book, "Between the Ears" to the kids almost every practice.

Christy Smiley helps give the woman's touch to three of her favorites.

Bluebird All-Star Coaching Staff (L-R) Chuck Ashburn, Mark Burr, Chris Owen, Christy Smiley, Greg Hatcher, and Scott Loucks.

**clockwise from top left**

The Arkansas Belles also use Mighty Bluebird Field. Coach Loucks has helped over 95 girls receive Division I scholarships.

Bluebirds pose for a photo at practice.

Bluebirds all pitch in to congratulate Coach Hatcher on another State Title.

Bluebirds at North Carolina Soccer Camp

We get them started
early at Bluebird Field.
Layne at 1½.

Yes, we take a day off
every now and then. The
kids vacation in Florida.

**1999 U-9 STATE CHAMPIONS**
**MIGHTY BLUEBIRD SOCCER**

| Caroline Benton | Kelsey Hatcher | Amanda Johnson | Jessica Pruitt |
| Stacy Coonce | Holly Hilburn | Jessica Monarch | Courtney Sykes |
| Elizabeth Hackett | Erin Howland | Bethany Morrison | Haley Whisenhunt |
| | Amanda Janton | Mary Mulford | |

Coaches: Greg Hatcher, Gene Whisenhunt, and Leland Sykes

**2002 U-12 STATE CHAMPIONS**
**MIGHTY BLUEBIRD SOCCER**

| Abby Bloom | Erin Howland | Caty McMains | Calli Roberts |
| Annie DeCoursey | Amanda Janton | Bethany Morrison | Courtney Sykes |
| Kaylee Flowers | LeeAnna Magrath | Tracy Powell | Katie Udron |
| Kelsey Hatcher | | | Haley Wisenhunt |

## 2003 U-14 STATE CHAMPIONS
## MIGHTY BLUEBIRD SOCCER

| | | |
|---|---|---|
| Amanda Janton | Lindley Gaston | Rebekah Riner |
| Kaylee Flowers | Katie Udron | Bethany Morrison |
| Ashley Moskow | Kelsey Hatcher | Jonie Block |
| Lindsay Bridges | Caty McMains | Tracy Powell |
| Abby Bloom | | Annie DeCoursey |

Coaches: Chris Owen, Greg Hatcher, Adam May, Scott Loucks, and Christy Smiley

## 2003 U-13 STATE CHAMPIONS
## MIGHTY BLUEBIRD SOCCER

| | | | |
|---|---|---|---|
| Caroline Benton | Kelsey Burr | Amanda Janton | Ashley Moskow |
| Jonie Block | Annie DeCoursey | LeeAnna Magrath | Tracy Powell |
| Abby Bloom | Kaylee Flowers | Caty McMains | Rebekah Riner |
| Lindsay Bridges | Kelsey Hatcher | Bethany Morrison | Katie Udron |

Coaches: Chris Owen and Greg Hatcher

2005 BCI U-11 BCI STATE CHAMPIONS

# MIGHTY BLUEBIRD BASKETBALL

Front: Haley Filat, Larkin Hatcher, Kelsey Smith,
Back: Annie Stafford, Leah Rinon, Breanna Gordon, Whitney Beals, Haley Hatcher
Coaches: Mack Stafford, Greg Hatcher, Scott Loucks

2005 U-15 STATE CHAMPIONS

# MIGHTY BLUEBIRD SOCCER

Front: Kelsey Hatcher, Abby Bloom, Annie DeCourcey, Janie Black, Amanda Janton, Danielle Anderson, Haley Hatcher, Ashley Miess, Erin Warden
Back: Caitlin Lamb, Gaty McMains, Rebekah Riner, Brittany Hudson, Erin Johnson, Tracy Powell, Kaylee Flowers, Ashley Moskow
Coaches: Chris Queen, Greg Hatcher, Scott Loucks

## 2005 U-11 STATE CHAMPIONS
## MIGHTY BLUEBIRD SOCCER

### ARKANSAS STATE SOCCER ASSOCIATION

us YOUTH SOCCER

Front: Lauren Ashburn, Olivia Caillouet, Haley Hatcher, Samantha Mack, Haley Fliot, Kelsey Smith, Larkin Hatcher

Back: Greg Hatcher, Madison Lee, Leah Riner, Breanna Gordon, Annie Stafford, Megan Batek, Chris Owen

Bluebird Soccer Coach Chris Owen played professional soccer in Wales and brings a wealth of knowledge to the girls, both the Bluebirds and the Central Arkansas Christian Mustangs. Here he is (far left) with Coach Shackleford and the 2006 CAC Mustang State Championship Soccer Team.

CHAPTER

# 92

# Reward Excellence or Excellence is Lost

For most athletes that end up playing in high school, college, and on you will run across a coach who does not reward excellence, but will reward seniority, status, or worse yet rotate who is rewarded. I've always said reward excellence or excellence is lost.

If a coach puts only seniors on the All-Conference or the All-State team and doesn't reward the freshman, sophomore, or junior who may be the most deserving excellence is lost. These young kids who have been working their whole lives and who have won fair and square when they're not rewarded you send a message of why work there's no reward for it only a false reward, they'll be recognized when they are seniors. In the business world if you reward seniority instead of excellence you will get an apathetic workforce from top to bottom and your company will not produce the results that you desire. You'll have a bunch of old unmotivated employees. Reward excellence regardless of age, politics, status, race, and you will have all of your players battling it out and trying to achieve excellence because that is what's rewarded in your program.

In the most extreme cases if you don't reward excellence, excellence will leave the program. Anybody that's ever put forth their maximum effort and worked hard to become a champion knows that you don't want to be in a program where it is not rewarded and where it is not appreciated. These Warriors will seek out other programs where Warriors and their efforts are appreciated. Whether it's sports, at work, child raising, or simply the behaviors that you want, reward excellence and that's exactly what you'll get.

## Questions/Discussion

1. Has there ever been a situation in which you didn't pick the best or reward the best?
2. Why didn't you?

> You can rest when you're dead.

# Becoming Great – Overcoming the "Wait Your Turn" Attitude

Very few coaches really know how to make players great. The problem, especially in team sports, is that everybody is fighting over who gets the credit. In an individual sport there is no debate or jealousy because who plays is decided on the battlefield, and there are no politics in making decisions. In a team atmosphere you have a lot of subplots, emotions, and issues going on. Jealousy between underclassmen and upperclassmen, where a particular athlete is in their career, how talented the players are, and rivalry for who is going to be the star on the team are all part of the chemistry. Jealousies between parents and how a kid is programmed at home, are also determining factors in a player's development.

Coaches are also a big factor in whether a player becomes great. Coaches tend to coach the way they were coached. Some coaches played for coaches who, if a freshman and a junior were even or about the same, would always play the older player, feeling the freshman can wait their turn. Another coach would play the younger player knowing that they are going to get more years out of them and their potential is greater. Giving the young player the experience early if they earn it will make them great later. Also, believe it or not, some coaches sometimes can't relate to a great player because very few coaches, like very few individuals in the world, were great players themselves. There are only a select few that will end up going on to be truly great.

If you are going to be a great player, you better get used to overcoming all kinds of obstacles that may not be fair. Your coach may think that you don't need to have your day in the sun until you are in your junior or senior year. They will look back and say, I didn't get all those accolades until my junior or senior year, why should you? There may be other upper-classmen who feel that you must wait your turn like they did.

What people fail to realize many times is that the great ones may have been working and putting in extra hours after practice or after school for years just to get where they are. If you want to succeed and be a great one, you have to overcome all these obstacles by contin-uing <u>to be so much better than the competition</u> and continuing to perform and produce every day. Eventually other players, coaches, parents, and competition that you play will notice how often you get it done. After breaking through that very tough wall that holds so many back you will then be embraced and you will blossom; but first you must break down the barriers of people's past prejudices and experiences before the good times come. One of the common denominators of all the great ones is that they persevered through these times with unbridled determination. You can do it too!

## Questions/Discussion

1. Do you believe a person should play based on seniority or talent?
2. Do you think teams, schools, and companies reward people based on the time they been there versus the results they produce? If yes, why do you believe that?

# Dealing with Your Coach and Teammates

CHAPTER

# 94

# The Coach is the
# Most Valuable Player

We've all heard the excuse that this coach or that coach has all the horses, and that's why they won the championship. It's true that some coaches get lucky and get a bunch of great players that could be on the team. I have found that if you have two coaches with teams that have good athletes, the better coach will win the majority of the time and is certainly the most valuable player on any team. Take a look at major college sports and the professional teams. The Los Angeles Lakers could not win the NBA Championship until they got Phil Jackson. Great college coaches move to other programs, and those programs immediately become winners. When you're dealing with a large number of individuals, the real challenge in coaching is getting the entire team to move in the same cohesive direction.

Regardless of the level in coaching, in a team sport a coach's first and greatest goal is to get his team to all buy into their roles and play together for the common good. It doesn't matter whether it's nine year old soccer or the NBA. In nine year old soccer you've got parents wanting their kids scoring the goals, and in the NBA you have players wanting to score all the points. Getting a team to play together and to get rid of the petty jealousies at any level is a coach's first great obstacle to overcome. Then putting in a successful system and having the kind of practices that make these players better day in and day out is step number two.

Step three is working a team hard enough to know that they deserve to win, having them mentally prepared to win. The final piece is somehow getting all this done while having the players respect the coach and even want to win for the coach.

The coaches that I gave my absolute best for were the ones for whom winning for them was even more important than winning for me. When you have a coach that has that kind of stranglehold on his players, it means you have a coach that has put forth such an effort that they have gained the ultimate amount of respect from their players.

Have no doubt about it. If I were picking sides for a high school, college, or pro team and I could pick any player or coach in the world, I would start off with my first pick being the best coach.

## Questions/Discussion

1. How important is leadership in an organization?
2. Do you believe the coach influences every player, parent, fan, referee, opposing coach, etc?

# You Are Interviewing for Your Next Job Every Day

I was a 22-23 year old kid in my first or second year at Arkansas Blue Cross Blue Shield and getting started in the workplace. I went in to my boss and asked if I could interview sometime in the future for one of the account executive sales jobs, which was the highest level sales job in the company. At the time I was a group-marketing representative, which meant I was handling the smaller groups; and the account executives handled the larger groups.

My boss, Ed Choate, said something interesting that I never forgot and have often thought how true this is in sports as well. He said, "Greg, there will be no reason to interview for an account executive job when and if it comes open because you're interviewing for it everyday you come to work." What he meant was that the effort I put forth everyday doing my current job would determine whether they hired me for an open account executive position. For the most part there would be little I could say in an interview that would convince them I was the right person for the job if I hadn't been doing a great job as a group-marketing representative.

"Wow," I thought. "That makes so much sense."

In sports you may be the backup player that sees a little action or the guy that's on the bench that sees very little. When that senior graduates, the coach's mind, for the most part, is already made up as to who the replacement will be, based on their performance in practice and off the bench when they come into the games. A player can't walk into the coach's office and say, "Hey, I'd like to try out for this graduating senior's position," then just turn up the volume during the meeting and go out and start playing in practice the next day. For the most part it's what players have done prior to the opening that will determine who gets to play.

In every single sports season a coach will have a starting lineup, but you can't predict who will get injured, get kicked off the team for disciplinary reasons, lose interest in the game, or simply perform very poorly and lose their starting position. If you're one of those players that's not getting playing time, don't give up. It's how hard you are working and how good you look in practice everyday that will move you up to the spot where the coach will tap you next for that position. If you're a junior high player already in the starting lineup and you're playing very well, how you continue to play will determine whether you have a starting position waiting for you when you get to the varsity.

Without question your actions in all things whether it is sports, the workplace, or even how you've treated a particular girl or guy will determine whether you make the starting lineup, become the CEO or president, or get the boyfriend or girlfriend you want. Even when you die and go to heaven, there's no interview you can have with God when you get to the Pearly Gates that will help get you in. You've been interviewing for that position all your life.

Do the best you can everyday in all things because you are interviewing for every job you ever wanted in life each day with your performance.

## Questions/Discussion

1. Do you practice every day like you are interviewing for your next starting position?
2. Can you name some things that a high school player might be interviewing for every day at practice that most people wouldn't think of? (Name 10)

# You're On the Bench…
# How to Get Off of It

Sooner or later almost all players will find themselves sitting on the bench. Some players have had so little experience with this that they simply don't know how to respond. They lose confidence, and they can't figure out how to get off that bench.

Maybe you're a player who has started every game in your junior high and high school career, and now you are in college and there are a bunch of people just like you that started every game of their career. And you find yourself on the bench. Maybe you just came at the wrong time; maybe you are a freshman, and they're starting a bunch of sophomores at your position, and they're simply getting the nod because they have a little more experience. I have watched many a superstar in high school get frustrated to the point of quitting the team or just spending four years of frustration sitting on the bench. They were players who could play well as long as the coaches liked them and as long as they were confident and getting lots of playing time, but when those things didn't happen they simply didn't know what to do.

I've also seen a couple of tough cookies find some very creative things to do in order to get the coaches' attention. It's obvious to me that if you're not getting enough playing time several things need to occur to get yourself off the bench. The key fundamentals are:

Go see the coaches and ask them what areas you need to improve in. Write them down, and then go work like crazy on them and make sure the coach notices that you have worked hard on those items.

Be the first one to practice each and every day, working extra hard on your weaknesses and perfecting other parts of your game.

Be the last person to leave practice each and every day, again, working on those skills and working extra on fitness. Most importantly, work on improving your game and letting the coach and everyone know that you are paying the price to get better. Make it obvious that you want to get some playing time and help the team.

I want to share a couple of stories I have observed. This first one will help you understand how one of my close friends got playing time in college football. My friend Jamie Harrison was an excellent high school football player. He and I went to Alma College together where he played football. His freshman year he didn't letter; he didn't even get to suit out for the traveling squad games. You see, Jamie wasn't a top recruit of Alma's; he didn't have any brothers that had been great players there previously; and he was a 5'9", 180-pound defensive back. Alma had about 20 players that size competing for those positions. Jamie was probably, to be fair, better than at least half of those players; yet he found himself at the bottom of the rung due to the fact that the coaches didn't recruit him, and a lot of times they wanted to reward and play the players they had recruited into Alma. He wasn't the most serious player at the time, and that probably hurt him. The more he got passed over, the more frustrated he got; and he tended to be less focused and to lose confidence.

His sophomore year he came back out thinking that he'd get a break now since he had a little experience, but what he found was that the coaches still had new recruits coming in and new people that they kept passing him over for. The frustration grew, and he seriously thought about quitting football. He didn't even letter as a sophomore. When he came out his junior year he was more mature and more focused, and he became angry when he saw what he thought were some politics and some players getting playing time because they had better connections, whether it was the recruiting process or the fact that they had had brothers that were excellent players before them. Jamie was on the meat squad, the third team that goes against the first team and is supposed to tackle the starters lightly.

He decided he'd had enough, and when that starting running back came through the line into his area, he hit him as hard as he could hit him. The coaches blew the whistle and said, "Hey, take it easy on the starters, Harrison; you know we don't want them to be injured."

When the running back came through on the next play, Jamie popped him again. The running back got up and gave him a shove and told him to take it easy, that it was just meat squad practice. Sure enough, the next time they ran through again Jamie was there, knocking the heck out of him again. Basically, Jamie Harrison let them know that if they put him on meat squad he was going to play as hard as anybody else and that these starters didn't want to run against him.

The starting tailback complained that they had to get Harrison out of there or they were going to get hurt. The coaches and the other starters began to notice that that reserve junior over there was one of the hardest hitters on the team, if not the hardest hitter. Once the coaches started noticing that he had a reputation for being able to hit people hard, they also started to notice that he was the strongest of all the defensive backs in the weight room, and that he was either the fastest or the second fastest player on the team. The coaches hadn't noticed that throughout his freshman year and most of his sophomore year until he made it known that he was tired of sitting on the bench and he was not going to back down for anybody.

Although coaches like players that do what they tell them to do, respect in football is a little different. All football coaches, though they may be upset that he wasn't following the rules exactly, like very tough, hard nosed players that can hit. It was no coincidence that going into his junior year, Jamie Harrison was moved up from 18th or 19th defensive back to the backup position. In pre-season football he continued to hit the heck out of people and found himself in the starting lineup for the first game of the season. He went on to start those last two years, was the team's hardest hitter and earned two letters the hardest possible way at Alma College. But the example you can learn from him is: he had simply had enough and was willing to do anything to get the coaches' attention, and he decided to fight his way off the bench.

The second story is about me when I was playing soccer in college. Toward the end of my freshman year I thought I'd gotten good enough to be getting significantly more playing time. At the end of practice the coach would have us run 10 killers, which are cone drills where you run to a cone 5 yards out and back to the starting line, 10 yards, 15 yards, 20 yards, and 25 yards out, all without stopping. These cone drills were extremely exhausting, and the coach would have us divide up into two groups and the first group would run while the second group rested; then the second group would run while the first group rested. When I'd decided I'd had enough, I ran the cone drills with the first group and the second group. In other words, I didn't rest while all the other players got a rest. I won the first 19 cone drills despite running twice as many and getting no rest. On the 20$^{\text{th}}$ and last killer, one of the players beat me, and I took second. You see, most people run the last one the hardest. At the end of that 20th cone drill I threw up trying to win.

While I was throwing up at the end of the cone drills the coach said, "Take four laps around the field for the entire team." That is the equivalent of a mile run. I threw up just a little bit more and took off. You see, I was a pretty good distance runner. Not only did I win the distance running, but I also lapped the entire team after throwing up. When practice was over, my coach never said a word to me. He said, "Nice job" to our team captain who won the 20th line drill, never acknowledging me. But, from that point on he knew who wanted to play soccer and who the fittest player on the team was. My playing time went up and I ended up being a three-year starter my sophomore through senior years.

Sometimes you have to do some crazy things to get off that bench and to get your coach's attention. Most of the time the person who gets off the bench is the one who hates being there the most.

## Questions/Discussion

1. Have you ever done anything drastic to get off the bench? What was it? Did it work?

2. Once you get on the bench is it hard to get off of it? How can you make sure you never get there?

I truly believe justice prevails in time
with enough effort, most of the time.

# Leave No Doubt
# in the Coach's Mind

I've talked to people all my adult life who said they were good athletes or even great athletes in high school, but they quit playing because they didn't like the coach, or a coach screwed them over. There is no question in my mind that in some team sports such as soccer, football, basketball, and baseball different coaches have different opinions on players, especially if the playing ability is close. Some coaches prefer a running quarterback over a passing quarterback; some coaches prefer players who have speed, while others prefer players who have skill. There is even politics involved for coaches who may know a player's parents, or that player's parent may be on the board; and it is even possible that a parent may work at the school and have hired the coach. These issues can no doubt play a role in which players a coach chooses to start.

What you have to do as a player is realize that these things do happen and make sure there's absolutely no question in anyone's mind who's the better player. Even if they have a particular type of player they like, you've got to be good enough that if they play that player in the position you want, they'll move you to another position so that you find your way in a lineup. Champions find ways to get it done, and non-champions give up or find excuses why things didn't work out. I hate to be that abrupt, but there are some players for whom it just is not worth putting out the effort when these situations occur with the coach. However, if you truly love playing a sport, regardless of who the coach is at your school or university, you won't quit. You will keep trying and find a way to win a spot in the lineup. I have certainly gone through a couple of these situations myself, and the adversity I went through probably not only made me a much stronger person but a much better athlete. I worked harder, put in extra time, tried to make sure there was no way I could be left out of the lineup. Frustrating yes, but a real satisfaction when you get the job done. It's also a good lesson to learn because when you get out of sports and out of school the same differing opinions, the same politics, and the same style preferences will be made by bosses and the companies you work for. They'll be even more political and less objective than sports.

If you start running or giving up now in sports, you'll be running and giving up later in life. Stick your chin in the air and fight for the position if you think it's yours. You may not be successful immediately, and you may not be successful ever; but you'll become a better player and person for fighting and trying than you will if you give up. If you just can't bear it anymore, finish out the season and find yourself an individual sport where the lineups are determined by the players who beat each other in individual competition; for example, cross country, track, wrestling, swimming, tennis, or golf. All of these are individual sports where the determination of who is the best player is made on the field.

One final thought on college athletics: In high school you don't have a choice of who your coaches are and who you play for because that's the high school you go to, but when it's time to go to college you'll get a chance to choose your school and choose your coach. It's important to go to a college where the coach wants you, where you fit their particular style. Many players make the mistake of going to a school they really wanted to go to without considering the coach's preferences. If you're a passing quarterback and a coach wants a running quarterback to run the wishbone, you're going to have a bad experience.

Keep your eyes open and try to find a program that fits you if you're going there and you want to play sports. There's still some stubborn, bull headed players that pick their school and then decide they'll do whatever it takes to please that coach, and there's nothing wrong with that either. In the end if you work hard enough, and if you're good enough you can win over just about any coach because for the most part all coaches have trouble not rewarding a hard worker with some talent...and coaches want to win.

## Questions/Discussion

1. Do all coaches agree on who is the best player? Why?
2. What can you do to always protect your starting position?

CHAPTER

# 98

# Poor Coaches Want the Credit, Good Coaches Want to Win and Get Everybody Involved

As a player over the years you will run into your fair share of good coaches and your fair share of poor coaches. One of the things you must understand as a player is how to recognize each and what to do in that situation. I've run into coaches who have their system and they won't deviate from their system regardless of what players they have or regardless of the situation. For example, some basketball coaches may always play two guards, two forwards, and a center while other coaches may always play three guards, one forward, and a center. What happens if you have four good guards and one good center and no good forwards then you might have to change your lineup a little bit in order to win. I have found without question, though, the most overriding thing about coaches is sometimes their egos and their desire to want the credit for developing players and wins. Great coaches and great players understand how important it is to get everybody involved all going in the same direction in order to win. Poor coaches isolate themselves on an island and want everybody to do it their way listening to noone.

An example of one of the things that I found amazing about one of the best basketball coaches I've seen was a situation that happened with Coach Scott Loucks. His AAA basketball team was playing the #1 ranked AAAAA basketball team in the state and it was a one-point game at halftime. As Coach Loucks ran off the floor he ran to the stands and talked to a summer AAU coach who he had a lot of respect for named Bobby Alexander. Here he is in the middle of high school game and he's going to get any thoughts from Bobby Alexander because he knew that Bobby Alexander coached his team in the summer during AAU basketball and he also knew that Bobby Alexander knew his players as well as he did from his years of coaching them. Most coaches would have too big an ego or too much pride to look for some help, but Coach Loucks was exactly the opposite, he would have asked a Grandmother in the stands for her advice if he thought it would help.

The bottom line is that good coaches look for assistance from anyone that will help their team win. They're not afraid to copy someone else's plays or their system. They are not after who gets the credit. They're after winning. I've also seen coaches who always want to play upper classman because no newcomer could be possibly as good as a player that they coached the previous season. These new players couldn't possibly understand the game until they had been coached by them for a while. These same coaches typically don't want to learn from anybody else and therefore they get stuck on an island never improving because they never open their minds to self-improvement.

As a player you have to recognize both coaches, figure out what works and understand them. You will play differently for each of these coaches but it's important to understand their traits and learn from all of them. You'll never be able to control your coach, but you will be able to control how you respond to them and try to produce in the ways that are important to them. In the end, you can't control the coach you get, but it's important to recognize what type of coach you have, and what it's going to take to win them over. Some coaches want skill, some want size, some want effort, some want experience, some just want players they trained. Some want intensity, some like cocky kids, some like humble kids, some like them confident and outspoken, others like them to be quiet and just do what they say. There's a lot of truth that most coaches like players who were like they were as players, but they love someone who was even better than they were…the player they aspired to be.

Here's the key to winning coaches over…In the end they want to win. Be the player that helps the coach win and you'll find yourself in the game.

Note: I've seen a coach who didn't like a player who didn't play them much in the blowouts, but when the close games came the player they didn't like played the entire game.

## Questions/Discussion

1. Are you willing to get assistance from anyone in order to get better?
2. What does being coachable mean?

CHAPTER

# 99

# It's Time to Meet with Your Coach or Boss

Anybody who's been a player long enough will know that there may come a time in your career when a particular coach doesn't like your style of game, doesn't notice you, or just doesn't understand you. Or, possibly you don't understand your coach. Rather than sulking and being upset that you're not getting playing time, it doesn't hurt to go meet with the coach. Your coach was a player, too. They've sat on that bench, they've probably been a star, and they've probably been everything in between. All coaches like players who want to play, and all coaches like players who believe they are good enough to play. After all if you don't think you're good enough and if you don't want to play, why should the coach play you to begin with?

When it's time to have that meeting with the coach to find out what you need to improve on in order to get more playing time, have an agenda. Make a list of items that you want to discuss. After all, you may only be 14 or 15 years old, and a coach may be 45. The coach is a lot smarter than you and has had a lot more experiences. When you go in and start asking questions, the conversation may go completely away from the questions you wanted to ask or the concerns you have. When you go brain dead after the conversation has gone away from the subject, you can't remember what you came in to talk to him about to begin with. It's certainly not going to be impressive to the coach; you're not going to get your questions answered; and it just makes for a very unproductive meeting. Be well prepared. Know what you want to discuss. Have a pencil and paper ready, and write down the answers the coach gives you. Writing down these answers lets the coach know that you're listening and that you value his or her response, and most importantly it allows you to remember this information when you get home so you can work on the things the coach wants you to work on.

Too many times players are afraid to go talk to coaches. If you're too afraid to go talk to the coach, then you're too afraid to perform well at crunch time. I find that the better you get and the more you believe that you should be playing, the more confidence you'll have to go in and see that coach. I've sat on the bench at times in my career, and let me tell you, what I did was let everybody in the world know that I didn't want to be there. I was the first one to practice; I was the last one out. I went to the coaches and asked them what I needed to work on. I made my list; I worked on those things; and I reported back to them on the progress. I let them know how I was doing and when I was improving.

My college coach once told me, "One of the problems with you, Greg, is that you always see yourself as you're going to be before you get there." In other words, he was saying that I always saw myself as an improved player before I was actually that far improved, but I told him that was not the case. I said, "Nobody knows better than I when I have improved and have learned to do a certain thing because I'm watching what I do every second of every day."

The coach has to watch 15 or 20 players, so sometimes when I went to see him to tell him that I had solved this problem or I could do a certain thing, I would say, "Now you watch for it. You're going to see it." Sure enough, when he watched he would see it. I can assure you that he realized I could do those things a lot more quickly than he would have if I had not alerted him to them. If I had waited, it may have taken two or three more weeks for him to notice what I pointed out.

My coach never thought I was being a smart aleck because he knew how hard I worked and how serious I was about becoming the best. He also knew that I did exactly what he asked me to do. The coach that I had to work my way off the bench for is one of my very best friends today and a man I admire as much as any. It all started with a few meetings, a few written down agendas, and a few written down answers to my questions. These meetings helped propel me from the bench to a three and four year starter in different sports. The same approach works in business and in all relationships whether it is marriage, a friendship, etc. If there's a problem, go talk about it, have a plan and record your findings, and you'll find yourself improving very quickly.

## Questions/Discussion

1. Are you willing to change your game to the one your coach wants?
2. How hard are you willing to work?

> When you say "thank you," two people feel good...the receiver and the sender.

# Be Appreciative and Say "Thank You"

In sports as a player you have so much to be appreciative and thankful for. Generally the coaches that are out coaching you are doing it for little or no money at all. Your parents drive you to and from practices and games missing their own personal workouts or personal time for themselves. They have removed themselves from the spotlight and now are just fans of yours trying to help you become the best you can be. All of these people, coaches, parents, school administrators, they're really all in this for one thing and that is the satisfaction of feeling good about helping somebody else. Many times the most satisfying thing they will get all year from being a coach or a parent is a thank you in person from you or a thank you note of your appreciation for all their hours of hard work.

As a coach I can tell you that for the most part you don't get near as many thank you's as you get complaints over a kids playing time or criticism over the loss that the team may have had. Sometimes one thank you note, whether it be from a player that's currently playing or years later from a player who writes to let you know that you changed their lives is all it takes to keep a coach going for another season. I'll also tell you that as a coach, you would do anything in the world for those appreciative players. Let your coaches know that you appreciate them and you'll find that you'll feel good letting them know that; they'll feel good hearing that and they'll even work harder to help you even more. Thank you notes are a forgotten art in today's world and especially from young kids, but they mean the most to coaches. I've received letters from players ten years after they've played for me that have brought me to tears and I've received nice little thank you notes from young players that were extremely sincere that I would do anything in the world to help even more today.

This appreciation and thank yous don't just go to your coaches and to your parents, but they also go to the players that you play with. When someone throws a great touchdown pass to you or a great pass in basketball that allows you to make a lay-up or a nice jump shot don't celebrate taking all the credit yourself by spiking the ball or throwing your hands up after the made basket, find the player that made the great pass and as you run down the field or the court point at them and tell them "great pass" and give them the recognition that they deserve. This gives your teammates the recognition they deserve, it makes them feel good and appreciated and they're a lot more likely to make a good pass to you again in the future. This type of harmony helps a team win. No team ever wins where a bunch of individuals are battling over who's scoring the most or what the statistics are. The teammates that get just as much satisfaction out of making a good pass to help somebody else score versus scoring themselves are the real winners. It all starts with attitude and that includes appreciation and thank yous to all people involved.

The best coaches in the world understand that they can't win by just having a good relationship with their parents or with their players. They understand that there are numerous people involved, from the parents to the administration, to the professors or teachers, to the media, to the referees, to the janitors that clean their gymnasiums, or the maintenance men that take care of the football field. All of these people are an integral part to their success. It's critical to get out the pen and paper and thank all those involved if you want to have a winning program. After all, any winning organization is exactly that, a winning organization, not just a winning coach or player. I've never had anybody get upset with me for thanking them or appreciating them too much, it's always made me feel good and I can assure you the same result will occur for you.

## Questions/Discussion

1. How many Thank You notes did you receive last year?

2. Can you name the people that sent them to you?

3. Did you feel better about the person that sent you the Thank You note? Why?

# 101

> Adversity makes some people break;
> it makes other people break records.

## Show Your Coaches
## Confidence When You Fail

When I was in college we had a third baseman that was an excellent baseball player, but he had some periods where he went through real slumps both in his hitting and his fielding. He was a good friend of mine and a person that I respected a lot. One of the things I noticed about him was when they hit a ball to him at third base and he made an error and fumbled it or threw it away, he didn't throw his glove down or cuss or kick in the dirt and draw a lot of attention to himself. Instead, he simply cocked his head back and shook his head a little like he was the best third baseman in the world, that this error was a fluke, and that he probably wouldn't make another one for the next 10 years. This confidence and the ability to blow off his error made the coach feel the same way—that the player was unlikely to make another error, and therefore he should leave him in the game. What amazed me about this player was that there was a period of time where he was in a horrible slump and maybe missed four out of every 10 balls hit at him; but sure enough, he acted like he'd never miss another one again. And sure enough, he stayed in the lineup.

One of my daughters has the same confidence, cockiness, or self-assuredness—whatever you want to call it. If we were playing basketball and she missed the first 20 shots of the game she would think nothing of it; and when it came time to take the game winner with the score tied, she would expect to have the ball. Needless to say, when the game is tied we give her the ball because she thinks she can put it in. If you develop that confidence that you can be counted on even after several mishaps, you'll be surprised how often the coach will trust you and not give up on you.

## Questions/Discussion

1. When you make a mistake in a competition, how do you react?
2. Does it show on your face?

CHAPTER

# 102

# Leaders Develop Relationships Before They Reprimand

As a coach I certainly make my share of mistakes. One of the mistakes I have made over the years is to get on players before I have a relationship with them. Once players know that their coach loves and cares about them and believes in them, players can be pushed and dragged to improve. Players who feel comfortable in their relationship with the coach can even handle being chewed out occasionally for making mistakes because they know the coach wants them to remember so they will not repeat that mistake. The player who knows his or her coach believes in him won't feel personally offended, embarrassed, or humiliated but will understand, "The coach may be mad at me right now, but he still loves me, and I just need to learn from this situation."

The same principle works for teammates. If you go down to the athletic club and pick teams and play with a bunch of people you don't know, you don't jump on one of your teammates for not making the proper pass or for not blocking out on the rebound or for making poor decisions. If you do, that player may think you are a jerk and not like you at all. However, if you are good friends with that player and you have gone through practices together and developed a relationship, when they make a mistake, you can say, "block out!" and they very well may appreciate you reminding them of the key point of the game. Even if you do it harshly, they will know you did it to help your team win. The bottom line is your team needs leadership and hopefully you will be a leader, but develop a relationship first.

## Questions/Discussion

1. Have you earned the respect of your teammates to the extent that you can be a team leader?

CHAPTER
# 103

# Don't Talk About Your Teammates or Your Coach Behind Their Backs

It is human nature to blame somebody else sometimes when our teams don't win or our personal performance was not good. We've all heard athletes say the coach didn't start the right lineup or didn't call the right game today, or so-and-so didn't play very well and cost us the game. We also know many negative wizards that create a lot of dissension on the team by being critical of others. Remember that this information almost always gets back to the other players or to the coaches. There's no way this kind of negative energy can help your team get better.

If you have something you can say to a teammate to help them next time, say it in a positive way, give them a pat on the back, and let them know that you know they'll come through next time. This is leadership, and your teammates will appreciate it.

After a loss, most players and coaches want to blame someone else. Look in the mirror first and ask yourself what you could have done physically, mentally, and from a motivational perspective to help your team win. Only after you've analyzed your own game and made corrections is it time to offer advice and suggestions to others. Learn to be a person that doesn't talk about other people and you'll feel better about yourself. You will get a lot more respect from your teammates and your coaches.

## Questions/Discussion

1. Have you ever talked about a teammate behind his/her back?
2. Have you ever been talked about behind your back? If yes, how did it make you feel?
3. Will your team suffer if this behavior occurs?

CHAPTER
# 104

# Starting Seniors and Senior Phase Out

Over the years of playing sports I learned what it means when coaches prefer to start upperclassmen or seniors over underclassmen; and I've also seen the exact opposite, which is senior phase out. As a player you need to be aware of these strategies and make sure you're not caught on the short end of either one. Many coaches are old-school and will play an upper-classman over an underclassman even if the underclassman's a little better. Certainly if an upperclassmen and an underclassmen are very close in their abilities, it makes sense to start the upperclassmen because they've paid their dues and they may bring a little more experience to the team. Where it becomes an issue is when an underclassmen is clearly better, but the coach continues to start the upperclassmen to maintain peace, satisfy team politics, or just reward a kid for being in their program a while. For the most part, the coaches who take this approach probably had coaches who did it the same way and are repeating the system. As an underclassman, you may think the coach should just play the best player. If you are better than the upperclassman, you want to widen the gap so it is clear that you are better. If you do this, eventually, and especially in the close games, the coach will find an excuse to get you in the game so you can help your team win.

If you're an upperclassmen starting, and there's an underclassmen very close to you in your abilities you also need to be aware of senior phase out. Coaches, especially at the college level where their incomes depend on winning, start phasing out a senior for a fresh-man or a sophomore even though that senior may have started for two or three years to help build the program for the future. If there's not a big difference between the players, the coaches' thinking is that if they play the younger player, they'll get two or three more years out of them. If the season isn't going to be a winning one anyway why not go ahead and build for the future so that they can have a good season next year? This strategy certainly makes sense for the long-term development of the team and in helping keep the coach's job in future years. The seniors who are a little bit better players than the underclassmen feel they should continue starting because they've been doing their job for years and are still better than those underclassmen.

The bottom line in both cases—starting upperclassmen and senior phase out— is that the coach does not simply play the best player if there is not a big difference in performance. If you, as an athlete, find yourself in either of these situations, you are the person who can make sure you don't become the victim. Just be sure that you are so much better than the competition that the coach doesn't have a choice. Most coaches will end up playing the best player and reward the players who work hard and continue to improve. If they don't, and there's nothing you can do to change this particular situation, just keep working hard to make yourself the best that you can be. There will be other opportunities that come up when all that hard work will pay off. Hang in there! Team sports are not always fair, but there are certainly lessons to be learned.

One of the best examples of a player who got benched but continued to be his best is Derek Fisher. In 2004 when Gary Payton signed a one year deal with the Los Angeles Lakers, he was a Hall of Fame player at the end of his career and had been a great player for the Seattle Supersonics. He immediately took Derek Fisher's job as the starting point guard for the Lakers and started throughout all the regular season games and the playoffs. Fisher never complained and continued to work hard and perform when he got in the games. By the time the Lakers got to the semi-finals and the finals of the NBA Championship, Payton was still starting, but Derek Fisher got more playing time; and it was Derek Fisher who was playing at the end of the games, not Gary Payton.

Despite Payton's Hall of Fame status, Fisher kept doing the little things to help the Lakers win and Coach Phil Jackson played him even though in this case he was the underclassman, or the non-Hall of Famer. When Fisher got in to play, he didn't complain; he just kept doing a great job when the coach had to have him in there.

We can all learn a lot from Derek Fisher. He was the fifth best player on his high school team and went to a smaller Division I college while all his high school buddies went to bigger schools. He was the shortest player who started on that team and the least recruited. But he outworked them all in college and ended up being the only player from his high school team who played in the NBA.

## Questions/Discussion

1. How do you make sure senior phase out doesn't happen to you?

"The efficient man is a man who thinks for himself,
and is capable of thinking hard and long."
—CHARLES W. ELIOT

CHAPTER

# 105

# Rarely Can a Parent Change a Coach's Mind, But a Player Can

Over the years of coaching and being a parent I've had the opportunity to hear from many parents voicing concern over their kids playing time, and I've watched many parents approach other coaches regarding a kid's playing time. Even as a parent I have had some discussions with coaches about my own kids, although I've never gone in and actually had a formal conversation with any coach as a parent. One thing I've learned is that coaches really don't like to be told by parents how good their kids are, and they don't want to be evaluated on whether they're playing them appropriately. The coach has a distinct advantage over the parents in that they get to see all the kids at practice every day, and they understand the dynamics of the entire team and should play the best people in order to help their team win.

There is no question that I have seen coaches play kids based on some political circumstances, or maybe not even play kids because they don't like one as well as another. Probably the most common thing I see is that if a coach was a certain type of player—say a Charlie Hustle player, or the type of player who didn't work that hard in practice but was a gamer, a superstar player, or a role player—that coach will identify with and like players who are more like them.

There are situations that present very real obstacles for players and parents to overcome. I would advise any parent to be extremely careful before they go to a coach and start

325

complaining about playing time for their kid, as this almost always backfires and leaves the coach with the impression that they don't have supportive parents. This can make the situation even worse because if your kid is in a close battle for playing time, the coach may decide to play the other kid even more because at least their parents are supportive and not complainers. Or, the coach may feel that if they play the kids they've succumbed to parental pressure, and it's not fair to the other kid whose parents didn't come in and complain.

Without question a coach can be influenced by parents, but a good one rarely will be. There are coaches who will play upper classmen over under classmen even if the under classmen are better just to be conservative and try to avoid parental heat, or maybe in their lives seniority is more important than talent. Much of this has to do with the way things were when they were players; they determine what's fair by the way coaches conducted things when they were playing. It's certainly true that sports is not always fair, but that's also the beauty in sports. It teaches athletes that they have to get so much better than the competition, then there's no way they can be left out. This is often true in the game of life in that things aren't always fair or equal, but we just have to keep working to get the desired result.

Today, as a parent, if my child's not getting the playing time they want I encourage them to go talk to the coach, find out what areas they need to improve on and then work on those areas. Any coach wants to play a kid that wants to play. Very few coaches will get truly upset with a kid for trying to improve and get more playing time. The best policy is to send the kid in and then let the kid change the coach's mind by demonstrating what they can do in practice and by letting their coach know their desire to improve.

## Questions/Discussion

1. Have you ever gone in to talk to your coach? How did it go?
2. Did you spend more time talking or listening?

"Individual commitment to a group effort—that
is what makes a team work, a company work,
a society work, a civilization work."
—VINCE LOMBARDI

CHAPTER
# 106

# Ladder 49

If you've seen the movie, Ladder 49, you probably really enjoyed the high action film. I certainly enjoyed the action in the movie, but I loved the movie for a different reason. As a 44-year-old coach the days of my going to practice every day with my teammates are long gone. I miss being in the locker room and traveling on the team bus, eating on the road, spending the night in hotel rooms, and most importantly going to battle on the field together. Those days will go by for most of you in four years of high school. A select few of you will get another four years in college, and one in 100,000 of you may get to participate in professional sports. Some of you may play team tennis or adult softball or some other sport which will prolong your participation, but it's not the same once you get out of organized sports.

What I loved about Ladder 49 was the camaraderie involved in being a fireman. Those firemen lived together; they shared their lives together, and bonded just like teammates. Their commitment to each other is even greater than that of a football team in that they're not just playing a game; they're risking their lives for each other and for the public. By coaching I feel like I get to have some relationship with the athletes and the other coaches, but Ladder 49 reminded me those beautiful years of time spent together on a team vanish quickly. Don't waste the opportunity to give it your all and participate in sports while you have the chance. You will develop some of your greatest friendships during these times that will last a lifetime. I've always said your best friendships are forged when you're doing battle together fighting for a common goal. I still know the people that I can truly count on in the crunch based on the way they responded when we played sports together and they are still my very closest friends.

## Questions/Discussion

1. How close are you to your teammates?
2. Which is more important to you, the sport you play, the relationships with your teammates, or both?

CHAPTER

# 107

# Be a Great Teammate

If you made 1,000 guesses you could never guess who I think is the greatest teammate of all time. He is a fictional character, and his name is Forrest Gump. When most people go to the movies they watch the movie and get some enjoyment out of it. My favorite movies are those that teach life lessons, and Forrest Gump was one of the most motivating movies of all time for me.

Forrest Gump was the teammate anyone would want to have. He was loyal, honest, straight forward, committed, and a great friend. Think about it. Forrest Gump is the kind of person we would all love to be.

He didn't make excuses for his liabilities; he did what he was told with a great attitude. He never meant anyone any harm but would stand up to anyone if they weren't doing right, including the Black Panthers when they messed with his beloved Jenny. He loved his mother and would drop whatever he was doing to be by her side. When he was hurt by his girlfriend, Jenny, his love was so deep that he had to run for months to get rid of the pain. When his buddy, Bubba, said he wanted him to be his business partner and Forrest Gump made a promise with him that they'd be 50/50 partners, he came back after Bubba's death to pay his relatives their 50 percent when he became a billionaire. When one of his buddies got shot in the military and was in danger, and everybody else was running for cover, Forrest just couldn't leave his buddy out there to die and ran back through enemy fire to get him. When Lieutenant Dan was left to die with his legs blown off, Forrest Gump was again there to save him.

When everyone called Forrest stupid or said he couldn't do things, he continued to just do what he promised to do. When Lieutenant Dan was lonely and in dire straits, Forrest came to visit him. Lieutenant Dan said that if Forrest ever became a shrimp boat captain, he would come and be his first mate; and sure enough Lieutenant Dan showed up good to his word.

Most importantly, once Forrest was a billionaire he came back to take care of Jenny, giving her a second chance despite the fact that she was ill with AIDS. He was a great father to his son. When the grass at the school needed to be mowed, Forrest mowed it (in spite of the fact that he was a billionaire) for free because "it needed to be done." I don't know how you get to be a better teammate, friend, husband, son, or father than Forrest Gump. There is something to be learned in almost all situations if you just look.

## Questions/Discussion

1. What type of teammate are you?
2. How would your teammates describe you?

CHAPTER
# 108

# Don't Let Your Parents Call the Coach

Until a child is about 10 years old it is certainly understandable that a parent may call a coach every time there is a problem or if a kid is going to be late or when there's a concern. After age 10 it would be best for the player to go in to talk to the coach if he or she is going to be late for practice, if there's a question to be asked or if there is any particular concern for the player. Certainly parents can help guide their child, but any coach will appreciate talking to the player more than to the parents. Coaches are pretty smart individuals, and they know whether a parent supports them or not. They can tell by the kids' actions at practice what they are being taught at home. If a kid is not happy with their playing time or they want to get across a point to a coach, the coach is not only more likely to listen to the kid but will consider it more sincere, and will probably be a lot more likely to do something about it if the kid makes the request.

For example, I've coached players who when I've pulled them out of the game and they're sitting on the bench say, "Coach, put me back in, put me back in." When a kid says that to me, I'm not offended. I just know I have a kid that loves the game and wants to play. If a parent were to come and tell me that, I would think that we have a meddling parent who doesn't care about the other kids and only cares about their child. In other words, coaches will factor in the age of the child and understand where their heart is.

If a high school kid came to me as a coach and said, "Hey I'm not getting enough playing time. What do I have to do to improve?" I would feel that I have a kid that really wants to play. And if that kid goes out and does the assignment I give them to work on, I'd be a lot more likely to play them. However, if a parent came in and said their kid wasn't getting enough playing time, almost any coach would think, "No wonder the kid isn't any good. Their parents fight all their battles for them, and when something goes wrong Mommy or Daddy come to the rescue.

One of the temptations for parents is to protect their children. It's a natural instinct for them, especially mothers. I would tell any player, "Whatever you do, don't have your mother call the coach when there's a little issue." I've had mothers call and say, "Please take it easy on the kids today; they have a tough test tomorrow." Or "they have a tough game in a few days." Any coach who receives that call is going to think that neither the parents nor the child is very committed or tough. You have to remember that coaches are Warriors; they're people who live their lives with very few excuses and most likely have battled through many tough circumstances. These coaches aren't looking for an easy way out or a cushion to fall on, and they're trying to teach your kids to be the same way. These kinds of calls to coaches generally infuriate them and can cause them to lose confidence in your child.

In the movie Hoosiers there is a scene where a father shows up dragging his teenager by the arm and says, "Coach here's my boy. Do whatever you want with him; just make a man and a basketball player out of him." He drops him off and off he goes. That's the kind of parent a coach wants, one that shows total support but is not meddlesome and isn't afraid for his kid to have to learn a few things through the school of hard knocks. In the end your kid will be better, and you'll have done them a lot of favors.

Finally, I've watched many kids go off to high school or college programs. At each level it gets a little tougher; but the longer I watch the more I am convinced that when it gets close, the difference between player A and player B often is their parents and the support the players get and what they're told at home. When their little superstar runs into the first difficult task of sitting on the bench or competing for a high school or college job, do the parents tell them to get out there and get in the gym earlier and work harder? Or do they suggest that they're not getting the breaks, or things are not going their way, or things are not fair? If it's the latter, you can pretty much assume that that kid will be sitting on the bench in most situations while the first parents' kid will hang in there and eventually see playing time. There are exceptions to all these rules, but very few. The bottom line is, fight your own battles on the field and with the coaches, and they will respect you for it and you'll respect yourself.

## Questions/Discussion

1. Have your parents ever called the coach about your playing time? If so, did it help?

# Be a Warrior

"In life as in a football game, the
principle to follow is: hit the line hard!"

—THEODORE ROOSEVELT

CHAPTER

# 109

# What is a Warrior and Why I Love Them

Every coach now and then gets to coach a kid who is truly a Warrior. Most of the time these kids were born competitive, they get some success, and then they become even more competitive eventually becoming a Warrior. A Warrior is someone who dives for the loose ball on the basketball court, who will slide tackle in soccer, who will lower his head and run you over in football, who will run while they're throwing up, who will take the inside pitch in baseball in the shoulder so that they can advance to first base, the boxer who continues to battle with his face bloodied, these are athletes who truly enjoy the competition and refuse to ever quit.

One of my all time favorite movies is Rocky. In the original movie Rocky was truly a Warrior deciding that it was not about winning or losing, but giving it his all. My favorite moral of that movie is that you can be a winner and still lose the fight. I'll never forget him saying in the movie that if I can just go the distance against the champion that that is something that Rocky could live with. He was scared, unsure of what the outcome was going to be, but the Warrior in him led him into battle to do all he could do and take the consequences. Another favorite movie of mine is, The Last Samurai, with Tom Cruise. The Last Samurai and Rocky are movies that every athlete needs to see because we will all be put in situations where the odds look insurmountable, but do we have the courage to get in there and battle? A Warrior loves to play the best competition even if they have just a minute chance of winning. But the Warrior will fight until the very end knowing that at any time their opponent might reach the end of their rope and the Warrior can survive just on their intensity and competitiveness.

I've watched many games where a team dominates another and they just give up and then all the wheels fall off and the better team annihilates them in competition. This never happens when you're playing against a Warrior. A Warrior may get beat but they're going to make sure that you pay a price for winning. They're going to be more physical, they're going to battle, their goal is to get better and make you know that at least you were in a good fight.

Over the years when I coached AAU basketball, we would play teams that would be beating us by 20 or more and they would take off the press to show mercy. I would go over to the coach and tell them to put the press back on us, how in the world are we ever going to get better? I want my kids to spend a lot of time in the fire and see if they're going to give up or if they're going to fight. For the Warrior there is no option, they always come to fight until the final whistle blows.

## Questions/Discussion

1. Are you a Warrior? Why or why not?
2. Do you battle to the end, even when you know you're going to lose?

CHAPTER

# 110

# My First Warrior

I'm the father of five kids and my oldest daughter is Kelsey. Kelsey is currently 15 about to turn 16 and I have twin daughters that are 12, a 6-year-old son, and a 4-year-old girl at the time I write this book. I've coached a lot of kids over the years and not because she's mine, but because of all that I have watched her do over the years I would say that Kelsey Hatcher is the first true Warrior from the Hatcher family that I've coached. At age four she ran a four-mile road race running 90 percent of the way and walking a little bit at times. I knew I had a winner when I watched her walking and someone ran past her and she stopped walking and started running to try to pass them back up.

Later in that year I went to run a two-mile race in Eureka Springs, as I ran a lot of road races back then and Kelsey went with me to run. We ran together and it was a race that had an age group division of fourteen and under and around fifteen to twenty in the girls division. Kelsey and I took off and were doing pretty well when a couple of sixth grade girls passed Kelsey going up a hill. I never said a word; I looked down as I watched her pick up the pace and pass these girls. This went on back and forth for the next half mile, they would try to pass her, she would refuse, and I never said a word just kept running quietly smiling to myself. By the time we reached the one mile mark Kelsey had control and went on to beat those girls and every other runner fourteen and under. They gave out the awards in the ten to fourteen age bracket and the five to nine age bracket and Kelsey received no award even though she had beaten all fifteen kids male and female who were under fourteen years old, but there was no medal for her because she wasn't eligible for any of those classes because she was just a four year old running this two mile race. At the end of the race the race director realized that the top finisher had gotten no award and brought her up for her special medal. I knew then that there was something burning inside that might make her just a little bit different.

Kelsey is not a super outspoken child, but yet she can be a leader. She has always played sports since she was four playing on a co-ed soccer team that year and then later moving to girl's soccer teams. She's always been the Mighty Bluebirds top goal scorer and turned out to be a pretty fine basketball player as well. What separated her were her discipline and her ability to workout despite having a slender and small frame. Today she has just finished her 9th grade year and weighs 116 pounds. She was the top cross country runner for the senior high team as a freshman and was named All-State. In track she won 3 state titles as a freshman in the 800, 1600, and 3200 meters and set the All-Time State Record in the mile. She won all three events with very little rest in between and after throwing up several times after winning the mile. Her track coach, Kevin Kelley, called it the most courageous performance he's ever witnessed first hand.

In basketball she led her team to the Regional Championship starting at shooting guard as a freshman, leading the team in scoring with 13.1 points per game, being named All-District, and most importantly hitting a 3 pointer with her team down by 2 with 5 seconds to go in the Regional finals. The team made it to the final four at state before losing.

In soccer, she led her team in goals and assists as a freshman and they never lost a game once she joined the team following the basketball season. The team won the State Championship with Kelsey leading the team in goals and assists through the State Tournament. I guess you could say she had a fine freshman year.

She's a Warrior because she'll go shoot baskets on Christmas day. She'll get up and run or work on her soccer skills before she goes to school, and she'll always do it with a great attitude.

What makes Kelsey her absolute best, though, is when we play the most important games and we're in the toughest situations. That's where Kelsey shines the most. She takes the penalty kicks in soccer; she makes a lot of big three pointers in pressure games and she wants the ball when the game's on the line. When our team is beating the tar out of somebody she's probably at her worst. She's not the type of player that wants to get five goals or get 30 points against the weak opponent. At that time she's happy to spread the ball around and let others have success or maybe she just doesn't focus as much because we're winning and that's what she's really after. It's not that she's a ball hog in the big games; it's just that she wants to win and she steps it up a few notches in those games.

Despite her success in many of her sports she still has a long way to go mentally as all high school kids do, and this book is written with her in mind to help her get smarter between the ears. God has given her the physical gifts, the rest is up to her.

## Questions/Discussion

1. How are you between the ears?
2. Do you believe the mental part of the game is as important as the physical part? Why or why not?

> Always bear in mind that your own resolution to succeed is more important than any one thing.
> —ABRAHAM LINCOLN

# The Cantigator

Have you ever heard a coach say execution is the key? Well maybe this story will help you take execution to a new level. When I was a freshman in high school I met the famous Ed Bentley from Albion High School who was an All State Wrestler. Some wrestlers win their matches by decision nearly edging out their opponents on points. Ed was the kind of wrestler that pinned you and ended the match early. Ed had a patented move called the Cantigator, which involved taking his opponents arm, putting it behind his back, and then coming around to the side and then rolling him over on his back on that arm that was pinned behind his back. He would go to tournaments and pin opponent after opponent with his Cantigator move.

I'll never forget the time he had pinned a couple of opponents in the Cantigator and someone asked him to show that move on a side mat with over 100 people standing and watching including his opponents that he would see in the next rounds. He carefully and slowly showed everyone how to do the Cantigator move. Sure enough, the very next match he put that same Cantigator move on his opponent who had just watched him demonstrate the move, and the match was over. The point was it didn't matter if you knew it was coming; he could execute it because he'd practiced it over and over again and had the fundamentals perfect.

Whatever your sport is, before long everybody will pretty much know what you're going to do. The key is can you execute it against the very best defense? Can you execute it when your opponent knows it's coming? Have you perfected your skill so that it's unstoppable? When you have practiced long enough and hard enough that you can tell your opponent that it's coming and still execute it you will find yourself at the top of the heap and be a champion.

My good friend, Coach Loucks, always says he wants his teams to play defense good enough that they can steal the ball from the opposing team in basketball and then just roll it back to the point guard and say let's start all over again and stop them over and over again. Certainly most defenses don't do that, but wouldn't it be neat to get yourself good enough to do that just every now and then and challenge yourself? Remember, practice and execution to perfection are the keys. Come up with your Cantigator move and become a show stopper against your opponent.

## Questions/Discussion

1. Have you ever changed the rules of the game to make things tougher on yourself?
2. In what other ways do you challenge yourself?

CHAPTER
# 112

# Life is an Hourglass

One of the things that kept me motivated in my life was the understanding that life is not a clock where the hands just keep going around and around and around on the clock and you get a new day each day. For me, life is like an hourglass. It is a big hourglass, but the bottom line is when you flip that hourglass over and the sand starts dropping through there's no chance to redo the day of life that God gave you. When you get to high school there's no chance to get your ninth grade year over or your eighth grade of junior high back. You only get one chance to do each of these little time phases of life. When I was in high school I started to finally get a grasp of this, and I think I fully understood it by college. In other words, during those four years of high school I wanted to be the best that I could be in my schoolwork and the sports that I played. It's important to give your best during those years and not look back and say, boy, I wish I would have gone out for this sport, or I wish I would have worked harder, or I wish our team would have won the championship. The time to do it is now.

When you get to college, it's no different. You always want to put forth your very best so you don't look back at your college years and say I wish I would have done this or I wish I would have done that. When I got older and got in my first job the same applied. Each phase of life is a different season and you want to do your very best along the way. Once that season is over it will certainly help you mentally not to have to look back and have regrets. It also is a foundation on which to build for the future. If you're successful in junior high you'll probably be successful in high school; if you're successful in junior high and high school you'll probably be successful in college and so on and so on. Each chapter of your life that you build you want to continue to put forth maximum effort and do the right things.

Today the chapter in my life that I'm on is being a father and watching my kids play. I enjoy being a father and I enjoy going to all my kids' games, coaching them, and encouraging them along the way because I will only get to do it one time for each child. As I dictate this chapter I only have three years left with my oldest daughter. To her it's an eternity, but to an experienced person watching the sand fall through the hourglass it will go by very quickly. Each of my kids will come along the way and that sand will fall and I will never get another chance to do it again. Nor will they. As an athlete, a student, a parent, a grandparent, you never get a chance to do it again, so be sure to give it your best.

There will come a time later in life for me when it's time to die. When that time comes I even want to do my best in that situation. I recently went to see my old coach who is 82 years old who has been a great mentor for me for 25 years. When I went to see him he asked me to sit down with him and read verses in the Bible. He told me what would happen if he didn't make it through his chemotherapy treatment and how I would be a pallbearer at his funeral. He told me that he loved me, and he told me what the important things were in life. Yes, even on his death bed he still was giving it his best leaving behind no regrets and still teaching me one more lesson, this time how to die. Be sure to live your life to the fullest at each stage, and you will not have wasted the great life God gave you.

## Questions/Discussion

1. After reading this chapter, will you look at life as an hourglass?
2. Can you think of something in life you only get one chance at that you wish you'd given more effort? How does that feel?

# 113

"There are two kinds of people,
those that are mentally weak and those
that are mentally strong."
—JOHN GRUDEN, NFL FOOTBALL COACH

# There Are Two Kinds of People

There are two kinds of people in this world, those who are mentally weak and those who are mentally strong. The sad part about all of this is that by the time you are an adult you probably are one of the two. How you were raised makes such a difference. Did your parents allow you to say can't or did they tell you it was a word that was not allowed to be used in their household, only the words I'll try? When things got rough when you were growing up did your parents run over and hug you and bail you out, or did they tell you to get up and jump back in the ring?

I've found that no matter what the age of the kids I'm coaching you get what you expect. Needless to say I expect a lot out of my athletes which means that I asked them to do a lot. The more you ask them to do the more proud they are of doing a job that was difficult and doing it well. It's funny how things work, but kids actually want to pay the price for success. The key is not to coddle them early in life and to set expectations high and not settle for less.

I'm most proud of the fact that I have raised children who aren't afraid to try new things that will take some risk no matter how silly it might be. Have you ever met somebody who is scared to ride this ride or scared to do that? So many people won't even enter the ring because they are afraid of failure. Encourage your children, athletes, and family members to try new things at an early age. I still have friends today that will only eat five or six different items because they determined long ago that they don't like anything else. Their taste buds have changed long ago but they simply don't enjoy the pleasures of other foods because they simply won't try. I know others who won't enter an arena that they're not experts in because of the fear of failure. Somewhere along the way somebody taught them it was better to not try than to try and fail.

Mentally tough people are those that when faced with difficulty or adversity have built a life and a foundation on battling through those tough times, which gives them even more confidence. These players are mentally strong and will be a success at whatever they do. Take risks, be a rock and be tough. For the most part mental toughness is having the discipline and courage to attempt the things that we are all scared to do but to know that the most important part is to try. Toughness is having the character to accept the consequences of things not going your way in return for the chance of success or for standing for an important ideal.

## Questions/Discussion

1. Are you mentally tough or weak? What can you do to improve either way?
2. Who is the most mentally tough athlete you can think of?

# 114

> "Pain is temporary. It may last a minute, or an hour, or a day, or a year, but eventually it will subside and something else will take its place. If I quit, it lasts forever."
> —LANCE ARMSTRONG

# Competitive Warfare

Over the years of coaching I've watched how some kids figure out immediately how to compete while others simply don't figure it out as quickly if at all. As the father of five kids I also notice immediately the difference in my kids and their nature in regard to competitiveness. Haley, one of my 12 year old twins at the time that I write this book is not only fascinating to me, but to all of our coaches as we prepare for any game. She always sizes up the competition before we play. She always wants to know who we're going to play before we go to any game. I always tell her the same thing…that we're going to be playing the loser. She gets frustrated and wants to know the team name and as soon as we get to the gymnasium or soccer field she is analyzing that opponent and figuring out the best way for her team to win.

If I divide the teams up at practice and we're playing and her team's not winning she asks me to redivide the teams or she tries to make changes herself. She has even come over to me in the middle of a game when I was about to make a substitution in soccer and told me, "Dad, that's a bad idea to make that substitution if you want to win." In other words, from the time she was 7 or 8 years old she was determining what would give her and her team the best chance to win, which is extremely rare for kids that age much less a girl. It's probably no surprise that she is one of the most competitive kids that I've ever coached, and her team has the highest winning percentage of any team I've ever coached. At the time I write this book her soccer team has never lost a game to girls her age, only to older teams or boys' teams. That's over 150 games without a loss.

On the flip side I have kids who we can put out there in a game of 3 on 3 basketball and they each are guarding their particular man. Their team might be losing and the person they are guarding hasn't scored a point in three games, yet they continue to guard them and not jump off of them to help stop the leading scorer on the other team.

Some kids just don't get it; for example, they will start a game of 3 on 3 and each chooses who they are going to guard. Maybe the best player on one team is guarding the weakest player on the other team and they continue to lose game after game without ever mentioning to their teammates that maybe we ought to switch who guards whom or double up on somebody else to prevent them from scoring. This happens a lot to young kids, especially girls, who simply go about doing their job but not worrying about the big picture and the end result of winning. To be good at competitive warfare you have to constantly look at the game as if you're a coach and try to figure out what is the best strategy for your team to win. In other words, size up the competition, take the leadership and make the necessary adjustments to have your team win. This type of attitude is between the ears.

When we were playing in the state tournament this past year in the 14-year-old age division we moved Haley up to serve as a substitute even though she was only 10 years old. In the second game in the state tournament she came up and asked me if she would be starting in the second half. The very fact that she could even ask me and Coach Owen such a question put a smile on our faces and made us laugh. She evaluated things and thought she was good enough and was ready to let us know that. It also shows that she has the courage even when playing on a brand new team for the first time with kids four years older to make a request if she thinks it would help the team win. As it turned out Haley made a lot of contributions in that tournament with some key passes and her play, but her most valuable asset was her attitude. The next time you go out to play 3 on 3 in basketball, pool or checkers, or whatever it might be, be the kind of player that's willing to make changes and take leadership roles to figure out what's going to give you the best chance to win. This will work in sports, business, school, or anything, even relationships. Anything that you want you better learn how to compete and figure out the best strategy to win because life is all one big competition.

As an athlete I never would have said that I had the best body ever made to compete, but I've always felt when looking at any game or evaluating any sport I could figure out the best strategy to win. This asset has helped me win many more games in business, in life, and on the sports field than any other asset I have. Competitive warfare is figuring out what gives you the best strategy to win and having the courage and the muster to implement it whether it's popular or not.

## Questions/Discussion

1. Do you evaluate every contest before you enter it?
2. Do you size up the competition and develop a strategy?

# Epilogue

As I stood on the sidelines looking out on the soccer field my eyes filled with tears. The Mighty Bluebirds were down 7-0 with 10 minutes to go. What once was a dynasty was no longer the same team of girls. We had stayed too long. We were like a former world champion prize fighter who thought he could still do it at age 45. The signs were all there a year ago, but because we were champions we were able to win another state championship by competing on what we'd done in the past having enough stud players to lift our team to victory.

I'd seen it happen to all the other soccer teams before us, but for some reason thought it wouldn't happen to my precious Mighty Bluebirds. When girls get to high school and they get ready to turn 15 and 16 things change. They are now playing high school soccer, and though the level of competition is not as good as club soccer it's more fun because they're playing for their school and with their friends. Practices are shorter and easier, and most of all it's something new. These girls have been playing club soccer some since they were four years old; and the time to stop playing club soccer, at least in the state of Arkansas, occurs about the ninth grade. Not because club soccer is not good anymore, but because there are no more teams to play in Arkansas and the population is simply not large enough to support it.

As I looked across the field I only had three original starters left from our team just a year ago. Two were injured and five decided not to play or focus on other sports, and one simply switched teams. For a 15 or 16-year-old girl traveling away on the weekends all the time is not what these teenagers are looking for unless they're really hard core. Our hard core players were still there, but they were surrounded by good kids many of whom had joined the Bluebird Organization recently, and were not seasoned veterans that we had trained for years.

We realized that our job is to train these kids so that they can be handed off to a high school or college coach and be at the top of their games. Our girls that had been in the program are already trained well enough to be collegiate players. They just have to have other collegiate players surrounding them. Soccer requires eleven players plus four or five good ones off the bench. As I looked across the field I realized that I had coached these Warriors for somewhere between six and eleven years, two soccer seasons each. Some of these girls had played 22 seasons for me traveling and competing, winning almost every tournament they entered and taking on all comers from surrounding states.

I realized then how much I would miss them, miss competing with them, miss training them, miss traveling with them, and talking with them. When I looked at Annie DeCourrsey, one of the hardest working players I'd ever coached, my eyes filled with tears. As I looked at Caty McMains, one of my smallest players, but a tough competitor at defender, my eyes got wetter. When I looked at my daughter, Kelsey, who I had coached for all 22 seasons I realized it was over. Things would never be the same again. She was grown up and it was time for her to move on to bigger and better things. Hopefully she would look back too and realize the wonderful times we had traveling and playing soccer, and I was very proud of the women she and the other girls had become.

Right then and there I knew it was time to pull the plug. I would not let the state's greatest soccer team and its greatest players go through any more of this. The coaches and I talked during the game and tried to see if there was any way we could make a final season out of it, but there simply was no way. We only had three or four girls at practice each day because they were juggling their high school sports and other things they had going on, and it simply wasn't fair to them. So we moved on to the next chapter in their lives, and that was to start doing individual training with them and get them ready to play the collegiate sports they would play.

Coach Loucks said, "You don't lead 800 men into battle against 30,000." It's not that we don't have the courage, and it's not that these players wouldn't fight. It's just better to retreat and build them and prepare them for the next battle, which I'm confident they will surely win, to move on and become great high school and collegiate players. It's time to enjoy and sit back and watch the next chapter of their lives as they move on.

A lot of people may think that I coach to win, but it is truly the practices that I live for and preparing them to get ready for their next challenge and battle and watching them grow. We'll get them ready for the next hurdle…we'll start "Between the Ears."